Uncertain

'We now live in a whitewater world of unpredictability. Change occurs at a rate that the human mind is not prepared for. Arie Kruglanski's groundbreaking book is the place to go to discover how to embrace uncertainty and turn the stress of whitewater to your growth and benefit'

Martin Seligman, author of *The Hope Circuit*

'One of my very favourite psychologists in the world tackles a subject that is both timeless and timely. Drawing on four decades of research and reflection, Arie Kruglanski shows us that though uncertainty is inevitable, how we react to it is not'

Angela Duckworth, bestselling author of *Grit*

'This is the book we've been waiting for. With his tremendous spirit, wit, knowledge and wisdom, Kruglanski gives us a book that helps us understand and navigate the uncertain world we live in. It's both based on science and filled with humanity – with deep compassion and benevolent guidance. It is a book for our time'

Carol Dweck, professor of psychology at Stanford University; author of *Mindset: The New Psychology of Success*

'If you're not sure if you need this book, then you do. Original, insightful and thought-provoking, the world's expert on the psychology of uncertainty reveals what science can tell us about our lives on the razor's edge'

Daniel Gilbert, Edgar Pierce professor of psychology at Harvard University; author of the *New York Times* bestseller *Stumbling on Happiness*, host of the PBS television series *This Emotional Life*

'I enthusiastically recommend *Uncertain*. Arie Kruglanski is one of the most prolific writers in modern psychological science. Here, he explores the relationship that we, as humans, have with uncertainty. He presents his fascinating research programme on the need for closure. His writing is deep, full of humour, and so many great stories of people who sought too much (or, at times, too little) certainty. The book further provides a guide for developing self-insights into your own need for closure, so that you make better decisions in life. If there's anything I'm certain about, it's that you'll love this book'

Ayelet Fishbach, author of *Get It Done: Surprising Lessons from the Science of Motivation*

ABOUT THE AUTHOR

Arie W. Kruglanski is an award-winning professor at the University of Maryland, College Park, and is recognized as a worldwide leading expert and authority on human motivation. Famed for his interest and studies in domains of human judgement and decision-making, the motivation-cognition interface, group and intergroup processes, and the psychology of human goals, his work has been published in over 400 articles, chapters and books and his papers have appeared in major psychological journals. He has published opinion pieces in the *Guardian, Huffington Post, National Interest, Conversation* and the *Washington Post*. His background has enabled him to be a founding co-PI of START (National Consortium for the Study of Terrorism and Responses to Terrorism). He is currently a PI on the psychological study of Syrian refugees in Europe and the Middle East.

Uncertain

How to Turn Your Biggest Fear into Your Greatest Power

ARIE W. KRUGLANSKI

MICHAEL JOSEPH

MICHAEL JOSEPH

UK | USA | Canada | Ireland | Australia
India | New Zealand | South Africa

Michael Joseph is part of the Penguin Random House group of companies
whose addresses can be found at global.penguinrandomhouse.com

First published by Michael Joseph, 2023

001

p.37: © Granger, Historical Picture Archive/Alamy Stock Photo; p.41: © Pictorial Press Ltd/Alamy
Stock Photo; p.44: © Austrian National Library/Interfoto /Alamy Stock Photo; p.52:
© Sueddeutsche Zeitung Photo/Alamy Stock Photo; p.54: © Kristoffer Tripplaar/Alamy Stock Photo;
p.106: © Album/Alamy Stock Photo; p.121: © Dov Cohen, Faith Shin, Xi Liu, Peter Ondish, et al.,
Personality and Social Psychology Bulletin (43(11)) p.10, © 2017 by the Society for Personality and
Social Psychology, Inc. Reprinted by Permission of SAGE Publications

Set in 13.5/16pt Garamond MT Std
Typeset by Jouve (UK), Milton Keynes
Printed and bound in Great Britain by Clays Ltd, Elcograf S.p.A.

The authorized representative in the EEA is Penguin Random House Ireland,
Morrison Chambers, 32 Nassau Street, Dublin D02 YH68

A CIP catalogue record for this book is available from the British Library

HB ISBN: 978-0-241-46769-5
OM ISBN: 978-0-241-46770-1

www.greenpenguin.co.uk

MIX
Paper from
responsible sources
FSC
www.fsc.org
FSC® C018179

Penguin Random House is committed to a
sustainable future for our business, our readers
and our planet. This book is made from Forest
Stewardship Council® certified paper.

To Hannah: My safest haven, and most secure base

Note: I am indebted to Molly Ellenberg and Noam Yanay
for help in researching the materials for this book.

Contents

Introduction: Escaping and Embracing Uncertainty   1

PART 1

Escaping Uncertainty

1 Measuring Your Need for Closure   15
2 The Price of Premature Closure   26
3 Who Needs Certainty?   48
4 Adult Attachment   75
5 Cultures of Certainty and Uncertainty   88
6 The Power of the Situation   104

PART 2

Closure's Consequences

7 The Pitfalls of Black-and-White Thinking   127
8 Among Others   142
9 Self-confidence and Self-doubt   165

PART 3

Embracing Uncertainty

10 Accentuating the Positive   183
11 Making Good Things Happen   210

CONTENTS

12 The Best is Yet to Come   231

13 The Allure of Detachment and Mystery   255

14 Living with Differences   276

Conclusion: Avoiding and Approaching Uncertainty   294

Notes   299

Bibliography   325

Index   349

Introduction:
Escaping and Embracing Uncertainty

It so happened that as I set out to write this book about uncertainty, people worldwide were experiencing it in massive doses during the COVID-19 pandemic. Just about everyone's plans and routines had been turned topsy-turvy. To be clear, I didn't decide to address uncertainty *because* of the pandemic; in fact, I had committed to this book way before it happened. Life was humming along, with its mundane worries, joys and challenges. The pandemic changed all that dramatically. By the time I started writing, uncertainty was a defining part of everyone's everyday experience. Living in its shadow while also contemplating its nature allowed me to see aspects of uncertainty I had never before considered. This new reality somehow broke my mindset about uncertainty. It challenged the common perspective about it to which I too had formerly subscribed. The new insights I garnered were a personal silver lining to what was otherwise a trying and constraining time.

This book distils, then, what I have learned about uncertainty, not only over the last few years, but over a lifetime of research and study. For as much as my views have developed, my interest in uncertainty has been a constant. From the early 1980s through to my present-day role as director of the Motivated Cognition Laboratory at the University of Maryland, it has been a subject of personal and professional fascination. The pioneering work on the human need for closure I conducted with Tali Freund, Donna Webster and

Adena Klem in the 1980s and 1990s brought uncertainty into the mainstream of psychological study. Since then, we've carried out hundreds of studies the world over to explore this fundamental aspect of the shared human predicament – our relationship with uncertainty – and the scale we developed to measure people's desire for certainty and closure has been translated into twenty different languages (that I know of) and is used across Europe, and in the Americas, Asia, the Middle East and Africa. Why this fascination? For two reasons really: uncertainty affects almost everything we do, and our reactions to uncertainty have a wide-ranging impact on broad social phenomena from love to politics and beyond.

In this book, I'll share with you everything that I've learned in the hope that you may gain a better understanding not just of the uncertainty that characterizes our lives but also your own personal relationship with it. As you'll learn, each of us is different in the way we respond to uncertainty, but we all have the capacity to harness the remarkable gifts that uncertainty can offer and face down the worst fears it brings.

The myth of the dark unknown

To most people, uncertainty carries exclusively negative connotations, and the idea that people desire certainty seems an obvious truth. This belief is so commonplace among both laypeople and scientists that we rarely, if ever, pause to question it. Indeed, it's a trope lying at the very bedrock of our culture. We find it in the sage advice of the fictional figure Albus Dumbledore, headmaster of Hogwarts School of Witchcraft and Wizardry, who declaimed that 'it is the unknown we fear when we look upon death and darkness, nothing more,' and in psychologist N. R. Carleton's assertion that 'fear of the unknown may be a, or possibly is the, fundamental fear,'[1] as well as in art and literature. 'We fear that which we cannot see,' remarked Tite Kubo, a Japanese manga artist,[2] while author H. P. Lovecraft wrote that 'the oldest and strongest kind of fear is fear of the unknown'.[3]

The widespread anxiety experienced by people during the COVID-19 pandemic seems to support the view that uncertainty is frightening and threatening. As Kathleen Parker, a *Washington Post* columnist, noted on 13 November 2020: 'Drinking is on the rise and smoking is making a comeback ... Google searches for "anxiety" in the past week reached a 16-year high.' When COVID started to take hold, millions of people around the globe began experiencing severe angst about the unprecedented situation they found themselves in. Data from across the world attested to a significant spike in reported distress tied to the pandemic, with the World Health Organization (WHO) reporting a 35 per cent increase in the prevalence of distress in China, 60 per cent in Iran and 45 per cent in the US. In the Amhara region of Ethiopia, a threefold increase in the frequency of depression and anxiety relative to the pre-pandemic rate was recorded.[4] At the time of writing, figures from all corners of the world indicate the same thing: wherever you look, people are deeply troubled and disconcerted.

Causality or correlation?

Yet the global rise in both uncertainty and distress does not prove that the former necessarily caused the latter. Scientists never tire of explaining that correlation does not mean causation. Just because two things happen simultaneously, or closely together in time, does not mean that one is the cause of the other. For instance, it has been found that in major US cities the greater the amount of ice cream sold, the more murders are committed. Does that mean that eating ice cream makes you more likely to commit murder or that committing murder whets the appetite for ice cream? Both possibilities appear ludicrous, and they are. Instead, the summer heat, a third factor, could both whet an appetite for ice cream and be a source of frustration that incites aggression.

Or consider the finding that the number of churches in a city is linked to the amount of crime. One could speculate that (Catholic) churches help absolve us of guilt, and so disinhibit our indulgences, which makes crime possible. Or perhaps crime induces guilt, hence the greater need for churches that offer a way to absolution. Both explanations seem far-fetched. Indeed, there is a much simpler explanation, which relates to a city's size. The larger the city's population, the greater the number of churches, and also, unrelatedly, the opportunity for crime.

So the fact that people experienced angst and uncertainty during the pandemic doesn't mean that the two are causally related. The pandemic generated both uncertainty and angst, but the angst does not come from the uncertainty as such; it comes from fear of negative outcomes, the bad things that could happen because of the pandemic. Trivial, irrelevant uncertainties don't evoke distress at all. Uncertainty about the weather produces a barely noticeable change in our emotions, and so does uncertainty about the outcome of an athletic competition between teams we don't care about or political elections in a faraway land.

Even when uncertainty is about things that do matter, any

angst evoked is not caused by the uncertainty itself but by the bad news that may be linked to that uncertainty, whether it's the increased likelihood of severe illness, death, the loss of loved ones or a job, restrictions to our freedom, and so on. Pause for a moment and ask yourself: Would you rather have a 90 per cent chance of contracting the virus or a 50 per cent chance? Most people would opt for the 50 per cent chance, even though, as with the toss of a coin, the outcome here is completely uncertain. The 90 per cent chance, while much more certain, is intuitively much less preferable and more anxiety-provoking. So it is not the uncertainty as such that is troubling but the adverse consequences that the pandemic makes more likely.

Uncertainty: objective and subjective

Uncertainty is the rule rather than the exception when it comes to our lives. There is simply no way of knowing what comes next. 'Prediction is tough, especially of the future,' quipped Yogi Berra, an American baseball player known for his pithy and paradoxical statements. Perhaps the reason why prediction is so precarious is that what has come before can never be repeated and can never, in itself, fully determine what will happen in the future. The sixth-century BC Greek philosopher Heraclitus highlighted this sense of flux, pointing out that 'No man ever steps in the same river twice, for it's not the same river and he's not the same man.' Far more recently, the twentieth-century philosopher Karl Popper discussed at length what is known as the fallacy of induction. No matter how many white swans you may have seen so far, the generalization that 'all swans are white' (or indeed any other generalization made from experience) is unwarranted, because the very next swan you may encounter could be black. Benjamin Franklin famously remarked that 'in this world nothing can be said to be certain, except death and taxes', yet we might wonder about these two as well. Who knows? In short, human lives are suffused with uncertainty. And any certainty we experience can be banished by unexpected events.

Take the striking story of Travis Roy, a gifted college hockey player who in the eleventh minute of his first game for Boston University (BU) crashed into the boards at high speed and snapped his fourth and fifth cervical vertebrae, which left him paralysed for life from the neck down. Crashing into the boards is nearly inevitable in hockey. It happens in most games. It is something professional players expect to happen. Yet sometimes the unexpected transpires. You do not expect your car to collide with another on a route you have travelled without a hitch countless times. You do not expect your simple backache to be diagnosed as a life-threatening disease.

But the Travis Roy story goes beyond illustrating life's inevitable uncertainty. Its inspirational power derives from what this young man did when confronted with a completely unfamiliar situation. Before the accident, his life seemed comfortably laid out, full of promise and professional success. Yet all that was gone, erased as if by a magic wand, deleted as if by a single click on a computer's keyboard. And yet, facing the utter unknown, Roy showed what he was made of. Following a tough rehabilitation, he resumed his studies at BU and obtained his degree. He then devoted his life to inspiring others by giving motivational speeches, setting up the Travis Roy Foundation and raising millions of dollars for spinal-injury research. He had a major impact on others, offering a ray of hope and dispelling the darkness of despair. Through his life of service and devotion to people's well-being, Roy showed abundantly that what might seem to be a total disaster might conceal a silver lining.

The Travis Roy story carries an important lesson about the distinction between objective and subjective uncertainty. Objectively, we know that anything can happen at any time, but subjectively we may feel secure that we are safe and that things will unfold pretty much as we envisioned. What happened to Roy shows the objective uncertainty that rules our lives. Yet Roy's subsequent resilience demonstrated his *subjective* confidence that, despite the tragedy, his future was in his own hands.

In facing a familiar situation, we behave 'inductively': we assume that whatever usually happens will happen and that our days will go as planned. Getting into our car in the morning, we expect to arrive at work without glitches, and when making an appointment with our dentist we assume that she will be there to treat us. What makes a new situation different is its unknown character; we have not encountered anything like it in the past, so we have no personal expectations of what it will be like.

Yet we can develop expectations based on what others tell us. We can learn from their experience and knowledge and base our beliefs on their assessments. Consider information from experts about our varying degrees of vulnerability to the COVID-19 virus. People whose expected outcomes were depicted as particularly dire should have been more troubled than people whose likely outcomes were less severe – and they were (and, as infections with the COVID-19 virus persist, still are). For instance, older people, whose likelihood of surviving the pandemic was depicted by experts as lower than that of younger people, were typically much more anxious and concerned. They tended to avoid public places, carefully observe lockdowns and comply with directives about social distancing. A Pew Research Center Poll of 18 March 2020 found that 33 per cent of people who were sixty-five or older viewed the pandemic as a major threat to their health, as compared to 25 per cent of people aged eighteen to twenty-nine. In other words, it is the differences in the *certainty* of negative outcomes about which we have learned from experts that matter rather than *uncertainty* per se.

However, expert information wasn't the only determinant of people's subjective view of the likelihood of outcomes during the pandemic. Based on their personality, motivations and life history, people either accepted the dire assessments of others, minimized them or downright ignored them. There were striking differences in this regard during the pandemic. Whereas some people isolated themselves thoroughly, given the same information others travelled carefree, attended social events and expected to be safe from infection.

The uncertainty malaise

Though some people remain unperturbed in uncertain situations that we might generally depict as dangerous, others feel anxious in uncertain situations that to most seem completely safe. For example, some people feel ill at ease in between projects, when they are uncertain about what they should be doing. They feel upset about an unanswered email or phone call. They constantly worry about their kids' whereabouts. In short, they are anxious about mundane uncertainties that to others may seem innocuous. Why do they dread uncertainty so much? It is likely that their malaise stems from a *conditioned anxiety*. Because in their past uncertainty was associated with negative outcomes, now any uncertain situation makes them anxious. In the same way that an animal (say, a dog) can be conditioned to certain cues in the environment (e.g. their owner putting on a coat) and anticipates what comes next (being taken for a walk), so we humans can also be conditioned to certain states, like uncertainty, and anticipate a positive or negative event in its wake. Anticipation of a negative event may occur if in the past uncertainty was consistently tied to adversity. A child who was scared of being abandoned by her parents or being abused by adults or felt anxious about violence that could strike unexpectedly (e.g. in times of war) might come to fear uncertainty. In subsequent uncertain situations she might quickly 'fill in the blanks' by imagining catastrophic scenarios.

So it is the negative thoughts conjured up in uncertain situations that create the anxiety. Realizing this can be significant and useful; it helps us understand who can deal with uncertainty constructively and who is devastated by it and why. Moreover, it suggests how we all can learn to cope with uncertainty, acquire the ability to face it calmly, explore its hidden potential and discover its silver lining.

Coping with uncertainty

Given that the dread of uncertainty stems from pessimistic thinking, a strategy for dealing with its adverse effects can be encapsulated in a succinct piece of advice to accentuate the positive and eliminate the negative thoughts that it evokes. Put simply, this means thinking good thoughts and refraining from fear or self-pity. Of course, this is easier said than done. Fortunately, psychology has come up with a number of trusted ways to banish defeatist thinking, covering the entire lifespan from the crib to the deathbed. In the chapters that follow I will unpack those insights, while exploring the many impacts of uncertainty on our lives and well-being.

In a nutshell

My long-standing fascination with the topic of uncertainty stems from my interest in closed-mindedness, a sense of overconfidence that leads people to disregard pertinent information and pertinent advice. In numerous studies my colleagues and I have carried out over the last forty years we have demonstrated repeatedly that closed-mindedness comes from the need for cognitive closure. That need motivates people to flee uncertainty and to latch on to whatever ideas, theories or conceptions promise certainty.

But from living through the pandemic experience, I realized that there is more to uncertainty than the will to escape it, and I discovered to my surprise that a lot of the research social psychologists have been carrying out over the past few decades has fundamentally been about our reactions to uncertainty. Like Molière's M. Jourdain in the 1670 play *The Bourgeois Gentleman*, who, famously, was 'speaking prose for . . . years without knowing it', psychology 'spoke' about uncertainty and its effects without explicitly acknowledging it. In this book I connect the dots and tie together the profound insights, intriguing findings and effective practices that

ESCAPING AND EMBRACING UNCERTAINTY

social psychology has come up with regarding the challenges and opportunities that uncertainty offers.

Uncertainty and you: how to use this book

The aim of this book is to help readers understand their reactions to uncertainty, their potential consequences and what can be done about them. As a first step, in Chapter 1, I invite the reader to measure their own attitude to certainty and uncertainty through our need-for-closure scale. I recommend that all readers undertake this assessment – it will help you develop a deeper self-understanding as you navigate the rest of the book.

Some readers will want to read the book from start to finish, but readers are also free to pick and choose chapters according to their interest in different aspects of uncertainty. To assist readers in making this choice, the book is divided into three parts: Part 1 ('Escaping Uncertainty'), comprising Chapters 1–6, lays out the *manifestations* and *causes* of people's reactions to uncertainty. Part 2 ('Closure's Consequences'), Chapters 7–9, deals with the *consequences* of those reactions for people's thinking, decision-making and social relations. Part 3 ('Embracing Uncertainty'), Chapters 10–14, offers various strategies for addressing uncertainty and offers practical suggestions for coping with uncertainty in different areas of life (parenting, adult relationships, career). However, in order to assess how you typically react to uncertain situations, let us begin by taking a look at the need-for-closure scale.

PART I

Escaping Uncertainty

1. Measuring Your Need for Closure

We are all different in the extent to which we crave certainty and need closure. Much of this book is about those differences, their causes and their consequences on our reactions to people and situations, and you may wonder where *you* fall on this psychological continuum. Do you find uncertainty unpleasant, or appealing? Do you try to be rid of it as quickly as possible, or do you enjoy it and relish the possibilities it might offer? In the chapters that follow you will find out *why* you might crave or avoid closure the way you do, and *how* this might impact your life, personal relations and political preferences. However, first let's find out a little more about the self-assessment exercise that will enable you to find out how you typically react to uncertainty and to determine the specific sources of your overall attitude towards closure.

In 1990, I defined the need for closure as the desire for 'a definite answer on a given topic, any answer . . . compared to confusion and ambiguity'.[1] And in 1994, my doctoral student (and now psychology professor) Donna Webster and I developed a questionnaire designed to measure this. The questionnaire consists of forty-one statements and the respondent is asked to agree or disagree with them and to what extent, from (1) strongly agree to (6) strongly disagree. For example, one of the statements is 'I think that having clear rules and order at work is essential for success,' and someone who strongly agrees with this statement (1) obviously likes and desires certainty. In contrast, someone who strongly disagrees with the statement (6) prefers to avoid closure and keep their options open.

Some of the statements are reversed (marked on the questionnaire with R), for example, 'I think it is fun to change my plans at the last moment.' Strong agreement with this statement (6) indicates a need to avoid closure rather than a need for closure. These statements are assessed through reverse scoring, so a 1 would be scored as a 6, a 2 as a 5, and so on. This means that the higher the total, the higher the need for closure.

Dimensions of needing closure

If you have a high need for closure, you probably like order and predictability in your life. You are probably decisive and communicate your ideas clearly, without too many hedges and qualifications. Also, once you make up your mind, you are unlikely to be dissuaded by contrary arguments, information and points of view. In fact, you are likely to be irritated by disagreements with your opinions and be somewhat impatient with people who see things differently.

It is possible to determine whether someone is generally high, low or intermediate in their need for closure by calculating their score on the need-for-closure questionnaire, but it is also interesting and informative to find out in what specific ways this need for cognitive closure manifests itself. In the original scale, Donna Webster and I[2] suggested that the need for closure can manifest itself in various attitudes and preferences: a preference for *order* and for *predictability*, *decisiveness*, discomfort with *ambiguity* and *closed-mindedness*. These all represent ways in which an overall desire for certainty affects what we like and how we think and behave.

16

For instance, *order*, which is a state in which everything (around the house or in the office) has a place and is in its place, avoids the uncertainty (of where things are) that chaos and disorder create. The statement 'I believe that orderliness and organization are among the most important characteristics of a good student' is one of several that measure the need for order. There are ten such statements in the scale. They are indicated by the letter a. Adding an individual's responses to these items yields an overall score on the need-for-order element of the total need for closure (with ten being the highest).

The statement 'I prefer to socialize with familiar friends because I know what to expect from them' is one of eight statements that measure the desire for *predictability* (indicated with the letter b). The tendency to be *decisive* (letter c) rather than hesitant is an important characteristic of someone who has a high need for closure. Examples among the six statements that tap into this element of the need for closure are: 'When I have made a decision, I feel relieved' and 'When I am confronted with a problem, I'm dying to reach a solution very quickly.' Discomfort with *ambiguity* (d) is measured by nine statements, among them 'I feel uncomfortable when I don't understand the reason why an event occurred in my life.' The final element of the need for closure is degree of *closed-mindedness* (e). Among the eight statements assessing this is 'I do not usually consult many different opinions before forming my own view.'

The full need-for-closure scale is given overleaf, but it is also possible to do a shorter version consisting of the fifteen items in bold. By summing up your responses to these statements you can still work out your need-for-closure score; however, the different elements within it will not be illuminated.

Long version of the NFCS scale (Webster and Kruglanski, 1994), improved by Roets and Van Hiel (2007)

INSTRUCTIONS: Read each of the following statements and decide to what extent you agree with each one according to your beliefs and experiences. Please use the following scale:

1 = Strongly disagree   4 = Slightly agree
2 = Moderately disagree   5 = Moderately agree
3 = Slightly disagree   6 = Strongly agree

1(a)	I think that having clear rules and order at work is essential for success.	1 2 3 4 5 6
2(e)	Even after I've made up my mind about something, I am always eager to consider a different opinion. R	1 2 3 4 5 6
3(d)	**I don't like situations that are uncertain.**	1 2 3 4 5 6
4(e)	**I dislike questions which could be answered in many different ways.**	1 2 3 4 5 6
5(b)	I like to have friends who are unpredictable. R	1 2 3 4 5 6
6(a)	**I find that a well-ordered life with regular hours suits my temperament.**	1 2 3 4 5 6
7(b)	When dining out, I like to go to places where I have been before so that I know what to expect.	1 2 3 4 5 6
8(d)	**I feel uncomfortable when I don't understand the reason why an event occurred in my life.**	1 2 3 4 5 6

9(e)	I feel irritated when one person disagrees with what everyone else in a group believes.	1 2 3 4 5 6
10(a)	I hate to change my plans at the last minute.	1 2 3 4 5 6
11(b)	I don't like to go into a situation without knowing what I can expect from it.	1 2 3 4 5 6
12(c)	When I have made a decision, I feel relieved.	1 2 3 4 5 6
13(c)	When I am confronted with a problem, I'm dying to reach a solution very quickly.	1 2 3 4 5 6
14(d)	When I am confused about an important issue, I feel very upset.	1 2 3 4 5 6
15(c)	I quickly become impatient and irritated if I cannot find a solution to a problem immediately.	1 2 3 4 5 6
16(c)	I would rather make a decision quickly than sleep on it.	1 2 3 4 5 6
17(c)	Even if I get a lot of time to make a decision, I still feel compelled to decide quickly.	1 2 3 4 5 6
18(b)	I think it is fun to change my plans at the last moment. R	1 2 3 4 5 6
19(b)	I enjoy the uncertainty of going into a new situation without knowing what might happen. R	1 2 3 4 5 6
20(a)	My personal space is usually messy and disorganized. R	1 2 3 4 5 6
21(d)	In most social conflicts, I can easily see which side is right and which is wrong.	1 2 3 4 5 6

22(c)	I almost always feel hurried to reach a decision, even when there is no reason to do so.	1 2 3 4 5 6
23(a)	I believe that orderliness and organization are among the most important characteristics of a good student.	1 2 3 4 5 6
24(e)	When considering most conflict situations, I can usually see how both sides could be right. R	1 2 3 4 5 6
25(b)	**I don't like to be with people who are capable of unexpected actions.**	1 2 3 4 5 6
26(b)	I prefer to socialize with familiar friends because I know what to expect from them.	1 2 3 4 5 6
27(a)	I think that I would learn best in a class that lacks clearly stated objectives and requirements. R	1 2 3 4 5 6
28(e)	When thinking about a problem, I consider as many different opinions on the issue as possible. R	1 2 3 4 5 6
29(d)	I like to know what people are thinking all the time.	1 2 3 4 5 6
30(d)	**I dislike it when a person's statement could mean many different things.**	1 2 3 4 5 6
31(d)	It's annoying to listen to someone who cannot seem to make up their mind.	1 2 3 4 5 6
32(a)	**I find that establishing a consistent routine enables me to enjoy life more.**	1 2 3 4 5 6
33(a)	**I enjoy having a clear and structured mode of life.**	1 2 3 4 5 6
34(e)	I prefer interacting with people whose opinions are very different from my own. R	1 2 3 4 5 6

35(a)	I like to have a place for everything and everything in its place.	1 2 3 4 5 6
36(d)	I feel uncomfortable when someone's meaning or intention is unclear to me.	1 2 3 4 5 6
37(e)	I always see many possible solutions to any problems I face. R	1 2 3 4 5 6
38(d)	I'd rather know bad news than stay in a state of uncertainty.	1 2 3 4 5 6
39(e)	**I do not usually consult many different opinions before forming my own view.**	1 2 3 4 5 6
40(b)	**I dislike unpredictable situations.**	1 2 3 4 5 6
41(a)	I dislike the routine aspects of my work/studies. R	1 2 3 4 5 6

Notes:

1) Items in bold make up the short version of the scale.
2) The letter next to the number of the item indicates the different elements in attitudes and preferences around the need for closure: a = order, b = predictability, c = decisiveness, d = ambiguity, e = closed-mindedness.

Computing your need for closure

To compute your need-for-closure score you simply add up the numbers (from 1 to 6) that you checked in response to each item. Remember to reverse out scores for statements marked with R.

If your score falls somewhere between 205 and 246, you

are high on the need for closure; if it falls between 41 and 82, you are low; and if it falls between 83 and 204, you are intermediate. In the same way, you can compute your score on each of the elements of the need for closure. For instance, if you checked mainly 5s and 6s on the preference-for-order subscale (a), your preference for order is high if it falls in the range 50–60; if you checked mainly 2s and 1s, your preference for order is low, with a score range 10–20; and if your preference-for-order score falls in the range 21–49, you are in the intermediate range on this element. You can calculate where you stand on all the elements of the need for closure in a similar way. The scores for preference for predictability can range between 8 and 48, those for decisiveness between 6 and 36, for discomfort with ambiguity between 9 and 54, and those for closed-mindedness between 8 and 48.

The benefits of self-knowledge

Why would you want to know where you stand on the need-for-closure scale? What use might such knowledge have? In a nutshell, it provides self-understanding that may guide your actions and reactions in lots of different situations. For instance, an awareness that you have a high need for closure may motivate you to be more ready to listen to someone else's point of view. Awareness that you are low on the need for closure and inclined to avoid closure may illuminate your reluctance to make commitments to ideas, people or institutions.

What I personally find most useful is the possibility of compensating for a high or low need for closure. Knowing that I possess a high need for closure allows me to detach myself somewhat from my overly 'definite' opinions and tone them down and take them less seriously than would otherwise be the case. It tempers my inclination to answer all emails immediately and helps me stop and think rather than decide on the spot about important matters. And it mitigates my tendency to dismiss out of hand other people's judgements, tastes and preferences that differ from mine.

Self-awareness of where we stand on the need for closure may inspire us to try to understand the reasons for our attitudes towards closure and certainty. And understanding those may help us to change our overall attitude towards closure if that attitude appears on inspection to be rooted in past problems and negative experiences in our personal or professional life. Socrates' famous statement 'To know thyself is the beginning of wisdom' is particularly relevant to this aspect of our personality.

I should emphasize that being high or low in the need for closure is neither all bad nor all good. Each tendency presents challenges but also has advantages. Though premature closure can result in costly mistakes, people with a high need for closure are committed to their friends, their faith, their family or their country. They inspire reciprocal commitment and devotion, which can be viewed as positive and having pro-social advantages. Likewise, although people with a low need for closure may appear indecisive and ambiguous, they are open to new ideas and the exploration of uncharted territories. Each psychological state involves trade-offs. Wisdom consists of knowing when a given inclination is detrimental and when it is beneficial. When does our aversion or attraction to uncertainty benefit us and when is it likely to do us harm?

If you pause and consider the people around you, at work

or outside of it, you might reflect on where colleagues, friends and family sit in their need for closure. Is that person in the contracts department frustrated when last-minute changes are requested? Perhaps it's their high need for closure that enables them to deal with the detail and punctuality of their job so efficiently. And that person in the design team who always arrives late for meetings yet can somehow generate creative ideas out of nowhere – perhaps their low need for closure leads both to these strengths and to these weaknesses. From a management perspective, it is worth considering how certain personality types may thrive in particular roles while others struggle. Likewise, in families and friendship groups, you may sometimes groan at a friend who likes things 'just so' and always wants to meet at the same place rather than try somewhere new, but they may also be the one who remembers to get the group together and organizes the outings that are so key to sustaining relationships.

Summary

Everyone sits somewhere on the need-for-closure scale. Some people desire closure intensely, while others prefer to avoid closure and instead relish ambiguity and not committing. When leaders of nations are high in their need for closure or low, the implications can be momentous and of historical import. President George W. Bush's decision to commit the US to the wars in Afghanistan or Iraq, for instance, could have stemmed from the deceptively simple closure-affording character of war as a solution to a problem – you either 'win' or 'lose'. President Clinton's unethical relations with Monica Lewinsky nearly cost him his presidency, and could have stemmed from his apparent need to avoid closure and not seeing such relations as clearly immoral and inappropriate.

We all are impacted in a major way by our inclination to avoid or approach uncertainty. Because our lives are full of judgements and decisions, our need for closure affects nearly everything we do. Self-knowledge could come in handy in situations where our desire for certainty and closure blinds us to crucial considerations and makes us disregard relevant arguments and information. It could also be helpful in identifying the situations in which hedging our decisions because of our aversion to certainty and commitment could be counter-productive. Lastly, being able to recognize others' tendencies and the specific elements within them in relation to closure can help us in our interactions with them, possibly enabling us to be more tolerant of their vulnerabilities as well as appreciative of their strengths.

Once you have determined your typical attitude to uncertainty and closure, it can help you understand how such an attitude might colour your reactions to people and events, and recognize its impact on your reactions and behaviours. These issues will be addressed and illustrated in the chapters that follow.

2. The Price of Premature Closure

Freezing on prior conceptions

Being disagreed with is tough, especially when you're convinced you're right. When the issue is important to you, it's even tougher. The experience is familiar. We become impatient and irritated. How could someone intelligent and of sound mind, we ask ourselves, hold a view that is so plainly incorrect? What's wrong with these people anyway?

When faced with disagreement we often become defensive, not just with others but also inwardly towards ourselves. Have you ever caught yourself, in an argument, trying to suppress an inner voice whispering to you that your antagonist might have a point? That they might be right and you wrong? Rather than listening and learning, we often become entrenched in our opinion, rationalize it in various ways and reject out of hand alternative views or perspectives. It doesn't help much if the alternative information is credible and relevant. Once our mind is made up, it is difficult to unmake it. This seeming irrationality, deep-rooted in our psychological make-up, has been responsible for calamitous mistakes of historic proportions.

The Yom Kippur surprise

On 6 October 1973, the eve of the Jewish Day of Atonement (Yom Kippur), Egypt and Syria launched a surprise attack on

Israel, starting the Yom Kippur War. The country's civilian and military leadership was caught off guard. It is said that Moshe Dayan, the tough Israeli minister of defence at the time, contemplated the 'Samson Option': the use of the nuclear weapons Israel was rumoured to hold, to fend off the catastrophe.

Anxiety was felt in almost every Israeli household. I was in my early thirties and living in Tel Aviv, working as a professor at the university there, and like those around me I was thoroughly dismayed and shocked by what transpired. Things were happening with lightning speed; I hardly had time to gather my thoughts – my Day of Atonement had ended before it had begun. The day after Yom Kippur, 8 October, I was on my way to the Sinai Peninsula. As a psychology officer in the reserves of the army, I had been summoned to assist the struggling Israeli troops.

Unlike other sneak attacks in recent history, for instance the German attack in 1941 against the Soviet Union (Operation Barbarossa) or the Japanese attack on Pearl Harbor in 1941, when the element of surprise was explained by a lack of adequate information or an elaborate deception, the Yom Kippur attack should not have come as a surprise at all. Israeli intelligence had received ample indication that an assault was coming. Detailed warnings about the coming attack had been given by Ashraf Marwan, known by the code name 'the Angel', an exceptional Israeli spy. Marwan was the son-in-law of the late Gamal Abdul Nasser, the former president of Egypt; he was also a trusted emissary of President Anwar Sadat, who initiated the attack. The information he provided was therefore exceedingly rare and invaluable; a gift from providence, you might say. Yet it was completely ignored. Why?

Two figures in Israel's military intelligence rejected the

warnings: the Director, General Eli Zeira, and Colonel Yona Bandman, who was responsible for Egypt and North Africa. Despite Marwan's warnings, they held on to a strategic assessment known as 'the conception', which stated that without a fighter force capable of attacking Israeli air bases, and without surface-to-surface missiles capable of reaching Israel proper, Egypt could not launch a major military strike. By the time they recognized their error, it was too late – Israel was under attack and a big question mark hovered over its very existence.

Greeks bearing gifts

One of the most well-known tales of all ages, recounted in Virgil's *Aeneid*, is the story of Troy and its tragic demise. Following Odysseus' cunning advice, the Greeks who had besieged the city for nine years built a large wooden horse and concealed warriors within it. It was presented to the Trojans as a parting gift, signalling the Greeks' intention to desist from the siege and sail home. King Priam, the ruler of Troy, for whom the horse symbolized great victory, wanted to bring it into the city and to Athena's temple. Others dissented; they recommended burning the statue or opening it up with axes to divulge its contents. Surely it was worth seeing what was inside?

There were ample omens that the Greeks were up to no good, and even voices that had divined their specific plan. Laocoön, a priest of the Temple of Apollo, cried in vain that the Greeks might be hiding inside. Clangs of armour sounded from within the structure, and human moans emanated when it was hit by a spear. Yet Priam remained closed-minded and fixated: things were as they seemed. What happened next was a horrendous tragedy for the Trojans. Their city was burned to the ground, its warriors were slaughtered and its women raped and turned into slaves for the Greeks.

Storming the US Capitol

Fast-forward to 6 January 2021. On that day, a riotous mob stormed the United States Capitol in Washington, DC, in an attempt to overturn Donald Trump's defeat in the 2020 presidential election. For several hours, the rioters occupied and vandalized the Capitol building, from which lawmakers and staff had been hurriedly evacuated. Over 140 police officers were wounded and five people lost their lives in the tumultuous confrontations that defined it.

Shockingly, the US Capitol Police had specific intelligence at least two weeks prior to 6 January that supporters of President Trump were planning an armed assault on the Capitol. Despite the attack being planned 'in plain sight' online, security assessments by the intelligence arm of the Capitol Police continued to view the threat of violence as 'remote' and 'improbable'. Because an event of this kind was so unprecedented, security officials seized on the idea that it wouldn't happen and became impervious to information that it would, freezing on this as the hoped-for closure. The price of their mistake was enormous. The storming of the Capitol shook America to its foundations and exposed the fragility of its democracy to the world at large.

Shooters' error

The psychology of freezing because of prior conceptions applies to everyday prejudices and discriminations that are based on stereotypes, something that occasionally results in tragic mistakes. On 4 February 1999, an unarmed West African immigrant, Amadou Diallo, a student of computer science at Bronx Community College, died at the hands of four New York City police officers. They fired forty-one shots at him as he stood in the doorway of his Bronx apartment building. How could trained police officers make such a terrible mistake – or were they callous racists?

An alternative possibility was their psychological need to escape the dangerous uncertainty that the situation evoked and the anxiety-fraught questions it raised. What business might a Black man have out and about at almost one o'clock in the morning? The first stereotypic idea that may have popped into the officers' heads was that he was up to no good, and probably armed and dangerous at that. If so, time was of the essence, and a quick judgement had to be made. Accordingly, the police officers interpreted an innocent movement as reaching for a weapon. One officer may have then opened fire. The rest may have followed suit because the shooting validated their own suspicions.

In the same way that Zeira and Bandman and the Capitol Police seized and froze on their conceptions and Priam on his, the New York cops seized and froze on the initial stereotype that came to mind. They reached an unfortunate judgement and acted upon it. And an innocent man died as a consequence.

Idealization

Freezing on conceptions isn't limited to violent events; it under-lies errors whose consequences can be benign, even pleasant. An interesting example of freezing on overly positive concep-tions while ignoring or suppressing information that contradicts our views, an 'inconvenient truth', as it were, is *idealization*. Social psychologists Thibaut and Kelley in their classic book *The Social Psychology of Groups* (1959) discuss the over-idealization of deceased husbands by their widows. In an earlier study, Dickinson and Beam[1] describe how widows tend to recall their marriage to their deceased spouse as 'sexually golden'.

Thibaut and Kelley discuss in these terms the 'Rebecca Myth', named after Daphne du Maurier's novel about a departed wife of that name whose idealized memory casts a long shadow over the husband's marriage to a new, and in herself remarkable, spouse. The 'Rebecca Myth' can be found at play in any organi-zational context, for instance when employees show resistance to new managers because of their idealization of their prede-cessors, or vice versa. Idealization, or freezing on unrealistically positive aspects of a person, also underlies infatuation, having a crush and falling in love. We become convinced of the wonder-ful qualities of the object of our attraction while ignoring or suppressing any information to the contrary. We are 'blind' to what other people see as obvious; our heightened need for clos-ure makes us freeze on a distorted view of our beloved, and often we end up paying a heavy price for our misconception.

It is not only people that we can idealize; we idealize ex-periences as well. A trip to Paris that has been marred by a combination of rainy weather, a sore throat and long hours of waiting in line in front of the Louvre may be remembered as romantic and wonderful, fitting in with the general schema of the 'Paris trip' with which the negative aspects of the visit are inconsistent.

Idealization of people and experiences, and acting on stereotypes and prior conceptions, cover a wide variety of things that at first blush seem diverse and unrelated. Yet on deeper consideration they reveal the same psychological dynamic: freezing on a conception and ignoring relevant information, leading to an erroneous judgement. This is how science works. It peers beyond the surface of things and aims at their essential core; it formulates common rules that apply to disparate entities and events. No two drops of water are exactly uniform, yet they all conform to the H_2O chemical structure. The 1,000-lb gorilla and a feather couldn't seem more different, yet both observe the laws of gravity. This is the case with diverse examples of reaching a false certainty by freezing on available conceptions and forming biased memories and judgements as a consequence.

But what causes this? What causes people to fall prey to a cognitive fixation that can produce disastrous consequences? What goes wrong with our information-processing system that allows it to happen? How does it fit with the presumed rationality of humans?

The confidence paradox: ignorance-based assurance

As I mentioned in the introduction, my interest in the psychological study of certainty and uncertainty goes back to the 1980s. Like many psychologists at the time, I excitedly embraced what became known as the cognitive revolution. Its guiding assumption was that humans are rational calculating machines, just like computers. The brain was assumed to process information on the basis of logical algorithms. This 'cool' new approach promised to explain all human behaviour with information and logic. It ushered in a heady optimism about people's rationality. A new age of reason seemed to be dawning.

Guided by this perspective, I designed experiments to examine the ways in which people's confidence depends on their knowledge. For, in the rational world assumed by cognitive science, the more knowledge people have, the more confidence they should have; and the less knowledge they have, the less confidence. Presumably, if they were aware that they lacked knowledge, they would appropriately downshift their level of confidence, right?

I couldn't have been more wrong. Precisely the opposite turned out to be the case. My experiments created conditions that limited participants' ability to process information when presented with a task, for instance forming an impression of a person from brief biographical information. Such experimental restriction made it difficult for participants to learn, contemplate and think. I did this by imposing strict deadlines on the completion of the task, creating time pressure; by having the participants perform the task against a background of loud noise generated by a rickety computer printer; and by making them fatigued from having had to perform a difficult assignment beforehand. These difficulties, I reasoned, would cause people to be less able to process any information they received, and so they would be less assured with regard to the task at hand. Yet time and time again they were *more confident*, not less. Their level of confidence was higher the less knowledge they had. That cannot be true, I thought to myself. Surely I am missing something.

Yet, these results weren't a fluke or a statistical anomaly.

They turned up consistently in study after careful study. I struggled with the puzzle for months on end, utterly confused. My rescue came unexpectedly and from a direction I had not anticipated.

When is 'enough' enough?

As my teaching schedule at the time included a course on how science works, I immersed myself in the philosophy of science as part of my preparation. In those days, this topic generated great excitement in the academic community, stimulated by the seminal contributions of trail-blazing thinkers: Karl Popper, Thomas Kuhn and Imre Lakatos, among others. These scholars focused on a simple question: How can scientists be confident that their hypotheses are *true*? How do they confirm or refute their hypotheses? Strictly speaking, it is not possible to be sure of even the simplest proposition; all our scientific theories could potentially be wrong, even those that have been previously tested by myriad studies. There is no guarantee that the next time they are tested they will again be supported by observation. As the great philosopher of science Karl Popper stated, all human knowledge is pretty much guesswork, or conjecture, which so far has worked for us.

In a very real sense, 'The future's not ours to see,' just as the song has it.

Yet people, scientists included, do form confident beliefs that most of us accept as given. So how do scientists do it? How do they know when to stop the information search and call the hypothesis true or false? How many swans should we inspect before concluding they are all white (or not)? There

34

had to be a 'stopping mechanism' that brings the inquiry to a halt and makes us feel that we know what is what, I thought. I searched high and low for such a mechanism in all the philosophy of science writing I could find. Alas, to no avail.

The answer lies *outside* the realm of scientific rationality, in the court of psychology, whether rational or not. And it is simpler than anyone might have imagined.

The exploration stopper

The revelation – my 'aha' moment, as it were – was that people stop exploring and data gathering when they *feel* they have enough information. But where does this feeling come from? And the simple answer is that it comes from the *desire* to have certainty and to stop exploring. For human beings, the stopping mechanism is psychological. Nature (through human evolution) has equipped us with this as a way of conserving mental resources and ensuring timely actions. At some point our minds find closure and adopt an assured belief. This frees us from deliberating interminably and obsessing without end. Once we have formed a judgement, we can move on to what comes next.

The importance of having closure

The need for cognitive closure serves an indispensable function. It is an essential psychological mechanism without which life as we know it would be impossible. Living entails making endless decisions requiring a degree of certainty. When we cross a busy street, we want to be sure that the road is clear;

when we buy groceries, that they are fresh; when we send our kids to school, that they will be safe; and when we heed our doctor's advice, that she is knowledgeable and trustworthy. If we are wrong on any of these counts, we will pay a high price for our mistakes. Yet without certainty, we would be in limbo. Not knowing what to do, we might suffer 'analysis paralysis' – all thought, no action. Potentially, the information-gathering phase before making a decision could be endless. No objective sign can tell us when we have gathered enough evidence to be sure we have made a correct decision. Yet if we never make up our minds, events will surely overtake us. The world will not wait until we are ready. If we don't decide, unfolding events will decide for us.

It would be nice if things were different. If we received a sign, say from a satellite, a mega computer, or a drone, about how much information we need to be sure we have made an accurate judgement. Unfortunately, this is an impossible pipe dream – to err is human, after all – but the news is not all bad. Even though we cannot peer into the future, nature has endowed us with the next best thing: a *subjective* mechanism that 'whispers in our ear' that 'enough (information) is enough'. The need for cognitive closure is such a mechanism. It stops our search for information and instils a degree of certainty that enables decision and action.

In confronting mortal hazards on a daily basis, facing scary predators bigger and stronger than themselves, our hominoid ancestors often needed to make rapid fight-or-flight decisions when assured, unwavering judgements were essential, so evolution favoured individuals whose desire for certainty was sufficiently strong that they could swiftly decide to avoid such dangers. As a result, they survived and propagated. Of course, evolution allows for considerable variety among members of our species. Some populations may have found themselves in environments fraught with peril and such environments may have lent a selective advantage to people capable of quick decisions. In less challenging conditions, people may have evolved very differently; their selective advantage may have come from physical attractiveness, strength or artistic creativity. Their descendants may therefore have been less desirous of certainty and closure.

Pavlov's dogs

The need for closure and certainty isn't unique to humans. As with many other behaviours, it exists in some shape or form in other animals as well. Ivan Pavlov's seminal and widely known (though from a contemporary perspective ethically questionable) work on experimental neurosis in dogs demonstrates it strikingly.

The discovery of this phenomenon was quite accidental. One of Pavlov's assistants noticed something curious. When she administered an electric shock to a dog at one location on its skin and then moved it to another, the animal broke down and became immensely emotional. Another assistant noticed a related phenomenon. When a dog was conditioned to expect food when presented with a circle and no food when presented with an ellipse (a figure difficult to distinguish from a circle), it also had an emotional outburst. Yet another assistant noticed that when there was a long period of time between a bell ringing and the food being offered to the dog, creating a state of uncertain anticipation, the dog exhibited the same emotional behaviours.

These studies, and others conducted with different animals such as pigs, sheep, rats and goats, show that uncertainty and confusion can be highly unpleasant to animals, especially when associated with a possible negative event (like an electric shock) or the possible elimination of a positive event (like food). So, in an important sense, animals also manifest the need for closure. Whereas humans often flee unpleasant, danger-fraught uncertainties by freezing on prior conceptions, animals display their anxiety in confusing, aversive (that is, to them unpleasant) situations through their behaviour, by squealing, violently shaking and showing a visible readiness and motivation to escape them. In both animals and humans, certainty is required in order to know what to do or where to go to get what we want (food, for instance). And when the stakes are high and inaction isn't an option, uncertainty can be truly unnerving.

The quest for certainty

The experiments I mentioned earlier in which we introduced time pressure, noise and fatigue showed that a need for closure can arise when processing information becomes difficult and therefore effortful and unpleasant. In such situations, we strive to form a cognitive closure that gives us confidence and allows us to escape the drudgery. This produces the paradoxical result that time-pressured, distracted or fatigued people who process *less* information are more confident or self-assured. They strongly desire to be certain, so they convince themselves that they are.

The same thing can happen under the influence of alcohol,[2] in that it induces a kind of 'alcohol myopia'.[3] Because careful processing of information becomes difficult and unpleasant when our thinking is impaired by alcohol, we process less information and become cocksure of our opinions rather quickly. This makes a lot of sense, doesn't it? When thinking requires more effort than we are willing to expend, we would rather avoid thinking. And we do so by convincing ourselves, unconsciously, that thinking is no longer necessary, that is, by escaping into a feeling of certainty and cognitive closure.

Avoiding extensive deliberation and seeking closure when our mental capacities are taxed through the influence of alcohol, fatigue or excessive heat, or are 'squeezed' by time pressure, often leads people to act impulsively, with dire consequences. I deal with some of those more extensively later, but here are a couple of examples. The World Health Organization estimates that roughly 55 per cent of domestic abuse perpetrators were drinking alcohol prior to carrying out an assault, and a recent study found that, on average, overall crime increases by 2.2 per cent and violent crime by 5.7 per cent on hotter days with maximum daily temperatures above 85°F (29.4°C).*[4] Given the warming of the planet,

* World Health Organization (2005). Alcohol and interpersonal violence: policy briefing. https://www.euro.who.int/__data/assets/pdf_file/0004/98806/E87347.pdf

39

these findings and ample other research showing that violent behaviour increases with heat issue a stern warning about what might lie ahead and highlight the importance of understanding the psychology of uncertainty and people's tendency to escape it through impulsive actions.

Is such closure-seeking behaviour irrational? To answer this, consider that rationality has been defined as choosing a means that serves a goal, that is, it advances the objective you desire to accomplish. Striving for certainty when certainty is what you desire (because uncertainty is unpleasant) is quite rational. Calling it irrational assumes that you desire something other than certainty, say to avoid a mistake, which might be more effectively achieved by collecting further information and postponing closure. Yet sometimes we crave certainty more than we worry about mistakes. And because there is no way of truly knowing how much information to gather, all we have to fall back on is our need for cognitive closure, the voice in our head that tells us 'Enough.'

Most of the time, this inbuilt desire for closure and certainty serves us well. We safely cross busy streets, pass our exams and graduate from school. We carry out our work with relative competence; occasionally, too, the process of reaching closure leads scholars to formulate useful scientific theories, promoting human progress. But sometimes this need for certainty and closure also trips us up. It might push us to make a hasty decision and lead us to commit regrettable mistakes. Wisdom lies in knowing ourselves and the conditions which push us prematurely towards closure. But what conditions make certainty so appealing in the first place?

Thinking back to the studies and examples I described earlier, all these conditions relate to the negative consequences of uncertainty. In the experiments that I carried out, the time pressure under which the participants were put meant they were running the risk of missing a deadline and failing the task. Processing information in a noisy environment was difficult and unpleasant and this motivated people to end the experience as soon as possible. The same happens when we are too tired to think straight or become cognitively lazy under the influence of alcohol. A more profound reason for craving certainty is when our existence or our safety is uncertain. A case in point is a pandemic where terrible illness and death are thought to be likely. In short, wanting certainty is part of human nature, but craving certainty and closure arises when there are perceived negative consequences of uncertainty.

The fragility of assurance

William James, sometimes referred to as the 'father' of scientific psychology, speculated that at birth human infants experience a 'buzzing confusion', a chaos without rhyme or reason – uncertainty incarnate.[5] This fog gradually lifts as the child is socialized into their family and community. They acquire knowledge that lends meaning to things and gives them coherence. They assign names to objects and to the relations between events. They identify causes and consequences of actions that guide their behaviour. But the knowledge that buffers children and adults from chaos is itself limited and tentative; uncertainty is but a heartbeat away. As Professor Donald Campbell, a renowned psychologist, lamented, 'Cousin to the amoeba, how can we know for certain?'[6] Even science cannot deliver certainty. Whether we like it or not, our certainty is ephemeral and our knowledge – all our knowledge – is potentially subject to revision.

Uncertainty, large and small

If uncertainty is the rule, and if we are supposed to 'fear the unknown', we should be fearful and crave cognitive closure all the time. Obviously, we do not. Not all uncertainties are born equal. Some are about major issues, matters of life and death: Will the enemy attack? Will the epidemic spread? Will a recession strike? A fundamental uncertainty that affects everyone is 'existential dread', an incomprehension of mortality, an inability to imagine what happens after death. Many everyday uncertainties, however, are mundane and trivial, 'small stuff' that we should not 'sweat' over: Why didn't we get a response to that email? Did we remember to lock the door? Will it rain tomorrow? Is the boss in a foul mood? For most people, excluding those diagnosed with obsessive-compulsive disorder (OCD), these minute uncertainties may bother us, make us antsy momentarily, but they rarely become a major, persistent worry.

Naturally, we react more strongly to uncertainties that matter more. In most cases, we would react more strongly to uncertainty about a medical diagnosis than to uncertainty about the following day's weather. It's more interesting to ask, however, *how* we react: what do we feel, think and do when an uncertainty that matters greatly sets in? When an uncertainty has potentially devastating consequences it is natural to want to end it, to escape the dread. For millions of people around the planet, the COVID-19 pandemic raised monumental questions about (possibly mortal) danger to their health, the potentially crushing impact on their economic security and their ability to see their loved ones. Under conditions like this, people's need for certainty and closure rises. Intriguingly, not everyone reacts in the same way. Whereas some people virtually fall apart, others find the strength to carry on. Nothing exemplifies this better than Viktor Frankl's story of hardship and horror in a Nazi concentration camp during the Second World War.

Finding meaning in adversity

Viktor Frankl, an Austrian psychiatrist and a Jew, spent three years in Nazi concentration camps, among them Auschwitz, the infamous death camp, where 1.1 million people lost their lives. His life circumstances and those of his fellow inmates were horrific beyond imagination. The likelihood of survival was slim in the extreme. The slightest frailty, illness or

outward malaise meant you were destined for the death chamber. Inmates were starved, deprived of basic hygiene facilities and regularly subjected to wanton punishment. Yet even in these terrible circumstances, where the most dreaded outcomes imaginable were a near certainty, some indomitable people, like Frankl, managed to keep their humanity and hope alive. That was their great achievement: not letting the horrific situation break their spirit. As Frankl put it, no matter the circumstances, humans

> have a choice of action . . . Every day, every hour, offered the opportunity to make a decision, a decision which determined whether you would or would not submit to those powers which threatened to rob you of your very self, your inner freedom, which determined whether or not you would

44

become the plaything of circumstance, renouncing freedom and dignity to become molded into the form of the
typical inmate.[7]

Frankl managed to translate his experiences in concentration
camps, under existential uncertainty of major proportions,
into psychological insights of great value. He went on to lead
a highly productive life and helped many with his particular
form of psychotherapy.

Only a tiny fraction of inmates, however, were capable of
the kind of hope that Frankl managed to keep alive. For
most, the harrowing uncertainty activated a strong need for
closure. Some decided that survival necessitated inhumanity
to other inmates. Others became convinced that a humiliating death was their destiny. As Frankl recounts, many inmates
lost their capacity for empathy and their appreciation of
beauty and virtue. Many simply gave up and became depressed,
while some, certain of their fate yet eager not to prolong the
horror and uncertainty, committed suicide. Frankl survived
because he didn't yield to such negative closure. He believed
that devastation is not inevitable and preordained. He was
proven right.

When painful uncertainty strikes, people often escape it
by forming cognitive closure in order to end their agonizing
rumination. So what, then, enables some people, like Victor
Frankl, to smile in the face of adversity, to face down the terrifying unknown and find meaning and hope when others
see only tragedy and misfortune? Psychology provides
important answers to this question and I will explore its
secrets and lessons later in the book. But Frankl's amazing
ability to keep hope alive proves that not everyone responds
to troubling uncertainty with a flight towards closure. People

have different personalities and different capabilities. I will look at those differences and their sources in Chapter 3.

Summary

The standard human response to troublesome uncertainty is to seek cognitive closure. This may cause us to seize and freeze on prior conceptions, which can result in undesirable or even tragic mistakes. Yet our capacity to crave closure allows us simultaneously to make decisions and initiate actions; it is therefore responsible for much that is good and much that is problematic within our nature and behaviour. This mechanism is often activated by the unpleasant feeling that uncertainty can generate. The more unpleasant that feeling, the stronger our desire to escape it and reach certainty or closure. Not all people yield equally to this urge. Even under the most harrowing of circumstances, some of us are able to resist the siren call, the pull towards the certainty that all is lost. People differ widely in their attitudes towards uncertainty, yet we all require at least some certainty to navigate the innumerable decisions and choices that we perennially encounter. The need for closure is a mechanism that makes this possible.

In your experience

1. Can you recall a time when you confronted an uncertain situation that meant a lot to you?
2. Try to remember how you felt. What were you thinking? What did you wish for? How did you act?

3. Do you form impressions quickly? Do you ever change your mind about judgements you have made?

4. Now that you know some facts about the need for closure, would you react differently to that uncertainty? If so, how?

3. Who Needs Certainty?

It is often said that psychologists tend to study problems that they themselves have difficulty with. This generalization rings true in my own case, as I consider myself high on the need for closure. I exhibit all the characteristics and inclinations of someone who is uncomfortable with uncertain situations. I feel uneasy between projects when it isn't quite clear to me what I should be doing. I am quick to decide on what I would like to eat in a restaurant. I answer emails promptly and imagine the worst when I do not hear back quickly. I value punctuality and am myself punctual to a fault. One time I set up a lunch appointment with a colleague at a restaurant, arrived ten minutes early, waited five minutes and left, assuming my friend wasn't going to make it. She did, minutes later, and was surprised to find I was no longer there . . .

That said, I don't allow my closure-needing disposition to govern my life and drive all my decisions. When push comes to shove and important matters are at stake, I force myself to live with uncertainty and avoid 'freezing' on preconceived notions. As a psychologist who studies closure, I know better, and I am able to compensate for my aversion to uncertainty when it really counts. Yet if I am caught unawares, my impulse is to opt for closure, with all that this entails. When that happens, I certainly pay the price and suffer the consequences.

A couple of silly mistakes my family loves to tease me about say it all. The first happened on a winter afternoon when I went grocery shopping at a local shop. After I had wheeled my trolley into the car park an attendant offered to load the groceries I had just purchased into the boot of my car. So I got into the car, opened the boot and . . . immediately drove off with the boot wide open and completely empty! Sheepishly, I drove back to the store, where the stunned attendant wryly remarked, 'You really were in a hurry . . .' But I knew better: it was my high need for closure that had kicked in and led me to prematurely decide it was time to take off.

Another time, having relocated to work at my current university, I rented an unfurnished apartment and proceeded to assemble some IKEA furniture to make the place liveable. I started on a dining table and diligently worked on it the entire evening, following the instructions that came with it. Around midnight, the table was finally ready and I inspected it with pride. It surprised me, I must admit, that IKEA had provided more screws than were needed, but I quickly learned why when, under the weight of a couple of books, the construction collapsed. My need for (premature) closure had struck again.

People differ widely in their responses to uncertain situations. Some, like myself, find uncertainty upsetting and ambiguity unpleasant. Others enjoy uncertainty and find too much certainty constraining and boring. What kind of person are you? How did you get to be that way? Can you change? Would you like to? How might you do it? This and the following chapters offer evidence-based answers to these questions.

Genetics

Do you see yourself as aggressive, ambitious, liberal, conservative? Chances are that however you answered, this stems, at least in part, from your genetic inheritance. The need for cognitive closure is no exception. Research by Bobby Cheon and his colleagues at Nanyang Technological University in Singapore[1] has shown that people with a specific genetic make-up – possession of the 5-HTTLPR gene – have a higher need for closure, as measured by the scale given in Chapter 1, than those without it.* They are more upset by uncertain, ambiguous and unfamiliar situations and are more sensitive to signals of threat from an out-group.[2]

In Chapter 8, I'll elaborate on how the need for cognitive closure induces a positive orientation to our in-group, something my colleagues and I have called 'group centrism', which fosters animosity towards out-groups. Out-groups represent *otherness*; they confront us with different values, different standards, different norms of behaviour. They imply that our worldviews, attitudes and moralities aren't the absolute truths we may want them to be. To someone with a high need for closure, otherness can be confusing, if not downright threatening. Such a person may want to avoid it, escape it or reject it.

The intriguing genetic differences involving the 5-HTTLPR gene and its role in reactions to out-groups are consistent with differences in the need for closure and intolerance of uncertainty, and attest to at least one element of our orientation towards the unknown being 'hard-wired'. This is not the same as saying that we are bound by our genes; as human beings, we have the capacity to learn, adapt and develop beyond our genetically based proclivities – yet an initial understanding of how our genes may underlie our

---

* People who have a short allele (versus long allele) of the serotonin transporter gene (5-HTTLPR) are more upset by uncertain, ambiguous and unfamiliar situations. Other studies have shown that a different genetic make-up, including two Met alleles (versus two Val alleles) of catechol-O-methyltransferase (COMT) polymorphism is associated with lower cognitive flexibility.

attitudes, not just towards other people but to uncertainty more broadly, is a critical starting point.

Brain activation

Echoing genetic research, there is evidence of differences in brain function between people with a high or low need for cognitive closure. Research by Małgorzata Kossowska and her team at the Jagiellonian University in Kraków revealed that those with a high need for cognitive closure show greater activity in what is known as the N1 component of event-related potentials (ERPs),* which is linked to their ability to focus ('freeze', if you will) on a task and disregard extraneous information.[3] Put more simply, the special ability of high-need-for-closure people to focus and avoid distractions can be seen as an advantage. However, there is a downside – a reduction in cognitive flexibility due to excessive focusing, and 'freezing', on a given idea or perception and ignoring others. Research by Martha Viola and colleagues attests to this phenomenon and shows that reduced flexibility is mediated by decreased electrical connectivity between certain brain regions (the anterior cingulate cortex and the dorsolateral prefrontal cortex).[4] This decreased connectivity means that the brain regions do not communicate with each other. Consequently, the person is pretty much 'stuck' or 'frozen' on an idea, and unable to consider any alternatives. Combined, these studies show that our personal craving for closure and an aversion to uncertainty are in part determined by our natural brain mechanisms, which are shaped by our genetic make-up.

* Electric activity in the brain evoked by external events.

A tale of two presidents

Because of their genetic make-up, their attachment history and their culture, people differ widely in their reactions to uncertainty. Some of us are decisive and forthright; we dislike ambiguous situations and shun 'if's, 'but's and other nuances. Some of us are the opposite: we are comfortable with uncertainty, excited by the possibilities it offers and are in no hurry to dispel it. Such people take their time making up their mind and are prone to reversing their decisions. They readily 'flip-flop' in their views and don't mind appearing indecisive. But how do these different types of people actually behave? What do they do? How do they think?

Two recent consecutive US presidents, more than other eminent figures who come to mind, strikingly illustrate the contrasting open- and closed-minded styles: Bill Clinton and George W. Bush. Largely because of their divergent attitudes to uncertainty, the two seem virtual opposites of each other, so much so that David Frum in his biography of Bush (*The Right Man*) referred to him as 'un-Clinton'!

Clinton

Clinton is known for being open-minded to a fault. Hesitant and reluctant to commit to firm positions on issues, he has been unusually receptive to novel and esoteric (New Age) philosophies and unconventional perspectives. In an article for the *Washington Post* entitled 'At a difficult time, First Lady reaches out, looks within', Bob Woodward described how President Clinton and his wife, Hillary, had invited a group of popular self-help writers to Camp David to help them dissect what had happened in the first two years of the presidency and to search for a way back after the Democrats' devastating loss to the Republicans in the 1994 elections to the US Congress.[5] They met the weekend beginning Friday, 30 December 1994. Prominent among the invitees was Jean Houston, co-director of the Foundation for Mind Research, which is devoted to the exploration of psychic experiences as well as altered and expanded consciousness. Houston was apparently a believer in spirits, both mythical and historical, and held that her personal archetypal predecessor was Athena, the Greek goddess of wisdom, with whom she conducted extensive dialogues. The president's interest in her esoteric opinions attests to his open-minded attitude and his lack of concern for convention.

Commentators on Bill Clinton's political career marvelled at his chameleon-like ability to make himself over in the way most likely to appeal to voters. Columnist Nat Hentoff remarked, 'There is no Bill Clinton . . . he has no principles that he will stick to when the going gets rough. His great passion is to be popular.'[6] For example, on the issue of US involvement in the Gulf War, Clinton stated, 'I guess I would have voted with the majority if it was a close vote. But I agree with the arguments the minority made.' A glaring attempt to have your cake and eat it! Clinton manoeuvred in order to avoid alienating others and creating potential enemies.

However, Clinton's open-mindedness had genuine benefits. It afforded him the ability to empathize with others, to see their pain and appreciate their points of view. These made him a skilful mediator and an outstanding communicator and persuader. It enabled him to comfortably listen to opposing points of view and to implement new ideas with ease and charm. So, whereas critics faulted Clinton on his indecision and lack of principle, his open-minded personality ultimately contributed to his successes, although it also opened the door to his failings.

Bush

'Open-minded' is hardly how most people would describe George W. Bush. The differences between him and Clinton span diverse domains. One of these concerned promptness. Where Clinton was notoriously unpunctual, Bush was impeccably punctual. Their outward appearance and demeanour, too, differed drastically. Clinton had no qualms about holding forth in the Oval Office while in sportswear. Bush would never be seen at work without a jacket and tie, even on weekends. Where Clinton was often characterized as an atheist, Bush was devoutly religious. Where Clinton was informal with his staff, Bush was highly formal. Clinton was all about shades of grey; Bush was all about black and white. His speeches betrayed a fundamentally dichotomous belief system. He often lectured about good and evil, right and wrong, morality and sin, cleanliness and mess. He dichotomized people as either friends or foes and famously warned international leaders that those who weren't 'with us' would be seen as 'against us'.

Clinton surrounded himself with leading intellectuals with complex styles of thinking and nuanced perceptions. According to David Frum, 'conspicuous intelligence seemed actively unwelcome in Bush's White House'.[7] Instead, he preferred plain-speaking folk whose opinions were simple and clearcut, leaving little room for qualification.

The decision-making styles of the two presidents differed vastly as well. Clinton agonized over his decisions and often reversed them; Bush made his swiftly and unhesitatingly. Asked by an elementary-school student whether he found decision-making difficult, Bush's reply was telling: 'Not really. If you know what you believe, decisions come pretty easy. I know who I am. I know what I believe in, and I know where I want to lead the country . . . I've never been one to try to please everybody all the time. I just do what I think is right . . .'[8]

The differences between Bush's and Clinton's personalities had a deep impact on their relationships with others.

Bush inspired intense loyalty among his staff, despite the low levels of public approval for his leadership in the last years of his presidency. Observers of the early days of his administration commented on the remarkable cohesiveness of his staff, the almost complete absence of leaks and how smoothly the White House message machine ran.[9] In contrast, Clinton's relations with his staff were complicated. Joe Klein, in his 2002 biography (*The Natural*) remarks that Clinton's staffers' reactions to the president were a mixture of awe and disappointment. On the one hand, there were his admirable intellect, his thorough familiarity with policy issues at a level of detail that people found amazing, his encyclopaedic knowledge and a native charm that few could resist. On the other hand, Klein comments on his 'harshness' and 'brute insensitivity', suggesting that he lacked personal commitment to others on his team.[10]

It is interesting to compare Clinton and Bush because they are polar opposites when it comes to need for closure. Other recent US presidents occupy intermediate positions on the need-for-closure continuum. President Trump, for instance, was relatively open-minded; he was not beholden to any particular political ideology. At the same time, he strongly favoured views that served his personal interests (staying in power, growing his financial profits), though it was unclear whether he actually subscribed to those views or merely used them as a tool to persuade others. President Biden is more a pragmatist than an ideologue, and in that sense he too is open-minded to any solutions that promise to work, yet at the same time he is a man of principle who sticks to his guns when push comes to shove. So was President Obama, who nonetheless advanced innovative notions such as 'leading from behind', or having a 'reset' with Russia and the Muslim world, moves that were sometimes described as 'naive'.[11]

Growing up with a secure base

Although our genes and the brain processes influenced by them play a crucial role in our attitude towards uncertainty, our personal reactions to stimuli and events are also strongly affected by the social environments in which we find ourselves, both past and present. Nature combines with nurture to determine who we are. As a case in point, our response to uncertainty reflects to a considerable extent the circumstances in which we grew up. Critical in this regard is having reliable and loving support from our parents or other caregivers. Intriguingly, the dependence on nurture and love for the development of self-assurance isn't unique to humans. The discovery of this phenomenon in primates is a fascinating scientific story in itself.

Harlow's monkeys

In the 1950s, Harry Harlow, an experimental psychologist at the University of Wisconsin, carried out landmark experiments with infant rhesus monkeys. His work changed how scientists view the development of self-assurance. Harlow's studies were striking in their ingenuity. He placed eight newborn monkeys in separate cages, each with two doll-like figures that Harlow called 'surrogate mothers'. One was formed of a wire cylinder topped with a wooden head on which a semblance of a face was drawn. The other was similar, but the wire was covered with soft terry cloth. Both 'mothers' functioned as feeding devices via a nursing bottle with a nipple placed in the vicinity of where a mother's breast would be. Four of the monkeys were randomly selected to receive milk from the terry-cloth mother and the remaining four from the one made of bare wire.

The results of the study were astonishing. First, there were no differences in the *biological* development of monkeys whether they were fed from the wire or the terry-cloth mother. They imbibed roughly the same quantity of milk and gained weight at about the same rate, regardless of whether the feeding bottle was placed on the terry-cloth or the wire mother. The psychological impact, however, was strikingly different. Regardless of which figure was the one that was feeding them, the little monkeys spent significantly more time with the terry-cloth mother. They climbed on and clung to her often, whereas they spent hardly any time with the wire mother other than at feeding time. Moreover, when a stressful new stimulus was put into their cage, the monkeys predominantly turned for comfort to the terry-cloth mother.

To examine this, the experimenter introduced into the cage a mechanical teddy bear who walked and beat a drum noisily. The monkeys scurried in fear to the terry-cloth mother and clung to her. Even those who initially rushed to the wire mother quickly left her and clung to the terry-cloth one instead. Even more striking was the self-confidence that the infant monkeys seemed to acquire from contact with the softness of the terry-cloth figure. They became curious within a short while and eyed the device they had formerly found terrifying calmly and without fear. And after a few minutes of clinging, they often disconnected from their 'mother' and approached the teddy bear to explore.

In one variant of this experiment the monkeys were taken out of their cage and placed in a much larger room with unfamiliar objects such as a crumpled piece of paper, a gauze nappy, a doorknob and a wooden block. Again, the infants initially exhibited considerable fear and rushed to the terry-cloth mother, rubbing against her and clinging to her with all their might. But again their fear was soon assuaged and the reassured monkeys soon became playful, curious and exploratory. Not only did they go on to investigate the mother herself, they quickly detached themselves from her altogether, approaching the new object and beginning to treat it as an enjoyable plaything, something evoking no fear whatsoever. The Harlow experiments teach us something fundamental about the psychology of uncertainty and novelty: confronting potential threats with equanimity and relish requires self-assurance. In Harlow's studies, the little monkeys' self-assurance came from their physical contact with the softness of the terry-cloth figure, a feeling that resembled a sensation they had had with their natural mothers, from whom they had been separated. Maternal love, real or artificial, provided a grounding of psychological certainty to counterbalance the troubling uncertainty of their environment.

Mary Ainsworth and the 'Strange Situation'

About a decade after Harlow's groundbreaking experiments, Mary Ainsworth, an American-Canadian psychologist, made another illuminating discovery. It offered an important insight into how self-assurance develops in the human infant. Ainsworth's interest in this topic spanned her entire career, starting with her 1939 doctoral dissertation at the University of Toronto (under her maiden name, Salter). Her basic thesis was that 'where familial security is lacking, the individual is handicapped by the lack of what might be called a secure base from which to work'.[12]

The Second World War interrupted Mary Salter's work on psychological security. After graduation, she taught at the University of Toronto, before enlisting in the Canadian Women's Army Corps, where she reached the rank of major. After the war, Salter rejoined the faculty in psychology at the University of Toronto; there she taught courses in personality psychology and worked in the area of psychological assessment. A turning point came in 1950 with her marriage to Leonard Ainsworth and her departure with him to London, where he enrolled in a doctoral programme (in psychology) at University College London. This created an opportunity that would have a significant impact on Mary Ainsworth's career. Specifically, she responded to a job announcement in the London *Times* to work on research with John Bowlby, a child psychiatrist who studied the impact of children's separation from adult caregivers.

In 1951, Bowlby wrote: 'the infant and young child should experience a warm, intimate, and continuous relationship with his mother (or permanent mother-substitute) in which both find satisfaction and enjoyment'.[13] The affinity between Bowlby's theorizing and Ainsworth's earlier interest in the question of a secure base is striking. Strangely enough, she would realize only much later how fatefully important joining Bowlby's research unit would be for her career and her subsequent discoveries. And this was also true of Bowlby.

In 1953, Ainsworth accompanied her husband to Uganda on a job assignment at the East African Institute of Social Research. This allowed her to carry out her first observational study, on 'mother–infant' interaction, with local mother–infant pairs as research participants. She continued this work in Baltimore, where the couple moved after Uganda. Ainsworth noticed that children differed in the way they were attached to their mothers. Some were attached securely, whereas others were conflicted and anxious about their attachment. She discovered that these patterns stemmed from the way that the mothers had responded to their infants in the earliest months of their life. Children of mothers who were highly sensitive to their infant's cries and who responded quickly were more likely to develop a pattern of secure attachment to their mother than the children of mothers who were less overtly sensitive to their baby's distress.

Ainsworth's method of measuring how secure a given infant's attachment is to their mother has been particularly influential in subsequent research on human development. This method is known as the 'Strange Situation' test and it looks at how an infant reacts to a brief separation from their mother. The mother and the infant enter a laboratory where various appealing toys lie strewn on the floor. The infant typically begins to play with them and explore this novel environment happily. Then a woman unknown to the infant comes in, greets the mother and initiates interaction with the infant. At some point, the mother leaves the room and the child's reaction is observed. Typically, the child is upset by the mother's departure. They manifest a variety of stress-reflecting behaviours such as crying, tapping the door and showing signs of distress. Securely attached children are more visibly upset by their mother's departure, crying more than children whose attachment to their mother is anxious or ambivalent.

The mother remains absent for a few minutes and then returns. The children's behaviour at this point is more telling than their reaction to her departure. Even though initially they appeared to be less bothered by the mother's departure, anxiously and ambivalently attached children take a long time to return to their happy, exploratory state, instead clinging to their mother, whereas securely attached kids regain their confidence quickly. After a brief cuddle, they leave their mother's side and resume their exploration of the laboratory environment. For securely attached babies, just as for Harlow's infant monkeys, the supportive mother is a safe haven to whom they can turn when in distress; she serves as a secure base from which they can launch their exploration of the unknown.

In Baltimore, Ainsworth taught developmental psychology at Johns Hopkins University, before moving to the University of Virginia, where she remained until the end of her career. Her research into attachment continued and she developed a fruitful collaboration with John Bowlby. Their work had a fundamental impact on the understanding of child development and of children's sense of certainty and assurance.

Separation and uncertainty

Although Ainsworth's 'Strange Situation' test artificially creates a situation that is stressful for infants, a brief separation of a child from their mother is likely to occur often in real life. A long-lasting separation, however, is much harder to bear. Such separation can occur in a variety of circumstances, even, tragically, by government decree and as a matter of policy. Just such a decree was issued in April 2018, when the administration of President Trump in the US implemented a 'zero-tolerance' approach to immigration. Under this policy, federal agents separated children and infants from their families. The adults were prosecuted and held in federal jails or deported, and the children were placed under the supervision of the US Department of Health and Human Services and entrusted to foster homes or to relatives.[14]

According to reports, the number of separated children was over 4,300. As of October 2020, the families of 545 children had not been found and the children remained separated from their parents or guardians.[15] This situation is sure to have caused considerable and enduring stress to the separated children (and the adults). A medical report by Physicians for Human Rights, based on in-depth psychological evaluations of twenty-six people separated under the policy (nine children and seventeen adults), found ample evidence of psychological trauma, post traumatic stress disorder (PTSD), depression and anxiety. According to the report, in nearly all these cases the psychological distress experienced as a consequence of the separation warranted further intervention and therapy.[16]

Sadly, history offers many similar stories, one noteworthy example being the mass expatriation and movement of children during the Second World War in Europe. Extensive research has addressed the impact of the evacuation of young children from London and other major British cities in Operation Pied Piper at the onset of the war. This move was intended to protect the children (and in some cases their mothers) from the German bombings that were expected to devastate British cities. By the time war was declared, close to 2 million children had been moved to the countryside and placed in specially designated 'reception areas'. Unaccompanied children stayed with families who volunteered (for a fee) to take care of their needs for as long as required.

Even though the operation was well intentioned and the children were on the whole placed in comfortable surroundings, the impact of the separation from their parents was highly traumatic. John Bowlby studied these children as part of his research on child security and attachment and concluded that their level of stress from prolonged separation from their primary caregivers was higher than it would have been had they witnessed the bombings while in the company of their parents.

The psychoanalyst Anna Freud, who also carried out research with these children, arrived at a similar conclusion: as long as they stayed with their families, wartime hardships had little effect on children's well-being. However, when separated from their mothers, the children were clearly traumatized and showed signs of distress such as bed-wetting, aggressive play and uncontrollable crying; some refused to speak or eat. The impact of the separation trauma turned out to be long-lasting. Bowlby observed that years later the separated children experienced severe psychological difficulties that at times translated into deviant, even criminal, behaviour.

Though separation from parents is highly stressful, it is not the only possible source of stress children can experience. Conflicts at home, tension caused by an adverse economic situation, growing up in times of turmoil and trouble – all can affect a child's development and contribute to the underlying sense that bad things can and will happen. Research on the effects of war on children shows that the experience can result in all kinds of psychological problems, such as PTSD, depression and anxiety, as well as inducing a lasting fear of the unknown and anxiety in uncertain situations. Children who have experienced war may well exhibit excessive fears, cling closely to their parents, feel anxious about being left alone and sleeping in the dark, and suffer from severe separation anxiety.[17] Recently, Molly Ellenberg at the University of Maryland asked research participants to think back to their childhood. She found that adverse childhood experiences* bore a significant relationship to negative reactions to uncertain situations.† Furthermore, parental support, including involvement in participants' lives as children, their support for the child's autonomy, and warmth, were significantly related to positive reactions to the same uncertain situations.

So, adverse childhood experiences seem to shape our future attitudes towards uncertainty. For all I know, my own strong need for closure might stem in part from my early childhood in a Jewish ghetto (in Łódź, Poland) during the Second World War, from which most of the inhabitants perished in Nazi concentration camps. Let me also add, echoing the conclusions reached by John Bowlby and Anna Freud, that as I spent the duration of the war in the loving care of my parents (both of whom survived the war), I was spared any severe separation traumas or stress disorders of the kind that befell many children separated from their parents during the war.

---

* These included emotional, physical and sexual abuse, emotional and physical neglect, domestic violence, substance abuse and mental illness in the household, an incarcerated household member, parental divorce or separation, witnessed violence in the community, perceived discrimination, an unsafe neighbourhood, bullying and having lived in foster care.
† Including a blind date, a terrorist attack, the first day of school, a trip to a foreign country for the first time, the first day of a new job, economic recession, the birth of a new sibling, war and an undiagnosed illness.

Bereavement

At the time of writing, close to 6 million people worldwide have lost their lives in the COVID-19 pandemic. In the *Washington Post* of 19 February 2021, the journalist David von Drehle wrote about the oceans of grief these deaths must have caused. As he put it:

> The toll of COVID-19 is not some huge and faceless mass; it is the accumulation of 500,000 individuals each with a name, a way of laughing, a favorite song, a life story. Many of them are elderly, but the elderly are grieved. Many of them were in poor health, but the infirm can be missed. The pain has a peculiar quality sharpened by the very facts of the pandemic: funerals that could not be held, wakes that could not be convened; hugs that could not be shared.[18]

A major aspect of bereavement is the void that the departed relative or friend leaves behind. That void creates confusion and uncertainty. On 14 December 1861, Prince Albert, Queen Victoria's husband, passed away at the age of forty-two. The cause was typhoid, which he had contracted only weeks earlier. The queen's world crumbled in on her. Lord Clarendon, who visited her at Osborne in March 1862, reported:

> She talked upon all sorts of subjects as usual and referred to the sayings and doings of the Prince as if he was in the next room. It was difficult to believe that he was not, but in his own room where she received me everything was set out on his table and the pen and his blotting-book, his handkerchief on the sofa, his watch going, fresh flowers in the glass,

etc., as I had always been accustomed to see them, and as if he might have come in at any moment.[19]

Queen Victoria's bereavement was painful and long-lasting. It is as if she refused to accept his passing and attempted to freeze time around their former togetherness. You could view her reaction to the terrifying uncertainty that her husband's death created as being incoherent and dysfunctional, yet was it? Her actions sought to apply a reassuring sense of certainty to her surroundings, from the fixed nature of an established daily routine to the certainty that the environment he occupied while alive would not change. Recall Harlow's monkeys: even the *artificial* semblance of an attachment figure offered comfort.

Attachment figures like Victoria's Albert may reduce our fear of uncertain situations. They provide a safe haven and a secure base. Their loss reinstates the worry and magnifies it, and such a loss may highlight the harsh reality of negative events that could befall us, be it death or illness. People who generally fear uncertainty are especially sensitive to bereavement. Research by Paul Boelen of Utrecht University in the Netherlands supports this idea.[20] He found that people who are intolerant of uncertainty experience more grief and post-traumatic stress than those who are tolerant of it. A piece of research that echoes this comes from Lonneke Lenferink and her colleagues, who studied the impact on relatives of victims of the 2014 crash of a Malaysian plane (Flight MH17).[21] Relatives complained about a persistent sense of 'unrealness' and existential uncertainty and exhibited many psychopathological symptoms, including prolonged grief disorder (PGD), major depressive disorder (MDD) and PTSD.

Because people who have developed a secure attachment

can deal better with uncertain situations, they are likely to be more capable of making sense of their lives and reorganizing them after the loss of a significant attachment figure, someone they loved and cared for. Though they react emotionally to the loss, they are less likely to be overwhelmed by grief. Their optimism protects them against the devastating impact of loss and bereavement.[22]

God the saviour

In his highly acclaimed work *Sapiens: A Brief History of Humankind* Yuval Noah Harari notes how the human capacity to develop abstract ideologies which they can then communicate and share made possible the unification of large masses of people behind common purposes. Religion is one such unifying form of ideology, and a key element of most religions is a deity that always, and in all circumstances, protects believers from harm. In the same way that caring parents provide a safe haven and a secure base for their children, so does God for the faithful. In Christianity and Judaism, God is even referred to in familial terms. Christians pray to 'our *father* who art in heaven'; Jews pray to 'our *father*, our king' (*Avinou, Malkenou* in Hebrew). Other religions, such as Islam, do not refer to God in familial terms; nonetheless, the idea that God provides safety and security is as embedded in Islam as it is in Christianity and Judaism. This sense of a safe haven can be a source of strength and optimism in times of adversity.

America has long been among the world's most religious countries. The Pew Research Center reports that 55 per cent of US adults pray daily.[23] This figure is much higher than for other industrialized nations. For instance, in Canada the proportion of adults who (say they) pray daily is 25 per cent, in Australia it is 18 per cent, and in the UK just 6 per cent. In fact, as far as religiosity is concerned, America is closer to developing nations such as South Africa (where the comparable figure is 52 per cent), Bangladesh (57 per cent) or Bolivia (56 per cent), than to other Western countries or Europe more generally (22 per cent). It is tempting to speculate that religiosity, alive and well in the US to this day, lies at the root of the oft-vaunted American optimism that so impressed Alexis de Tocqueville in his classic book *Democracy in America* (1835).

The sense of a relationship with a benevolent and compassionate god provides believers with a feeling of security and well-being. People who have this intimate connection tend to have strength and confidence, and it stands them in good stead in times of crisis and uncertainty.[24]

At its most gratifying, love, including religious love, is a reciprocal affair. You are supposed to love God, and God loves you in return. The love of God is the mainstay of the Christian doctrine, while 'Jesus loves you' is a clarion call for commitment to the Christian faith. The secure base that comes from faith in a loving god allows us to confront adversity with equanimity. In the US, when people seek support in times of crisis their first point of contact, way ahead of mental health providers, is the clergy. In the general shock that ensued after the tragic 9/11 attack on the Twin Towers in Manhattan, more than 90 per cent of Americans reported turning to their religion for comfort.[25]*

---

* Using random-digit dialling three to five days after September 11, Shuster et al. (2001) interviewed a nationally representative sample of 560 US adults about their reactions to the terrorist attacks and their perceptions of their children's reactions.

The concept of caring parents, or indeed a caring god, providing a safe haven and a secure base does not, however, relieve us of personal responsibility. In either case, we're still expected to act on our own and to take responsibility for our actions. It's a kind of insurance policy, not a substitute for personal agency. The following story illustrates how this works.

A fellow was stuck on the roof of his house in a flood. He was praying to God for help. After a while a man in a rowing boat came by and shouted to the man on the roof, 'Jump in. I can save you.' The stranded fellow shouted back, 'No, it's okay. I'm praying to God, and He is going to save me.' So the man in the boat rowed on. Then a motorboat came by, and the person in it shouted, 'Jump in. I can save you.' To this, the stranded man said, 'No, thanks. I'm praying to God, and He is going to save me. I have faith.' So the person in the motorboat moved on. Then a helicopter came by, and the pilot shouted down, 'Grab this rope, and I will lift you to safety.' To this, the stranded man again replied, 'No, thanks. I'm praying to God, and He is going to save me. I have faith.' So the helicopter pilot reluctantly flew off. Soon the water rose above the roof and the man drowned. When he arrived in heaven and finally got his chance to discuss this with God, he exclaimed, 'I had faith in you, but you didn't save me! You let me drown. I don't understand why!' To this God replied, 'I sent you a rowing boat and a motorboat and a helicopter. What more did you expect?'

In Islam it is said that the Prophet Muhammad told a Bedouin, 'Pray to God, but tie the camel tight.' The moral of these anecdotes is that religious faith is no substitute for responsible decision-making. It provides a sense of optimism that allows us to confront adversity calmly, but the way we confront it is all our own.

The sense of a caring god who loves you and looks out for you is only one sense in which religion is helpful in dealing with uncertainty. It also offers the faithful a feeling of certainty and closure about the most fundamental issues of human existence. How the world came into being, what happens after death, how to ensure that God views you favourably and that you are headed (in Islam and Christianity) for heaven rather than hell; all these metaphysical matters of vital importance, and more, are contained in religious teachings of various sorts. Religions also tend to express and offer certainty by applying in all places for all time. For a religion to express true certainty, its meanings and teachings must apply eternally and universally, not locally or for a limited duration – otherwise uncertainty creeps back in. Hence a common feature of religious belief systems – as well as other ideologies, be they political or social – is to attempt to assert their particular brand of certainty over others.

According to noted British historian Edward Gibbon, the fall of the (Western) Roman empire in the fourth and fifth centuries AD was accompanied by a proliferation of religious cults, including Judaism and Christianity. Presumably, the chaos and uncertainty that occurred alongside the dissolution of the Roman world order evoked an intense need for certainty and closure. Further data supporting the positive relationship between seeking certainty and religiosity is widely available, both in academic research and in the world around us. Specifically, Vassilis Saroglou, a researcher at the University of Louvain in Belgium, found a positive relationship between religiosity and the need for cognitive closure, and in the week after the September 11 attacks in the US in 2001 some retailers saw a 40 per cent increase in Bible sales.[26] Similarly, during and immediately after the Second World War an appreciable increase in religiosity was observed in Canada and North America more generally. Historian of religion John Webster Grant wrote that after the war ended in 1945, 'Men and women who had shown no more than a perfunctory interest in the church before going off to war demonstrated on their return an enthusiasm that confounded all prognosticators.' Turning to religion in that period occurred irrespective of denomination and creed, attesting to a universal human need for certainty and stability following a period of chaos and mayhem.[27]

Religion is not the exclusive source of certainty and predictability, and in times of chaos and turmoil other sources also experience a boost in their appeal. Archival studies demonstrate that during the Great Depression and other economic crises, the publication and sales of books on astrology saw a significant increase.[28] Other studies demonstrate a rise in interest in horoscopes in times of uncertainty[29] and an increase in the tendency to believe in clairvoyance and other supernatural phenomena.[30]

Summary

Our reactions to uncertainty are determined both by our genes and by our childhood experiences. How our parents or other adult caregivers reacted to our discomfort and distress in the early months of our lives determines how secure we feel and how we react to life's tragedies and disasters. A major and highly upsetting uncertainty can be prompted by the loss of a loved one. Because our worldviews, values and perceptions are shared with people who are close to us who we trust and respect, we experience their loss as a fraying of our shared reality; our world has suddenly crumbled and our secure base of acceptance and support has vanished. When confronted with such a catastrophe we must draw on our inner resources of optimism and our internal faith that things will get back on track, that despite tragedy and sadness life is worth living. Having a sense of secure attachment helps us cope with loss and the uncertainty that threatens to engulf us. Religious faith also offers a buffer against the anxiety inherent in life's tragic situations. It assures the faithful that happenings occur in accordance with a plan devised by a benign deity that loves human beings and rewards human virtue.

In your experience

1. When you think back to your childhood, what kind of attachment do you think you formed to your parents? How did this affect your relationship with them over the years? How did this affect your relationships with other people?

2. If you are a parent, what is your parenting philosophy? What kind of attachment do you feel there exists between you and your children?

3. Have you ever experienced the death of someone close to you? What was your reaction to the loss? What was the process you went through?

4. What are the main sources of your self-assurance? Is it your family, your friends, your religious beliefs? Think back to times when reliance on these sources proved helpful to you in confronting a troubling uncertainty.

4. Adult Attachment

Do you consider yourself a warm person, or somewhat distant and aloof? Do you feel you need people, or do you prefer to do things on your own? Do you like social occasions, or would you rather be alone? Are you generally a trusting person, or do you tend to regard others with suspicion? These are the kind of questions that the science of adult attachment deals with and attempts to answer. It does so by researching the determinants of our personal confidence and sense of security. Our early-childhood experiences are largely beyond our control, so it would be troubling if these were determined solely by these: our lives would be predetermined and unfree. Fortunately, they are not, and our choices in life do matter. Embracing a religion is one such choice, navigating our adult attachments and relationships in a particular way is another – and, unlike childhood attachments, adult ones are at least somewhat under our control.

Being securely attached means having loving friends, loving partners and a loving family. Copious scientific evidence attests that these give you many psychological advantages. Securely attached adults have a generally positive outlook on human relationships. They are typically open to hearing both positive and negative information about their close ones' (e.g. their partners') behaviour. They typically put a positive spin on other people's actions. Giving others the benefit of the doubt, they empathize with the mental and emotional states of other people.

75

Let's look at a study by Collins and colleagues in which research participants were asked to read statements about potentially negative behaviour on the part of their partner.[1] Attachment style was measured by an eighteen-item Adult Attachment Scale in which the participants were asked to imagine, for example, that their partner 'did not respond when you tried to cuddle', 'did not comfort you when you were feeling down', 'left you standing alone at a party where you didn't know anyone' and 'wanted to spend the evening by themselves'.[2] The results were revealing. Securely attached people interpreted such statements in a relationship-preserving way, for instance by explaining their partner's wish to spend the evening alone by affirming: 'My partner is tired and just needs some time to relax at home.' Insecure people were likely to choose a relationship-threatening statement: 'My partner is losing interest in me.' Insecure people were also more likely to state that this situation would 'lead to argument and conflict' and were more likely to punish their partner and stir up conflict. Whereas secure adults trust their partners and interpret ambiguous situations in a positive way, insecure ones are distrustful and suspicious. As a consequence, they are constantly ready to break off relationships and walk away. Sometimes certainty can be found by ending a relationship.

Confronting uncertainty

Sometimes in science a theory is proposed but it isn't tested until much later. Albert Einstein advanced his Theory of General Relativity in 1915, but it was not successfully tested until 1919 (by Eddington); in fact, tests are still ongoing over a century later. Sometimes scientists simply do not have the tools needed to test a theory early on, so testing has to wait until such tools are developed. A similar 'time warp' effect happened with John Bowlby's prediction that linked someone's personal security and confidence to their current attachment to others. Specifically, he expected securely attached adults to be more comfortable with uncertainty. As a consequence, they would be more curious about new situations and have a lower need for cognitive closure. Bowlby advanced these theories in London in the 1950s, yet definitive tests had to wait for almost half a century. It was the Argentinian-born Israeli psychologist Mario Mikulincer who carried them out.

Mikulincer wondered whether Mary Ainsworth's discovery that securely attached children exhibit greater interest in exploration than insecure children held for securely attached adults. Would they be more curious and inclined to explore novel situations? Would they be less afraid of the unknown? Would they be more adventurous? These were intriguing questions. The insight that attachment promotes exploration isn't trivial or obvious. At first glance, it seems that the two things have little to do with each other. It took the genius of Bowlby to come up with the idea and the insight of Ainsworth to find a way of testing it with toddlers; then, years later, it took Mikulincer's ingenuity to show that the relation holds for adults as well.

Mikulincer found, specifically, that securely attached people exhibit greater curiosity. They feel more comfortable being inquisitive and exhibit a lower need for closure than insecure adults. Like the securely attached toddlers who quickly overcame a brief separation from their mothers and marched on to explore unknown environments, so did securely attached adults within their own spheres of interest.

How Mikulincer discovered these phenomena is not only fascinating but reveals something fundamental about how we form relationships with others.

Attachment and cognitive closure

In Chapter 2, I discussed how people with a high need for cognitive closure 'seize and freeze' on relevant information; this allows them to have closure quickly and to keep it permanently. High-need-for-closure people 'jump' to premature conclusions without considering the full panoply of evidence on a topic. Imagine meeting someone at a party and finding them to be fun, friendly and entertaining. Someone with a high need for cognitive closure would probably accept them at face value and form a positive impression of the individual. They would not consider that in other circumstances, for instance at work or at home, the same person might be irritable, impatient and dour.

The same holds for negative experiences with a new acquaintance. If the person appears angry or aloof, the high-closure individual might write them off as unpleasant and not worth knowing. High-closure people 'freeze' on initial opinions; they will not change that negative impression easily. They may hold on to it even if in later encounters the same person is cheerful and optimistic. Like Mr Darcy in Jane Austen's *Pride and Prejudice*, their 'good opinion once lost is lost forever'.

To test these ideas empirically, Mikulincer invited securely and insecurely attached people (as measured by a specific questionnaire) to his laboratory.[3] There he presented them with an ambiguous description of another person. Half the participants first received positive information about the person (e.g.

that she was friendly and intelligent); this was then followed by negative information (e.g. that the person was also stingy and callous). Other participants received the negative information first. The insecure participants behaved like people with a high need for cognitive closure: their judgement was predominantly influenced by their first impression. Participants who received the positive information first formed a positive impression of the hypothetical individual; participants who received the negative information first formed a negative impression. In contrast, the secure people paid equal attention to both types of information; they judged the person in the positive–negative sequence just the same as they did in the negative–positive sequence. Having considered all the information, they did not fall into the primacy trap. They did not draw different conclusions from the same evidence given in a different order.

Prejudice and stereotyping

When we are uncomfortable with uncertainty and ambiguity, or are naturally or environmentally conditioned to be so, we base our judgments on the most accessible information in our environment. Such information is often contained in social stereotypes that are prevalent in our culture. These may often be about groups (genders, ethnicities, races) that are present in a society. Hence, in their hurry to escape uncertainty, insecure adults are unduly influenced by stereotypes. When they encounter a new person from a given ethnic or racial group, they apply a stereotype of that group rather than carefully examining that person's actual characteristics. Another interesting experiment by the Mikulincer team illustrates this tendency.

Participants in the research were asked to mark a piece of writing. Some participants were told that the essay was written by a student from a negatively stereotyped group (Middle Eastern Israelis), while others were told it was written by a student from a positively stereotyped group (Israelis of European origin). Strikingly, the insecurely attached people gave higher marks to the composition written by the latter group, whereas the securely attached participants gave both exactly the same mark.

These results demonstrate another negative consequence of insecure attachment: the propagation of stereotypes and prejudices. Not only do insecure people have problems in their own close relationships, they also judge strangers in stereotypic ways that are likely to cause alienation and tension. Racism, antisemitism, sexism, ageism and homophobia are all based on negative stereotypes. The embracing of (mostly negative) stereotypes, which stems from people's discomfort with uncertainty, thus contributes to the societal tensions that polarize communities and tear them apart. Especially in times of great confusion and uncertainty, as during the COVID-19 pandemic, with millions of people feeling unmoored and insecure, we see an increase in racial tensions, negative stereotyping and the adoption of simplistic (and often ridiculous) notions that offer gratifying closure by holding someone (members of stereotyped groups) responsible for our misery. I will have more to say about this in Chapter 7, where I discuss the conspiracy theories that have proliferated recently in an unprecedented way.

So the social attachment that we manage to develop, the network of family and friends that we trust, can determine how we respond to uncertain situations. This can affect our social relationships, our political attitudes and, through them, the fabric of society itself. The nineteenth-century British philosopher John Stuart Mill believed that all social phenomena are rooted in the human nature.[4] The wide-ranging effects of social attachments testify to the deep wisdom of his insight.

Attachment and audacity

Success in life often depends on temerity. Whether in business, art, science, sports or politics, playing it safe and sticking to the tried-and-true path is unlikely to take you to the next level of achievement. Conservative caution is unlikely to deliver outstanding outcomes in whatever it is you are trying to accomplish. The road to greatness is paved with risks: success often requires daring. And daring means confronting the unknown, venturing into uncharted territories. The secret to daring is focusing on the positive or following our dreams. Way back in 2008, President Barack Obama talked about the audacity of hope. In doing this he hit the proverbial nail on the head. To be audacious, we need to be hopeful. And hope comes in part from us having a sense of a safety net in case of trouble.

A sense of a secure base encourages independence and exploration. This is true not only for the laboratory tasks that Mario Mikulincer used in his research but in real-life situations too. The more supportive the partner, the more independent and daring the supported individual. Two researchers at Carnegie Mellon University, Brooke Feeney and Meredith Van Vleet, demonstrated this empirically.[5] They found that people whose partners lent them support on a given occasion showed greater independence in various pursuits as much as six months later. Moreover, they were more successful in accomplishing their stated goals. And in a laboratory study carried out by the same researchers, participants whose partners were present and supportive persisted longer in difficult tasks, and reported a greater reduction in their stress and anxiety after having completed the activity. All in all, it appears that a secure haven and a safe base matter not only in early childhood but in adult life as well. It provides us with the strength to cope with life's challenges and gives us the courage to take risks and confront uncertain situations with confidence and optimism.

The Mikulincer–Shaver Partnership

It is perhaps unsurprising that research on attachment and its relationship to uncertainty is indebted to a special synergy, chemistry and, yes, secure attachment, within two pairs of scholars. The legendary collaboration between Mary Ainsworth and John Bowlby led to the initial formulation of attachment theory and inspired early insights and breakthroughs in this domain. It is unlikely that either Ainsworth or Bowlby could individually have made their important discoveries without the mutual stimulation between them. Similarly, work undertaken by Mario Mikulincer was profoundly influenced and stimulated by his long-term collaboration with another eminent psychologist, Phillip Shaver, currently an emeritus professor at the University of California, Davis.

Mario and Phil have many things in common. These include an interest in psychoanalysis, 'workaholism', a background in clinical psychology and a fascination with love

and attachment. Moreover, their personal styles are comple-
mentary, so their 'whole' is greater than the sum of their
parts. Mario is the hard-nosed experimentalist comfortable
with methods and results. Phil is the humanist and literary
buff. He delights in crafting aesthetically pleasing scholarly
discussions to add to the more than a hundred research
papers these two scholars have contributed to the burgeoning scientific literature on attachment.

In one of their landmark studies, Mikulincer and Shaver
asked two important questions. First: Is the sense of secure
attachment fixed and thus stable over the course of our lifetime and across situations, or could it fluctuate so that
anybody could feel at given times more secure than at others?
And second: Does the openness to novelty that characterizes
secure people affect their attitudes to others who are different from themselves?[6]

From personal experience and informal observations,
Mikulincer and Shaver hypothesized that secure attachment
is a feeling we can experience in some situations more than
in others. How can this feeling arise? they wondered. Can a
'secure state of mind' be induced without people being
aware of it happening? And can this unconsciously generated security promote openness to others different from
ourselves?

In psychological research, unconscious induction of psychological states is often accomplished through subliminal
priming. It works like this. The research participant is presented with a phrase or a concept on a computer screen at a
fast flicker rate, so fast that the brain cannot register it

consciously. Nonetheless, and as if by magic, studies show that even though participants cannot clearly identify what they have seen, its meaning does register in the brain. Moreover, it affects participants' later thoughts and behaviour. Through such subliminal priming, Mikulincer and Shaver evoked in the participants in their study the feeling of secure attachment by simply flashing words on a computer screen that represented the concept, such as *love* and *support*. They also included a control, flashing up words that had nothing to do with attachment, such as *table* or *boat*. Finally, there was a control group in which the participants received subliminally flashed positive words that were also irrelevant to attachment, such as *success*. The rationale behind this was that it would enable the researchers to infer whether the words had an effect because they pertained to attachment, or simply because they were positive in tone. If attachment has a special effect on openness to others, attachment words (*love*, *support*, etc.) should have a different impact than merely positive words (e.g. *success*).

The participants in Mikulincer and Shaver's study were Jewish students at the Bar-Ilan University in Israel. They were asked to evaluate either the personality of another Jewish student (an in-group member) or that of a Palestinian student (an out-group member) on the basis of personal information about the attitudes and interests of the student, provided, or so they believed, by the student themselves. The results of this unconscious induction were fascinating. Participants primed with attachment words were equally positive in their evaluations of the Jewish and the Palestinian students. In contrast, participants who were not primed with attachment words evaluated the Jewish student much more positively than the Palestinian student. These findings were replicated in various ways* in subsequent studies by the same team. Taken together, they convey an important message: a sense of secure attachment induces openness to out-groups that are normally viewed negatively and discriminated against by members of the in-group.

A full decade later (2011), the Mikulincer–Shaver duo demonstrated that subliminally priming participants with names of attachment figures significantly improved their creative problem-solving, which required open-mindedness and 'thinking outside the box'.[7] So the same open-mindedness that rids us of biases and prejudices also opens our minds to unconventional ideas that improve our problem-solving ability. Both apparently stem from the secure feeling that somebody out there 'has our back'.

Summary

'You're Nobody Till Somebody Loves You' is the title of an immortal song by Russ Morgan, Larry Stock and James Cavanaugh. Indeed, it seems people can cope with uncertainty and a flagging sense of self-assurance if they have a secure attachment to others. This is not only fundamental to humans but also to other species (like the rhesus monkeys studied by Harlow). The impact of attachment extends from the earliest months of infancy and persists throughout life. Having a sense of secure attachment encourages us to confront uncertainty with a positive state of mind. It encourages exploration, optimism and trust and impacts not only our personal relationships

* For instance, with secular versus Orthodox Jews who typically perceive each other as antagonistic out-groups.

but our tolerance of diversity. It reduces our vulnerability to stereotypes and increases our ability to live with others different from us. In today's highly interconnected world, where cultures, ethnicities and religions increasingly mix and rub against each other, these attributes are highly important, not only for ourselves but for society as a whole.

A crucial aspect of human nature is that we derive our sense of self, our self-confidence and the feeling that we matter from being accepted and respected by others. Some of the greatest social thinkers have stressed that our concept of self, and hence our poise and self-assurance, depends on how those we respect treat us. The great German philosopher Georg Wilhelm Friedrich Hegel wrote that 'to be recognized is to exist'. His formulation 'I that is We, We that is I' means that our sense of self is bound up with the way others see us. The American sociologist Charles Cooley expressed a similar idea in his notion of the 'looking-glass self', and the American philosopher and psychologist George Herbert Mead talked about the 'internalized other'. Attachment theory and research demonstrates empirically how our self-confidence develops in large part through our interaction with significant others from our infancy onwards and throughout our lives. It is a key component of our social psyche that strongly determines our reactions to uncertainty.

In your experience

1. When you look back over your life story, how have you changed over the years? Have you become more or less secure as you have matured? What do

you think accounts for the change in your sense of self-assurance?

2. Are there currently people in your life you feel you could rely on in time of need?

3. Can these same people rely on you?

4. What does the concept of friendship mean to you? What do you see as the limits of friendship?

5. Cultures of Certainty and Uncertainty

Do you follow trends in popular culture – music, fashion, films, TV shows – or do you feel alienated from the contemporary scene and happier in the culture of your youth? What are your sources of information – the mass media, social media, your friends? All these define the culture in which you are embedded and in which your worldviews, values and opinions are grounded. They also determine your attitudes to novelty and uncertainty. The experience of uncertainty, and that of certainty, has certain qualities. These can be valued or devalued in the culture you belong to. For instance, certainty has connotations of precision, predictability and stability, so a culture that holds these as valuable and important will also value certainty. Uncertainty, on the other hand, has connotations of freedom, opportunity, open-mindedness and excitement, so cultures that hold these dear also value uncertainty. Members of a culture abide by its values, and this shapes their attitudes to certainty and uncertainty.

Intriguingly, the influence of culture on our psyche is largely unconscious. You might think that you like order, tradition and convention simply because they are intrinsically valuable and feel that people who do not think the same are simply wrong, misinformed or unintelligent. Conversely, you might think that you like freedom, spontaneity and rock 'n' roll because of your unique personality. In both cases, it is likely that you are underestimating the profound influence of your culture on your values, tastes and preferences. We might think that the values hailed by the society we live in, such as democracy, freedom and equality, are far superior to values such as obedience to authority, self-sacrifice for the group and religious devotion. Yet members of a different culture may hold the opposite view and regard the second set of values as supreme. Our values are relative to the culture in which we live, and this relativism also applies to our responses to certainty and uncertainty.

The effects of culture

In 1968 and 1972 the Dutch cultural psychologist Geert Hofstede embarked on a remarkable transnational research project related to people's reactions to uncertainty. Hofstede distributed the same surveys to workers of IBM subsidiaries in seventy-two countries – 116,000 questionnaires in all. The questionnaires were appropriately translated into the languages spoken by the respondents. This Herculean project addressed several areas in which cultures differ, including uncertainty avoidance.

Hofstede's Uncertainty Avoidance Index (UAI) was contained in three items in the IBM questionnaire, each asking for degree of agreement or disagreement. These looked at employees' attitude towards rules, employment stability and stress. Attitude towards rules was measured by responses to the statement: 'The company's rules should not be broken even if the employee thinks it is in the company's best interest.' The employees' view of job stability was measured by responses to the question 'How long do you think you will continue working for this company?' And stress was measured by responses to: 'How often do you feel nervous or tense at work?' The participants' responses to these three questions were highly correlated with each other, so if they registered high agreement on the first question, they were likely to respond with high ratings on the second and third questions. This allowed the researchers to combine all three questions into a singular measure, the UAI.

Hofstede discovered substantial differences among nations. Among the highest uncertainty-avoidant were Finland, Germany, Greece, Guatemala, Japan, Mexico, Portugal and South Korea. In contrast, Jamaica, Denmark, Sweden and Ireland were among the lowest uncertainty-avoidant nations. The US and Canada scored in the mid-range.

Hofstede's work reveals that people who are socialized in different cultures come to hold different attitudes to certainty and closure. Members of some cultures are taught to appreciate clarity and precision; they are praised for orderliness and decisiveness. These then become values that give them a sense of competence and significance. For the same reasons, they are uncomfortable with ambiguity and try to avoid it. In uncertainty-avoiding cultures, thinking unclearly and imprecisely is disrespected and frowned upon. Being characterized as 'wishy-washy', 'indecisive' and 'unconfident' is pejorative and seen as disparaging. Of course, the term 'wishy-washy' is explicitly pejorative, but in some cultures in Asia and Africa too much clarity and decisiveness is regarded as boorish and impolite. By being very decisive, say about your like or dislike for a given piece of art, a film or a fashion item, you might insult someone who holds the opposing views and create awkwardness. Decisiveness and 'wishy-washiness' have some benefits, after all, and sometimes they represent a social strategy that works.

Cultural evolution

Why is it that some cultures avoid uncertainty whereas others cherish it? What might have caused these cultural differences? It turns out that some of the causes stem from the external conditions under which a culture has evolved. Other causes stem from internal developments and trends within the culture itself as they occurred over time and shaped the mentality of its members across generations.

Most of us will be aware of Charles Darwin's (1859) theory of evolution, in which he states that different species, including humans, have evolved through a process of natural selection in which individuals whose genetic endowments have equipped them to cope well with the environmental conditions survived and procreated, giving rise to the different species that exist today, each with its unique characteristics. Less well known, though quite well established, is the theory of cultural evolution. According to this theory, just as with living organisms (animals and humans), cultures evolve in response to the conditions they confront. In essence, cultures adopt norms and values that serve their survival and welfare.

A fascinating study about how external circumstances shape cultural norms was carried out by Michele Gelfand – a distant cousin and former colleague of mine at the University of Maryland, and currently a professor at Stanford – and her team of international collaborators. Using data from thirty-three nations, their work showed that the external challenges that cultures have confronted contribute to the 'tightness' of the norms they have developed. The more severe the challenges, the tighter the norms. A history of territorial conflict, resource scarcity, disease and environmental threats were all external challenges that led to tighter norms. Cultures where these threats were prevalent, like Singapore or Germany, highlight the value of order and punish people for any sign of deviation from normative ways of doing things. In Singapore, spitting in the street earns you a fine of up to a thousand dollars, and smuggling illicit drugs is punishable by death. In southern Germany, residents of apartment blocks observe a 'sweeping week' in which they assume responsibility for cleaning areas around their buildings. In contrast, cultures whose history has not involved major threats tend to evolve much looser norms. Citizens in 'loose' countries tend to be less punitive towards such things as littering, noise pollution or a lack of punctuality.

The relationship between norm tightness in a given culture and its attitude towards uncertainty is straightforward. Cultures that face aversive uncertainty, fraught with threats and possible disasters, develop a negative attitude to uncertainty. Indeed, Gelfand and her colleagues found that members of tight cultures also typically have a high need for cognitive closure. The need to cope with adversity could contribute to the development of the strict norms needed for the coordination of societal efforts to deal with threats, where there is no place for indecision.

Differences in cultural values related to certainty can lead to intriguing challenges in intercultural communication. When they came to negotiate the Paris Peace Accords (signed in 1973) that ended the Vietnam War, the US delegation rented a house for a week, whereas the Vietnamese delegation rented a house for a year. This striking difference expresses more clearly than a thousand words the story of American impatience and the country's need (and hence expectation) to reach closure urgently. The less certainty-seeking Vietnamese were in far less of a hurry. As the Afghan Taliban are known to say: 'The Americans have the clocks, but we have the time.' Indeed, their patience and tolerance of uncertainty seems to have paid off. In the summer of 2021, nearly twenty years after US forces invaded Afghanistan and routed them, the Americans left and the Taliban returned to seize power in the country that they had lost almost two decades ago.

Historical change

Cultural evolution can also happen because of internal developments within a society. A striking example is Western culture, with the premium it puts on clarity and precision. For many of us in the West, the value of clarity seems like an absolute truism, a complete no-brainer – clarity seems good, period. Interestingly, this has not always been the case. Until the seventeenth century, sociologists tell us, human communication wasn't expected to be crisp and precise but instead sophisticated and wise, elegantly crafted, full of metaphors and allegories, lyrical yet profound and insightful.[1] Linguistic expression was valued for being eloquent, vivid and evocative rather than clear. It was admired for its poetic flourishes, use of irony and innuendo; in short, it was valued for its ambiguity. Why, then, the change?

Scholars suggest it stemmed from successes in the explanatory nature of mathematically formulated physical sciences from the seventeenth century onwards. Influential continental scientists, philosophers and educators, the likes of Newton, Descartes, Locke, Hobbes and Hume, extolled the virtues of simplicity and precision. They saw these as essential in attaining truth and clearly demarcating right from wrong. The assault on ambiguous eloquence even extended to the derision of poetry as a silly entertainment immersed in sentimentalism and devoid of real meaning and value. Poets of the day, like Dryden, Addison and Pope, were swept along in the pro-clarity tide. They embraced the spirit of the time and held that the principles and form of poetry should resemble the axioms of mathematics, coming to believe that an excellent poet needed a mathematical head.[2] Poetry of the 'head' was hailed as the ideal, and poetry of the 'heart' and 'spirit' came into disrepute.

Yet nothing is for ever. The upheaval of the French Revolution of 1789 signalled discontent with the ideals of reason, enlightenment and the old world order, as did the detrimental consequences of the Industrial Revolution (poor working and living conditions, low wages, child labour and pollution). These brought to the fore the notion of the people, their suffering and their emotions, which ushered in the Romanticism of the nineteenth century which came to pervade the arts, literature and politics.

Ideal mental health: closed- or open-minded?

Whereas clarity of expression and thought is regarded highly in contemporary Western societies, this does not mean that the spirit of our times encourages closed-mindedness at any price. In modern science, for instance, both certainty and uncertainty are valued and each has a definite place. Certainty has to do with providing clear evidence for our theories and assertions. Uncertainty has to do with imagining new, previously unthought of possibilities and the generation of surprising hypotheses that question accepted 'certainties'.

Social ideologies, too, colour people's attitudes towards openness and hence uncertainty. In today's liberal democracies people generally applaud open-mindedness and tolerance and disparage rigidity and closed-mindedness. Alternative political orientations invite very different attitudes. These notions are illustrated by the contradictory ideals of mental health espoused by German writers from different periods. The Nazi-era German psychologist Erich Jaensch in his 1938 book *Der Gegentypus: Psychologisch-anthropologische Grundlagen deutscher Kulturphilosophie* (*The Antitype: Psychological-anthropological Foundations of German Cultural Philosophy*) hailed the traits of consistency, stability and confidence as signs of good mental health. According to Jaensch, a normal, psychologically healthy individual sees things clearly and this translates into the coherence of their ideas and worldview. The antitype, a psychologically feeble person, in contrast, is incapable of stable perception. Their views and political attitudes are changeable and fleeting. They are inconsistent and therefore should not be taken seriously.

Note that the decisiveness and confidence that Jaensch ascribes to mentally healthy people suggest a closed-minded individual with a high need for closure and an aversion to uncertainty, and the antitype describes an open-minded individual whose views are malleable and who finds uncertainty unthreatening, even congenial. Intriguingly, after the Second World War and the collapse of the totalitarian Nazi regime, the tables were completely turned. Since then, rigidity and closed-mindedness have been generally viewed by social scientists as undesirable and pathological, while open-mindedness and mental flexibility are hailed as positive qualities. No doubt this was prompted in part by the horrors of Nazi extremism and reflected a rejection of the rigid mode of thinking that underpinned it.

In 1950, Theodor Adorno, a renowned German philosopher and psychologist, published (with colleagues) an epoch-making volume carrying that very message. *The Authoritarian Personality* portrayed black-and-white thinking and the uncritical acceptance of tradition and convention as hallmarks of a pathologically dichotomous personality. These were seen as the result of an overly harsh and problematic upbringing and arrested psychological development, which produced a poorly adjusted, mentally unhealthy individual. From one extreme to another!

As we saw in Chapters 1 and 2, both open- and closed-mindedness serve important functions in different circumstances. For various reasons, each has been applauded or vilified in different cultures and ideologies, depending on the historical context. The challenge for us is to understand their different functions, to know when to keep our options open and when to shut our mind. Knowing ourselves, appreciating our own personality and inclinations (that is, our cultural or personal aversion or attraction to uncertainty) and factoring them into our decision-making process is a step towards meeting this challenge.

Closed and open generations

Historical developments that shape people's reactions to uncertainty impact their lives and change their attitudes. The Second World War brought turmoil and troubling uncertainty into millions of people's lives. In reaction, the post-war generation of the late 1940s and 1950s craved order and certainty. During the war, with the men away from home, women took on jobs and managed their families, but once the war was over the roles of men and women quickly reverted into traditional divisions. Men were reinstated as the bread-winners, the heads of households endowed with power and prestige. Women resumed their subservient status as men's 'little helpers' in charge of children and the kitchen. Society embraced uniformity. Young and old were (mostly) happy to conform to group norms and observe tradition and convention. The television set, now in many homes, paid into this uniformity by presenting accepted social patterns for all to see and emulate.

Things reversed dramatically a decade and a half later. The post-war period was a time of sustained economic growth in many parts of the world, including the United States, the Soviet Union, Western Europe and East Asia. After severe wartime austerity, prosperity returned. By the early 1960s, a young generation of Americans was the most affluent in US history. With wealth came confidence and the daring to buck convention, rebel against the established order and experiment with alternative lifestyles. The Woodstock Festival in upstate New York gathered more than half a million people together for 'Three Days of Peace and Music'. It came to symbolize the counterculture movement of the decade. In defiance of the rigid conventions of the 1950s, it celebrated free love, drugs and rock 'n' roll. In those heady days, novelty was king and uncertainty was embraced as the gateway to adventure.

The cultural diversity that sprang up in the 1960s manifested itself in, among other things, a proliferation of communes, experimentation with psychedelic drugs, a widespread anti-war movement (focusing on Vietnam), even New Left-inspired terrorism. All were signs of extraordinary open-mindedness. They reflected a spirit of exploration that shunned rigid order and convention. Instead, it embraced 'looseness' and the release of restrictions. In the UK a new music scene flourished and London won a reputation as the 'coolest' epicentre of innovation, with Carnaby Street flourishing as the home of mods, skinheads, punks and the New Romantics.

People born after the 1960s, for example the much-discussed 'millennials' of recent years, inherited some of the countercultural values of their parents, the 'baby boomers'. These subsequent generations have been primarily defined, however, by the sweeping technological advances that have transformed the world. Sometimes referred to as 'digital natives', they grew up with the internet and social media as their playthings. They saw a vast increase in international travel and witnessed economic globalization. Both developments promoted diversity and introduced alternatives to formerly sacrosanct ways of doing things. Less 'experimental' than their parents' generation, nevertheless they are often described as generally confident and open-minded and undaunted by novelty and uncertainty.[3]

In recent decades, opposing cultural views have increasingly clashed within the United States, contributing to the so-called 'culture wars' around such issues as abortion, homosexuality and equal opportunity for all regardless of race or ethnicity. Under the various stresses faced by American society, among them growing economic inequality, issues of immigration and the COVID-19 pandemic, such conflicting cultural views have grown ever more polarized, with each side becoming increasingly certain of their moral righteousness. Those on the far left have clashed with far-right movements (the likes of the Proud Boys or Oath Keepers) that blame various sinister forces for wresting America away from the Whites (the so-called 'White-replacement theory') and call for a violent response against the alleged enemies of

America. The result has been unprecedented tension and rancour between large segments of US citizenry and a political gridlock that has nearly paralysed the country's civic institutions and systems of governance.

Multicultural experience and tolerance of uncertainty

The flattening of the world, as Thomas Friedman, a writer at *The New York Times*, put it, and the swelling volume of international travel, have inevitably brought people into contact with members of different cultures whose appearance, behaviour and overall mentality are different to theirs. How does such multicultural exposure, which in itself introduces uncertainty and unpredictability, affect our reactions to the strange and the unknown?

This question was addressed in six studies carried out by Tadmor and colleagues, and their results show the important consequences that multicultural experience can have on people's stereotyping of other groups, and on their tendency to be prejudiced and bigoted towards members of these groups.[4] In the first study, participants were split into four groups. The control group was shown a film of geometric figures, and the three other groups were shown a film of pictures, music and film trailers illustrating different aspects of American culture, Chinese culture, or American and Chinese cultures combined. The trailers included cultural manifestations across domains, including architecture, home decoration, fashion, cuisine, entertainment, recreation, music, films, art and literature. Afterwards, the participants were asked to spend five minutes describing their impressions.

It turned out, unsurprisingly, that the participants who

viewed the American-Chinese presentation devoted more words and observations to these two cultures than other participants. Less obvious and highly interesting, however, was the finding that participants who viewed the American-Chinese presentation subsequently expressed a significantly lower endorsement of the racist stereotypic beliefs that African Americans, who were not represented in the films at all, were uneducated, violent, irresponsible, lazy, loud and undisciplined. It seems that a presentation that eliminated one ethnic stereotype made people relinquish their tendency to stereotype more generally and thus reduced their endorsement of (the unrelated) racist portrayal of African Americans.

Next, participants were asked to assume the role of a sales manager and evaluate six candidates for a job in sales. Three of the candidates (two low quality and one high quality) had names that might typically be inferred as belonging to a White person, and three (again, two low quality and one high quality) had names that could be taken to suggest a Black person. The results of the study again attested to the benefits of multicultural exposure. Whereas those who had viewed the Chinese-only and American-only presentations downgraded the high-quality Black candidate in comparison to the high-quality White candidate, those who had seen the American-Chinese presentation did not discriminate.

Though of great interest and social importance, these results did not reveal which aspects of the bicultural American-Chinese presentation had had the effect of reducing the participants' prejudicial behaviour. The hypothesis that this effect may have had something to do with a reduction in the participants' need for cognitive closure and uncertainty avoidance was put forward, and Tadmor and colleagues' third experiment provided empirical support for this. The participants in this study were Jews living in Israel. They were asked to write an essay about an Israeli experience or an experience with a foreign culture or their experience of the beach (the control condition). The participants who were asked to write an essay about their experience with a culture foreign to them scored lower on a scale designed to measure their need for cognitive closure (see Chapter 1) than the other participants.

But is this reduction in the need for closure *related to* the fall in prejudicial behaviour that was seen as a result of participants watching the bicultural presentation in the first two studies? The fourth experiment answered this question. The participants were again Israeli, and the experience they described of a culture other than their own was assessed in the Multicultural Experience Survey (MES), developed by Leung and Chiu.[5] The survey elucidates the amount of time lived in other countries, the level of exposure to other cultures, the number of foreign languages spoken, parents' place of birth and participants' favourite foods and musicians. The results suggested not only that people with a greater multicultural experience had a lower need for closure but that they were also less supportive of prevalent Israeli stereotypes towards Ethiopians and homosexuals. And it was the lowered need for cognitive closure that caused the lower endorsement of stereotypes by participants with more extensive multicultural experience.

Ironically, then, whereas for some people the *idea* of otherness evokes fear and induces closed-mindedness, *actual exposure* to otherness through multicultural experiences can reduce the need for closure, which in turn reduces suspicion of and negative attitudes towards members of other groups. However exciting and potentially important the findings of the Tadmor team are, though, a caveat is in order. The bicultural presentation viewed by the research participants was highly positive; they were shown beautiful artwork, impressive architecture, fashion, films and so on from a different culture. This raises the possibility that this resolved an uncertainty they might have had with regard to otherness by replacing it with a positive feeling, and that it is that 'warm and fuzzy' feeling that reduced their aversion to uncertainty. Of course, not all multicultural encounters might be as positive, and those that aren't are unlikely to have the same impact on uncertainty aversion. I will revisit the issue of multiculturalism and its various impacts and discuss it more thoroughly in Chapter 14.

Summary

We've seen that, beyond genetics and family dynamics, our reactions to uncertainty are shaped and even determined by our culture. Depending on what has happened in their long- and short-term histories, cultures differ in their attitude to novelty and uncertainty. Typically, periods of physical danger, economic downturn and other sources of strain on an individual's psyche promote a desire for certainty and stability. We want to feel that things will turn out all right, that we can confront adversity and prevail. Such circumstances generally give rise to closed-mindedness, normative tightness and a high need for cognitive closure. In contrast, abundant wealth, stability and security promote the development of cultures that are 'looser', more open-minded and experimental.

People's attitudes and opinions reflect those embedded in their cultures. This includes their feelings towards uncertainty and their tendency to fear it or embrace it. The fact that our reactions to uncertainty are culturally relative means that they are not predetermined or set in stone. We are not predestined to fear the unknown or to long to escape uncertain situations. Rather, our reactions to the unknown are subject to various influences that associate uncertainty with positive or negative outcomes. Moreover, exposure to different cultures can reduce closed-mindedness and intolerance of uncertainty, so it may reduce people's stereotyping of others and increase their openness to diversity.

In your experience

1. How do members of your generation generally feel about uncertainty? How much do they value precision, order and punctuality? How conventional do they tend to be?
2. How much do they value openness, informality and adventure?
3. How does your parents' generation feel about these things?
4. How often have you encountered members of a different culture? Did you notice any differences in the ways they respond to uncertainty and disorder compared to you? How did you react to those differences?

6. The Power of the Situation

We all tend to think of ourselves as special and unique, and in many ways we are. We have a unique life history, a unique family, unique hobbies, temperament and talents. And yet there are ways in which we are the same, especially when the circumstances are extreme. We all experience fear when threatened, feel upset when we fail, and pride when we succeed. We feel elated when in love, dejected by a rejection, encouraged by a compliment. One of the most important psychological discoveries of the last century is the *power of the situation* – events that happen to us at a given time and place. Traditionally, psychology and psychiatry focused on people's personalities and their particular characteristics as individuals. Of course, personality matters. We differ from one another in myriad ways and this translates into our different reactions to circumstances. But events can bring out similar reactions, especially when the stakes are high and bear on matters of great importance. To be sure, some situations have more power over us than others. Imagine you receive a job offer that represents a mere 'lateral move'; the new position isn't more interesting, lucrative or prestigious than the one you are currently holding. It is a case in which you would probably feel ambivalent, and your personality would be the decisive factor in what you would ultimately do. Some people would decide to stay, while others would choose to accept the offer and leave. This is an example of a weak situation that doesn't have a uniform outcome and which allows personality differences to guide people's choices.

Think now of a different situation, one in which the position you are offered commands a much higher salary and is much more prestigious and far more intellectually interesting than your current job. Most people, regardless of their unique personality, would view this proposal as an 'offer you cannot refuse' and be quick to accept it. This is an example of a strong situation that overrides individual differences between people.

The logic applies to how we react to uncertainty as well. Someone may be low on the need for closure. She may be blessed with having had a happy, securely attached childhood. She may have grown up in a culture characterized by openness and exploration. All this should predispose her to cope well with uncertainty. Yet when confronted with a strong uncertain situation with connotations of serious danger, as in the case of a war or a pandemic for instance, she is likely to experience anxiety and the desire to escape the uncertainty, just as everyone else would.

Our behaviour changes according to the different circumstances we confront.[1] This may make us seem almost like different people at different times. In some situations, we may feel confident and empowered, while in others we may feel weak, fragile and lost. In some situations, we may act bravely, like a paragon of courage (such as a soldier storming a hill against enemy fire), whereas in others we may tread cautiously and hesitantly (perhaps in proposing marriage to our chosen one). We act differently in our responses to specific pressures and the opportunities situations may offer because of what psychologists call 'situational affordances'. It is not that we are inconsistent or have multiple personalities;*

---

* For example as in the 1957 film *The Three Faces of Eve*, or Robert Louis Stevenson's classic 1886 novel *Strange Case of Dr Jekyll and Mr Hyde*.

rather, certain situations can activate thoughts and behaviours that often overcome our natural inclinations. Whereas our unique personalities are what make us different from each other, strong situations make us the same, or nearly so.

Psychology has revealed the malleability of our psyche. It has highlighted how our moods, sense of self, confidence, motivations and feelings can fluctuate widely even in the course of a single day. We may feel full of zest and ready to take on the world in the morning, devastated by bad news at midday but be back on our feet in the evening, in the loving company of family and friends. We can examine these fascinating dynamics of the human psyche by looking at research around our engagement with uncertainty.

Kurt Lewin and the social psychological experiment

Kurt Lewin's influence is a major reason why the psychological situation became the hallmark of social psychology. Lewin was an émigré from Germany who trained as a rigorous experimentalist, an approach that he applied creatively to the scientific understanding of social problems. His students, sometimes referred to as the 'twelve apostles', included brilliant scientists such as Leon Festinger, Stanley Schachter and Harold Kelley. (The last, I am proud to report, was my own mentor and a lifelong friend.) Lewin's 'twelve apostles' became major movers and shakers in psychological science. It is they who created the unique field of American social psychology as it currently exists. Its methods and perspectives shaped the way this discipline is practised worldwide.

Lewin's approach was based on the simple assumption that every behaviour happens in a moment, at a unique point in time and space. There are forces that operate on the individual at that moment and determine what they will end up doing. That is why Lewin's approach has been called 'ahistorical', in the sense that it no longer delved into the individual's past to understand their current behaviour. Unlike Sigmund Freud, whose psychoanalytic method required inquiring about a person's early childhood, Lewin's analysis centred on the moment, what he referred to as the 'psychological situation'. It is not entirely accurate to say that this approach disregards history, however; instead it assumes that the historical development that shaped the individual's personality results in a tendency to react to the moment in a given way.

Lewin assumed that everyone's behaviour is determined by factors in two categories: the person (P) and the environment (E). The 'person' refers to your personality as it is determined by your genes, your socialization history and your culture. The 'environment' refers to the immediate events and stimuli to which you react. For example, someone might be sensitive to rejection (such sensitivity representing the individual's personality, or the P-factor). In addition, the environment (E) in which she finds herself may include others who are critical and rejecting (e.g. an insensitive boss or hostile, prejudiced co-workers). Such a person might suffer more in those circumstances than someone who is less personally sensitive to rejection, that is, has 'thicker skin'.

Some personality and environmental forces are stronger than others. Someone with a paranoid personality sees rejection and persecution everywhere. Their personality is so strong that it overrides the situation. But situations can also be strong and force the majority of people, even those without a paranoid disposition, to behave similarly. Most people will try to escape a burning house, accept a salary raise, or be upset if they lose their job; they will react in similar ways regardless of their specific personality or childhood history.

Lewin and his students emphasized the environmental part of the equation and downplayed personality. Their approach, that of manipulating situations in an experimental setting, became hugely influential. Thanks to their work, such experiments were soon adopted as a principal methodological tool used by social psychologists. In these experiments, research participants receive different treatments in different conditions, that is, they find themselves in different psychological *situations*. Studies of the psychology of uncertainty have often used the experimental method: by inducing uncertainty in research participants, we can observe what effects it has on their thoughts, feelings and behaviours.

'Competition' can arise between personality and the environment when they carry conflicting implications for someone's psychological reactions. Consider a generally optimistic and upbeat person confronted with a deadly pandemic. Of course, such a situation invites largely negative emotional reactions. In this instance, contrasting psychological forces find themselves battling one another. The ultimate result for a given individual will depend on their relative strengths. Some people can remain optimistic; others may be overwhelmed by the situation and succumb to dejection. I will address these conflicts in later chapters, but for now let's look at the ways in which psychologists have used the experimental method to study the effects of situationally induced uncertainty.

Manipulating aversive uncertainty

In Chapter 2, I described experiments in which we manipulated the stresses of uncertainty by making it difficult for participants to process information. Adding time pressure induced the need for quick closure. Unpleasant noise introduced a distraction and mental fatigue further reduced the participants' ability to process information. By making the task harder, the participants were motivated to end the state of uncertainty by seizing and freezing on whatever information was readily available (such as first impressions or stereotypes). They achieved a sense of certainty simply because they wished to achieve it, in order to escape the difficulties we had imposed on their information processing.

These experimental studies of information processing under difficult conditions (what psychologists refer to as increased 'cognitive load') create conditions we often encounter in daily life. They are the experimental analogue of the everyday stresses many of us confront: time pressure to meet our deadlines, the noise of the neighbour's TV or the fatigue of long commutes to work. Most of us will be able to recall feeling highly irritated when, after a gruelling day at work, family members (a partner or a child) disagree with us, or when a friend's inability to decide on their order at a restaurant became truly annoying, or an ear-splitting noise in the neighbourhood interfered with our ability to think. Just as in psychological experiments with time pressure, noise or fatigue (among other stresses that overload our mental system) so in real, everyday situations these are times when our need for closure is likely to rise, inducing an aversion to prolonged uncertainty.

Some social psychological experiments have manipulated uncertainty more directly. Kees van den Bos, a professor at the University of Utrecht in the Netherlands, has been a leading researcher into what he called 'personal uncertainty', that is, the sense of insecurity we feel about all kinds of things that matter to us, our perceptions, feelings and relations with other people (Does she love me? Do they respect me?). In one set of van den Bos studies, the experimenter asks the participant: 'Please briefly describe the emotions that the thought of your being uncertain arouses in you,' and 'Please describe as accurately as you can what you think physically will happen to you as you feel uncertain.'[2] In the control group, the participants were not asked these questions, or indeed any which pertained to notions of uncertainty, so a sense of uncertainty was unlikely to be on their mind. Next, participants were presented either with a scenario in which they were allowed or not allowed to voice their opinion or with a vignette depicting a fair or unfair job selection procedure.

Van den Bos and his colleagues found that participants' reactions to these scenarios were noticeably affected by their experimentally induced uncertainty. Those for whom a sense of uncertainty had been evoked desired more of a say. They felt better when given a voice and worse when not given one than participants in the control group. They also judged the fair job selection procedure as fairer and the unfair job selection procedure as less fair than the control group. So even contemplating uncertainty makes a difference to our state of mind. It highlights the importance of positive values like fairness and prompts a stronger affirmation of those values. That is why van den Bos's research participants saw the fair procedure as *fairer* in the uncertainty (versus control) condition and the unfair procedure as less fair.

But why did the manipulation of uncertainty produce this effect? Put simply, it made participants feel weakened and disempowered. This was a serious negative outcome associated with the uncertainty. To overcome this unpleasant state, they sought to re-empower themselves by having a voice in a decision or by affirming their appreciation of fair procedures. So, in a state of self-uncertainty, participants use any opportunity to compensate for the unpleasant feeling and to restore to themselves a more positive sense of self, thereby re-establishing a sense of self-certainty.

Does the experience of fairness assuage people's negative reactions to a troubling uncertainty in real-world situations as well? Van den Bos addressed this question in research he carried out at a chemical plant from which the majority of employees had been laid off due to restructuring. It turned out that the remaining workers who thought that the lay-offs were fair expressed less fear about the future than employees who deemed them unfair. Again, the notion that the world is fair and is governed by transparent rules lends us a sense of control. In a fair world, we can feel empowered and confident of getting good outcomes if we play by the rules. This is not the case if outcomes are dispensed through some random, whimsical process. The belief in a just world gives people a sense of optimism based on the belief that people get what they deserve and deserve what they get, that 'the arc of the moral universe is long, but it bends toward justice', as Martin Luther King famously said. If so, fate is to some extent under people's control, and whatever uncertainty we experience will ultimately resolve itself into a desirable state of affairs.

As we've already seen, when uncertainty threatens, people seek reassurance by directing themselves towards positive things, such as others' support, a 'secure base' provided by people who accept them unconditionally (for example family and friends). A sense of assurance can come from our warm relations with the people who care about us, appreciate us and have our back. But, in addition, our internal security can come from our cultural worldview that the world is fair. Affirming such a view gives us a sense of reassurance and helps counter the anxieties that uncertainty can engender.

When we feel unsure about ourselves, our need for closure rises. People who disagree with us or who criticize our worldview and hence may seem to question our worth can be upsetting and annoying. It is found, for instance, that religious people who experience uncertainty are particularly negative towards those who criticize religion.[3] Similarly, people who report a strong tendency to avoid uncertainty are typically less tolerant of diversity, less open to new experiences and alternative lifestyles and more likely to advocate sending immigrants back to where they came from, as well as being more negatively disposed to having people of a different race live in their neighbourhood.[4]

Who hurts more?

It is interesting that self-uncertainty is particularly hurtful to people who generally feel good about themselves. For them, negative thoughts and possibilities are less frequently felt and so carry a shock factor. Canadian psychologists Ian McGregor and Denise Marigold explored this phenomenon in depth.[5] They first measured their research participants' self-esteem and then exposed them to troubling uncertainty. Participants were asked to think of an unresolved personal dilemma that made them feel very uncertain. (The study also included a control group in which participants engaged in activities that did not affect their sense of self.) The participants with higher self-esteem responded more quickly to questions such as 'I seldom experience conflict between the different aspects of my personality' and 'In general, I have a clear sense of who I am and what I am.' They also exuded greater certainty and less ambivalence towards socially important issues such as capital punishment and abortion. So, somewhat counterintuitively, evoking uncertainty in people with high self-esteem produced an overcompensation and an inflated sense of certainty.

It is a process we have seen before. A troubling uncertainty evokes the need for certainty and cognitive closure. This biases people's thoughts and information processing so that they end up becoming *more* certain. In psychology, such a process is called 'defensive'. It protects the person from troubling and negative thoughts about themselves.

Benefits of self-assurance

When self-doubt sets in, we can compensate for it by recalling our commitment to important values and to our cherished worldviews, reassuring ourselves of our worth. It has been shown in a number of intriguing studies that, once reassured, people feel more able to confront opposing views without feeling unduly threatened. In research experiments, participants' self-confidence is first deliberately shaken, either by a confrontation with someone whose worldview clashes with theirs, by being reminded of a moment when their own behaviour was inconsistent with their values or by being reminded of negative stereotypes of people like themselves (women, people of colour, Muslims, Jews). Either before such a confrontation or after it, participants are offered the opportunity to affirm an important value. Following this affirmation, the individual's self-assurance is restored and strengthened, and they become less defensive and more open-minded .

In one experiment by Cohen et al., people who were pro-choice discussed abortion policy with a pro-life advocate.[6] This created a conflictual situation that challenged the individuals' self-worth. However, allowing participants to endorse important social values beforehand lowered their defensiveness and increased their readiness to make concessions to their pro-life adversary.

In a different study, sexually active students were shown a video highlighting the risks of unsafe sex, which, understandably, challenged their sense of self-assurance.[7] What happened next was very interesting: participants who had been given the opportunity to self-affirm before watching the video took the cautionary information to heart. Their perception of the risk of their sexual behaviour was heightened. Not so the participants who were not given the opportunity to self-affirm; they became defensive and resisted the information. In practical terms, 50 per cent of the self-affirmed participants purchased condoms after watching the videos – twice as many as the non-affirmed ones (25 per cent).

Confronting existential terror

When major uncertainty strikes, the meaning we give to our life can threaten to crumble. We didn't invent that meaning all by ourselves. Humans are social beings whose reality is shared by others. Our personal sense of meaning, of who we are, is also part of a shared reality, a cultural system of values that we embrace and which guides what we do in order to feel significant. Our culture defines for us what counts as significant accomplishments. In Western cultures this might mean getting an education, acquiring a profession, being a good citizen, athlete, artist, friend or parent. In a different, more collectivistic culture, like those found in Eastern or Middle Eastern cultures, our sense of meaning and personal significance may entail safeguarding the family's honour, displaying courage and devotion to the community, and so on. In most cultures, exhibiting a readiness to fight for your country and put your life on the line for a sacred cause also lends significance.

However, when major upheaval strikes, the activities that have been lending us meaning and significance may no longer be available to us. The uncertainty that the coronavirus pandemic aroused has been fraught with consequences that have lowered people's sense of self-worth. It prevented millions of people from pursuing the things that made them feel significant. They were unable to carry out their work, attend school, cheer their teams or enjoy foreign travel. In short, they couldn't be who they liked to be and have the kind of life that they found meaningful. In such a powerful situation, the inner demons of our soul may come unshackled and threaten our well-being with dark thoughts, depression and anxiety.

Fear of death

People's personal demons differ widely. For some they consist of guilt, for others shame, fear of abandonment, loss of control or humiliation. The one fear common to most people is what psychologists call 'existential dread', the terror of death and the descent into nothingness. Awareness of our own demise is unique to the human species and is universal. We all know, deep in our hearts, that we are mortal, although much of the time we repress the thought.

Yet uncertainty surrounding death is not about the sheer likelihood of dying. It is not the uncertainty about our mortality that is so troubling. Existential uncertainty is frightening because it brings to mind a highly negative event that frustrates our most fundamental motivation: the instinct for survival. Unless we adopt the reassuring certainties of a religion and its assertions about an afterlife, we simply do not know what happens when we die; it is the greatest uncertainty we encounter, and contemplating this serves as a reminder of how fragile, weak and insignificant we really are. Now you see us, now you don't. Fear of non-existence can be compounded by worries about the way in which we will die, which could be suffused with pain, trauma and suffering. The dread of

non-existence is usually kept in check by our everyday preoc-
cupations. In pursuing the tasks that give our life meaning, we
distract ourselves from the terror of non-being. By doing what
our 'in-group' deems important and worthwhile, we defend
ourselves from the sense that we are nothing but insignificant
specks of dust in an uncaring universe.

Surprisingly, despite the presumed ubiquity of death anxiety,
the 2017 'Survey of American Fears' conducted by Chapman
University found that only 20.3 per cent of Americans are
'afraid' or 'very afraid' of dying, and fear of dying is forty-
eighth on the list of people's greatest fears. At the top of the
list is fear of corrupt government officials (74.5 per cent), followed by the American Health Care Act/Trumpcare (55.3
per cent). Americans' fears reflect the issues of the day, with
existential anxiety way down the list. Presumably because
death is so scary, it is suppressed in our everyday awareness.

However, although a conscious preoccupation with death
isn't pervasive, it is relatively easy to bring it to the surface
and witness its effects. This has been demonstrated in numerous studies guided by terror-management theory, one of the
most influential theories in contemporary social psychology.[8]
Researchers in this field have carried out ample creative
research aimed at understanding how people react when
their psychological defences against thoughts of death are
momentarily pierced, when thoughts of death and dying,
usually banished from awareness by our normal pursuits, are
forcefully brought to the forefront of our attention.

How do you experimentally create a situation in which
people contemplate their death? One thing you might try is to
explicitly ask them to do so. This simple method was employed
in hundreds of studies. In a typical terror-management experiment, participants are asked to do two things: 'Briefly describe

the emotions that the thought of your own death arouses in you' and 'Write down as specifically as you can what you think happens to you when you are dead.' Not surprisingly, these manipulations evoked considerable anxiety in research participants, but when given an opportunity to affirm their cultural worldview, participants' anxiety was assuaged.[9] One way of affirming your worldview is by expressing disapproval of someone who has criticized your culture or expressed negative views about your nation or someone whose behaviour deviates from cultural norms. In other words, by asserting that you are patriotic, an honest person, in favour of the values and ideals that your country holds dear, you reaffirm your sense of self-worth that was threatened by the thought of your own mortality.

In one particularly striking experiment, the investigators contacted municipal judges and recruited them for participation in a study on bond decisions (in American courts, bonds, like bail, are sums of money secured as guarantees that the person charged with a crime will appear for trial).[10] The judges were all given an instructional packet that included a case brief describing an allegation against a woman accused of prostitution and a bond form, both identical to those typically submitted by pretrial services to judges. In the packets given to half the judges there were also written down the two questions above (the manipulation of mortality salience). The results of this experiment were remarkable: judges who received the questions recommended a much higher bond (of $455 on average) than the judges who did not ($50 on average).

The investigators replicated this study with college students as participants and used a different way of manipulating the salience of mortality: a fear-of-death scale that included statements such as 'The idea of never thinking again after I die frightens me' and 'Never again feeling anything after I die upsets me.' Participants in the control group were given a standard scale assessing their degree of anxiety. The results strongly confirmed those of the initial study: students in the first group recommended a significantly higher bond ($400 on average) than students in the control group ($99).

These findings demonstrate that when people confront a situation that requires them to face their (usually suppressed) terror of death and dying, they self-affirm by recommending a higher punishment to someone (a prostitute, in this case) who apparently flouts the norms of their culture. As in the van den Bos and McGregor experiments, when a sense of personal uncertainty led people to affirm the cultural norm of fairness, numerous terror-management studies in which participants were made anxious through the requirement that they contemplate their mortality, produced exactly the same cultural affirmation. So our deep-seated fear of non-existence can be countered and reduced by affirming an important cultural value. This happens because it serves as a reminder of our worth as a member of our culture. This gratifies our motivation for personal significance and hence serves as an 'antidote' to the frustration and anxiety occasioned by thoughts of death.

Accentuating the social

A key aspect of who we are can be found in the groups or categories of people to which we belong: our nationality, ethnicity, religion, gender, and so on. These define what psychologists refer to as our *social identity*. Most people belong to cultural communities that have a given worldview and a shared perspective on reality. This view includes the values and standards by which we evaluate ourselves and other people. When our individual self-confidence is challenged, say we fail a test, our proposal is rejected or we are passed over for a promotion, we compensate by orienting to our groups and affirming our social identity.

In a study that looked at these processes, we surveyed twelve Arab countries and Pakistan and Indonesia.[11] We found that respondents who reported lower life success tended to self-identify more strongly as members of their collectivities (their nations or religion) rather than as individuals. This does not mean that religion/nationalism and failure are generally correlated with each other, nor that religious/nationalistic people are generally those who fail in life. Rather, it suggests that people whose lives aren't going well and who therefore experience insignificance and disrespect as individuals (and associated self-uncertainty) tend to embrace a collectivistic narrative (whether nationalistic, social or religious) that offers an alternative path to significance.

The connection between troubling uncertainty and becoming group-focused has also been demonstrated in several research studies.[12] In one experiment, participants were asked to write an essay that described their experience of failure or success. Subsequently, they responded to statements about their American identity: 'I am proud to be American,' 'I am emotionally attached to America,' 'The fact that I am American is an important part of my identity.' The participants who wrote about failure agreed more with all those statements, attesting to a stronger sense of collective (American) identity than those who wrote about their experience of success. Other studies came to the same conclusion. People who feel that their individual lives lack meaning and whose self-confidence is shaken are particularly keen to affirm their social identity. They value their group memberships more highly, especially to successful groups whose glory reflects upon their members.

These psychological processes play out in the here and now and in part explain the recent surge of populism in America and the success of Donald Trump's slogan 'Make America Great Again'. A study by Cohen et al. shows that between the 1970s and 2010 the self-perception of being middle class by poor White Americans has declined precipitously.[13] Being middle class, the writer Gertrude Stein observed, is the very essence of Americanism. For some, the loss of that identity means a loss of significance, a sense of humiliation, of feeling abandoned by the system, uncared for and left behind. The 'Make America Great Again' slogan very deliberately prom- ised to restore to blue-collar Americans their self-assurance and significance, hence their enthusiastic response to Trump's rallying cries, prompting him to exclaim at victory speeches in the 2016 presidential campaign: 'I love the poorly educated.'

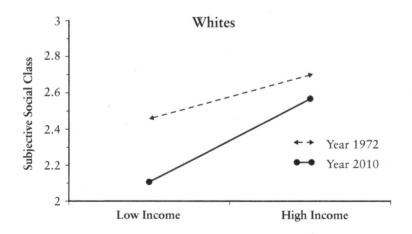

Summary

Whereas some people crave certainty and avoid uncertainty more than others, a sense of troubling uncertainty can be evoked by strong situations. Numerous experimental studies in which participants have been manipulated into feeling a disquieting uncertainty have demonstrated this. Extensive research on situational uncertainty makes two essential points: first, it is relatively easy to shake people's self-confidence by making them think about uncertain or anxiety-evoking situations, but second, it is equally easy to restore their sense of security and well-being by allowing them to affirm their worldview and their place in it. People can be resilient if their sense of a secure base and social support is readily available to them, and such a sense often comes from affirming their cultural worldview. Affirming the values of your culture makes you feel a valued member of a society and thus have worth and significance.

In your experience

1. Recall a situation that made you uncertain. How did you feel? What about it made you feel the way you did?
2. What about self-uncertainty? How did you feel and how long did the feeling last? What did you do?
3. Think about your friends and acquaintances. Who among them is particularly affected by uncertain situations? How do they react to those situations?

Who among your friends is unflappable in uncertain situations? Why do you think that is?

4. Have you been in situations in which your social identity (your nationality, your religion, your gender, your profession) seemed of particular importance to you? Try to identify what it was about those situations that made you particularly aware of your social identity.

PART 2
Closure's Consequences

7. The Pitfalls of Black-and-White Thinking

Black-and-white thinking

In my research on radicalization and terrorism, I came across what might seem a truly strange phenomenon. Lifelong atheists who had pursued a life of hedonism and luxury became devout fundamentalist Muslims, seemingly overnight. Others, who were fully committed neo-Nazis, embraced in astonishingly short order an extreme anti-Nazi stance and devoted all their energies to fighting the neo-Nazi movement tooth and nail. Later, I realized that the about-faces these people displayed reflect a unique mode of thinking in terms of polar opposites – juxtaposing good with evil, right with wrong, us with them, and classifying other people as being either for us or against us. Such black-and-white thinking, which dismisses shades of grey and believes in absolutes, is what prompts people to so radically jump from one ideological extreme to another. It is one of the most characteristic consequences of a need for closure.

When uncertainty threatens our sense of well-being it is only natural that we should seek to escape it. This translates into an intense pursuit of certainty. People can then become what Eric Hoffer called 'true believers'; they embrace dichotomous views that admit no nuance. Uncertainty avoidance promotes the feeling of 'seeing things clearly'. This is typically achieved by glossing over exceptions and suppressing evidence inconsistent with our 'incontrovertible' truths. Such dichotomous thinking characterizes the rhetoric of various ideological narratives (for example, nationalist or racist) that make sharp distinctions such as 'us versus them', 'good versus bad' and 'right versus wrong'. Black-and-white thinking is common because it affords us peace of mind. It dispels ambiguity and offers a blueprint for action. Black-and-white framing invites you to join the 'good guys' and fight the 'bad guys'. In return, you get to have your self-certainty restored and to feel that you are a good person who is doing the right thing.

Although it is soothing and reassuring, this type of thinking can be problematic. First, it typically ignores available information about complexities and nuances – shades of grey. We may be tempted to assume that someone who commits a crime is 'bad', that someone who contributes to charity is 'good', that someone whose career goes well is a 'winner', and that someone who's declared themselves bankrupt is a 'loser,' but if we bothered to look more deeply, we would soon discover that these simplistic labels are imprecise. Neglecting relevant information brings with it a risk. As with the historic tragedies caused by 'freezing' on prior conceptions that we saw in Chapter 2, it may result in serious mistakes, the sometimes disastrous consequences of premature closure. After all, things are rarely so categorical. Hardly anyone is purely bad or purely good. Indeed, those with extreme views tend to suppress information that, if only it were considered, would soften or moderate their opinion. Yet when we desperately crave closure, we are reluctant to think too much, instead cherishing clarity and simplicity.

Thinkers across the ages have been aware that subjective certainty is not to be mistaken for objective truth. John Stuart Mill criticized people's tendency 'to refuse a hearing to an opinion, because they are sure that it is false' based on the faulty assumption 'that *their* certainty is the same thing as *absolute* certainty'.[1] As Mill explained, refusing to engage with another person's contrasting opinion was a 'double injustice'; not only does it rob you of your right to express your view, it also deprives you of the chance to exchange your own view for a superior (and possibly correct!) one.

The eminent Welsh politician Aneurin Bevan, active in the UK in the 1940s and 1950s, coined the memorable term *imaginative tolerance* to describe the ideal approach towards others, recommending it as a constructive way to combat the inveterate subjectivity of our opinions. Philosopher Isaiah Berlin, meanwhile, advanced the notion of *value pluralism* and discussed at length the perils of placing one value or ideal (and by extension any belief system) above any other, thereby ceding our ability to react humanely to specific situations in an ever-changing world.[2] As he explained, personal freedom to do all that we want to do cannot *always* be a higher value than any other: if the wolf is granted unrestrained freedom, it spells death for the sheep. Instead, as moral human beings, we are forced to judge each situation as it comes, recognizing that our highest ideals – equality, freedom, compassion, and so on – may grow or diminish in importance depending on context. In short, we have to choose. Berlin's philosophy demands that if we are to be at our best as human beings, we must lose our reliance on the comforting certainty of rigid belief and value systems and the easy go-to answers they might provide – and this includes not just religion but also a vast range of political ideologies.

A more contemporary expression of this attitude can be found closer to home, in the field of psychology, as it is also central to Jonathan Haidt's moral foundations theory.[3] Haidt attributes many of the conflicts we see around us to individuals and groups placing one of six moral foundations above others (and retaining a fixed certainty in the moral rightness of doing so). These values (and their opposites) are: Care/ Harm, Fairness/Cheating, Loyalty/Betrayal, Authority/ Subversion, Sanctity/Degradation and Liberty/Oppression. Drawing on a huge range of international studies, Haidt showed how different societies tend to accord greater or lesser importance to these foundations – some Western societies, for example, may value liberty far more than sanctity, whereas the opposite may hold true for societies in the Far East. Yet underlying these problematic fixations that privilege one belief over all others, and sitting behind the questions posed to us from Mill to Haidt, is a deeper, ever-present motivation and dynamic: our psychological need to flee uncertainty and seek cognitive closure. Whether the situation is moral or political, it is our need for closure that will ultimately dictate outcomes. And it is our attitude towards it that will either cause havoc or help us find a way through the tangle of human affairs.

Escaping troubling uncertainty skews the way in which we process information. It prompts people to scan information selectively and exhibit a 'confirmation bias', that is, they selectively favour information that supports their views.[4] As a consequence, people who have the *least* information are often the most confident in their opinion. In a sense, then, ignorance is 'bliss', as it affords certainty. Unconsciously, these comfortable outcomes are more important to us than concerns about accuracy and precision. We lull ourselves into believing that our confidence is well grounded when in fact it is based on biased and restricted information.

These issues aren't just of academic interest. They underlie a host of everyday phenomena, including people's aesthetic and ethical preferences. Consider the former popularity of classic Westerns. They illustrate how gratifying morality tales with simplistic structures can be. In the classic Western, the hero is the 'good guy', portrayed as courageous, fair-minded and determined (as well as loaded with sex appeal), and their nemesis is an evil (and often ugly and mean-looking), depraved and cruel adversary whom they overcome at the (happy) ending so that justice prevails. As Stephen Kiss of the New York Public Library put it: 'Westerns sought to teach the good values of honesty and integrity, of hard work, of racial tolerance, of determination to succeed, and of justice for all. They were, in a sense, modern morality plays where heroes – strong, reliable, clear-headed and decent – fought their adversaries in the name of justice. At the show's end, moral lessons had been taught and learned.'[5]

The superhero genre, whose popularity these days is immense (with upwards of eight superhero films produced annually), also plays with the 'good versus evil' theme. As in Westerns, superhero movies, featuring characters like Batman versus the Joker, Superman facing off with Lex Luther, and Spider-Man confronting the Green Goblin, revolve around an upright hero who is fighting for the right cause against a central villain spinning dark plots against innocent humanity.

The inevitable happy resolution of these conflicts is of central psychological significance. As we have seen, the angst sometimes experienced in uncertain situations is produced not by the uncertainty as such but by the 'big, bad' thoughts that come to mind in those situations. That's why the happy ending the Western and superhero genres reliably deliver is so critical. Not only do they provide gratifying cognitive closure, they do so in a way that satisfies our yearning for positive outcomes. As our beloved heroes prevail, all seems well with the world. We just need to make sure we are on the side of right. Westerns and superhero films are, of course, simply a modern iteration of this phenomenon of seeking a sense of closure through narrative. We could argue that all books – indeed anything with a narrative structure – function in this way, from the earliest tales told by our ancestors to the latest novels, dramas or films. Stories gain appeal and trans-missibility by creating a state wherein the reader or listener craves closure, then follow a path that sustains that need before finally offering closure. (Perhaps you have in the past given up on a book as your need for closure was unfulfilled along the way? Or perhaps you kept going with it despite not enjoying it, just 'to see what happens'.) Some narratives play to our need for moral certainty; others to a reaffirmation of certain values, be they ethical, spiritual or political; others tap into a range of additional needs, such as a craving for connection (for example, romances where the reader follows a trajectory towards two lovers finding one another) or autonomy (such as in coming-of-age narratives, where the protagonist hopefully reaches a state of self-knowledge by the end of their journey). With any effective narrative struc-ture, our need for certainty is turned into a form of entertainment. By sharing stories, whether with our children or our friends, we not only diminish our fear of the unknown but build our tolerance for uncertainty and, ultimately, arrive at a reassuring sense of closure to boot.

The venom of excessive certainty

Not all dichotomous views are as innocuous and innocent as they are when played out in a Hollywood blockbuster, however. Black-and-white thinking can be the root cause of conflict-mongering and bellicose behaviour. It sharpens the differences between points of view and reduces the chances of compromise and agreement. In human history, dichotomous ideologies have been responsible for much violence and devastation, thanks to the stark choices they presented and the polarized attitudes they inspired.

Truth, held with unshakable confidence, has been a powerful legitimizing ideal throughout history, whether in matters of religion, philosophy or justice. In the name of truth, major wars have been waged and atrocities perpetrated, whether against early Christians in Rome or African Americans in the US in the twenty-first century. From the medieval crusades against the Muslims in the eleventh to seventeenth centuries and the European wars of religion in the sixteenth and eighteenth centuries, through to the early modern wars against the Ottoman empire and the current tensions between modern India and Pakistan, contemporary Islamist terrorism, White supremacist movements, and Hindu violence against Christians and Muslims (to mention just a few examples among many), endless bloody wars have been waged at the altar of faith and absolute truth, the denial of which could not be tolerated and was punishable by death, destruction and subjugation.

The pernicious effect of black-and-white thinking expresses itself pervasively in the negative stereotyping of various ethnic and religious groups. For instance, after the first and second world wars, Germans in American films were almost universally portrayed as evil and callous; 1940s and 1950s Hollywood movies persistently conflated Germans with Nazis. And certainty-craving American spectators, weary of war-induced confusion, happily accepted the message that Germans were generally depraved, bloodthirsty monsters. Symbolic features such as the black leather coat of Gestapo officers, the swastika and SS runes attached to German characters in American films signalled terror, helplessness and destruction. Similarly biased were depictions of Russian and Chinese characters during the Cold War as sadistic villains, and of Arab characters in the post 9/11 period as scheming terrorists.[6]

Rumours and conspiracy theories

The craving for cognitive closure in times of uncertainty often feeds another narrative phenomenon – rumours and conspiracy theories, those miniature (or occasionally lengthy and complex) stories that appear to offer conclusive explanations for why things are as they are. The 2020 coronavirus pandemic was a vivid example of this – with half the world's population (7.8 billion) online, the electronic spread of rumours was immense and immediate. Some alleged that the fever-reducing drug ibuprofen exacerbated COVID-19 symptoms. Others featured various fake cures for the disease: colloidal silver, vitamins, teas and essential oils. More extreme rumours alleged that the Chinese police were shooting people suspected of having the disease, that the pandemic had been deliberately propagated by the Jews or the Iranians, and that it had been ushered into the country by 'dirty' minorities.

A particularly troubling aspect of conspiracy theories is that they provide a basis for (and often explicitly issue calls for) violent action. As an example, certain far-right groups advocated deliberately infecting the minorities they deemed responsible for the pandemic with the COVID-19 virus itself. Infected people were encouraged to 'visit your local synagogue and hug as many Jews as possible', or to 'cough on your local minority'. Another post read: 'Cough on your local transport system.' And the Federal Protective Service (part of the Department of Homeland Security in the US) noted that White supremacists in the US presented the spreading of the virus as an obligation of those loyal to the supremacist cause who happened to contract it.[7]

In a set of studies published in 2017, Polish researchers Marchlewska, Cichocka and Kossowska measured a range of subjects' (all Polish) need for cognitive closure by using the need-for-closure questionnaire, then offered two groups of people – one consisting of people with a high need for closure, the other with a low need – a message about how the European Union had been financing refugees who came to Poland.[8] In addition, some people received examples of alleged reactions to the message by other Poles. Those reactions cultivated the sense of a conspiracy, namely that the European Union was trying to sow chaos in Poland in order to control it. People in the control group received no such message. All subjects were then asked to state the degree to which they believed in the conspiracy theory with which they were presented. It was found that people with a high need for cognitive closure believed in the conspiracy significantly more than those with a low need. No differences in conspiracy beliefs appeared in the control group between high and low need-for-closure subjects.

Conspiracy theories across time and space

The rumour mill generated by the COVID-19 pandemic was widespread and rapid because of the technology that powered it. Yet the desire to generate and accept rumours is hardly new. Time and again conspiracy theories have mushroomed in times of troubling uncertainty. The Black Death, the first large-scale plague pandemic in Europe, occurred in the mid-fourteenth century and had as a consequence the widespread persecution of Jews. Desperate to understand why they were afflicted with such loss and death, a sense of certainty came through scapegoating Jews, who, it seemed, 'had conspired with the Devil to plague Christianity with harm, calamity, and sicknesses'.[9] Historians also agree that the pervasive witch hunts that swept Europe in the later Middle Ages and early modern era were rooted in uncertainty introduced by the extensive cultural, religious, social and economic changes of those periods. These undermined people's former worldviews, introduced confusion into their belief systems and thwarted their ability to plan for their future.[10] History abounds with endless examples of conspiracy theories, including major recent ones, for example that Lee Harvey Oswald wasn't the only person who assassinated President John F. Kennedy, that the Moon landings were faked, or that the US and UK governments deliberately perpetrated the 9/11 and the 7 July 2005 attacks on their respective countries.

When aversive uncertainty strikes, people's need for closure rises, instilling a disquieting anxiety. In response, they spin and embrace closure by latching on to rumours and outlandish 'theories' in order to regain a sense of control and certainty. Though the concept of 'fake news' sounds distinctly modern, the tendency of people facing uncertainty to create and accept outlandish theories to explain various threatening events is as old as human nature itself.

Populism

Perhaps the most prominent and significant manifestation of black-and-white thinking in the modern age concerns the phenomenon of populism. The term emerged in the late-nineteenth century as part of a political movement characterized by a dichotomous narrative – put simply, it viewed society in terms of the people and an elite. Influenced by Romanticism, it portrayed 'the people' (folk) in superlative terms as pure, kind and trusting (even if naive). The elites, in contrast, were depicted as exploitative, corrupt and immoral. They were alleged to oppress the people and to do them harm. The populist narrative thus challenges people to rise up against the elite and depose them in the interests of justice and fairness.

Typically, the populist narrative addresses a nation, an ethnicity or a religion. The 'people' are therefore denizens of a state, co-ethnics or fellow believers. The 'elites', on the other hand, are characterized variously in different populist narratives. In an American context, the 'Washington establishment' has long been the evil elite of choice, the 'swamp' that Donald Trump promised to drain. In other populist rhetoric, the despised elites can be identified as 'the federal government', the 'military-industrial complex', 'the capitalists', the big banks, 'East Coast intellectuals', and so on.[11]

Political pundits and social scientists have suggested that populism is on the rise worldwide.[12] Whether in Europe, the

Americas, the Middle East or Asia, populist politicians (the likes of Marine Le Pen, Geert Wilders, Vladimir Putin, Rodrigo Duterte, Narendra Modi, Benjamin Netanyahu or Donald Trump) have enjoyed substantial popular support. To take several recent examples from Europe, the Alternative for Germany party in Germany (the AfD) was founded in 2013 yet initially failed to gain a seat in parliament. However, in subsequent years, support grew, and by 2017 they had gained 12.6 per cent of the vote and entered the Bundestag with ninety-four seats, becoming the largest opposition party in the process. In 2018, elections in two countries saw surges in anti-immigrant populist support: former centre-left politician Miloš Zeman's increasingly right-wing rhetoric brought him to power as president of the Czech Republic, while in Italy the neo-fascist leader Georgia Meloni became the prime minister.

There were similar trends in Russia, Poland, Turkey and Hungary. Pundits have noted that populist policies pose a threat to the neo-liberal world order that has been in place since the Second World War, and risk ushering dangerous tensions and discord into international relations.[13] If they are right, the current wave of populism could well constitute a movement of historical importance. But why is populism surging? What is the basis of its appeal and the reason for its increased attractiveness to people worldwide? And how can what we've learned about black-and-white thinking during times of uncertainty inform our understanding of it?

A major mystery that populism scholars have been attempting to unravel is its root causes. What attracts us to populist narratives and why? The explanations offered are predominantly centred on the frustrations and grievances of the 'people', assumed to be caused by the elites. Often mentioned are economic woes, political resentment, ethnic rivalries, the refugee crisis and geopolitical tensions. Leading scholars, such as the University of Michigan's Inglehart and Norris, have proposed that populism is a reaction to the so-called 'progressive' change in cultural values brought about by the trends of cosmopolitanism and multiculturalism.[14] These developments, which de-emphasized the values of nationality or ethnicity, threatened many individuals' sense that they mattered and were significant; those 'left behind' by globalization resented their diminished status and blamed the international elites for their humiliation. In response, they rallied behind the bracing politics of populism which promises to restore their sense of relevance.

The growing economic inequality in Western nations, analysed by Thomas Piketty, has exacerbated the rift between 'winners' and 'losers' and increased the threat of loss and disempowerment in large masses of people.[15] Much like conspiracy theories, of which this is a special case, the populist narrative is appealing because it gratifies people's twin needs for certainty and dignity/significance. These needs rise during times of unrest and change, as they induce a disquieting uncertainty about people's standing in society, their relevance and social worth.

Erica Molinario and I recently ran surveys designed to measure support for populism by focusing on two samples of people, American and Italian, including broad swathes of the political spectrum across both countries. The results revealed many differences between, for instance, the voters for Hillary Clinton and Donald Trump in the US 2016 elections, and between Italians voting in 2018 for the Democratic Party, the Northern League (Lega) and the Five Star Movement. What stood out particularly in both samples was that the need for cognitive certainty and closure and the need for personal significance were the strongest determinants of our respondents' support for populism. They carried far greater predictive sway than other possible factors, such as worries about economic security or cultural identity. It is not that these did not matter; they were influential *because* they activated the basic psychological needs for certainty and significance that the populist narrative is so adept at addressing.

Summary

When confronted with uncertain situations, people become prone to oversimplification couched in black-and-white terms. This finds expression in many domains. In the area of entertainment and aesthetic preferences, it promotes an attraction to 'morality tales' in which good battles bad and overcomes it. The great popularity of films and TV series that feature such dichotomies attests to their soothing power; they afford us escape from the angst-evoking uncertainties of the real world. Whereas escapism into the dichotomous world of good and bad can be innocent enough, the uncertainty-bred need for cognitive closure can inspire conflict and tension. It instils in us a readiness to believe in a different type of narrative – conspiracy theories that disparage whole categories of people. This, in turn, can drive populism, a formalized ideological form of black-and-white thinking that can catapult despots to power (and often has). These trends often inspire strife, violence and mayhem that can tear societies asunder.

In your experience

1. Do you believe in any stereotypes? What if you examined those stereotypes carefully? Are they really valid? If you looked at your stereotypic beliefs in a detached way, would you still believe them?
2. How about conspiracy theories? Are there any conspiracy theories that you believe to be plausible? Is there sufficient evidence for them? Can you conclusively prove them wrong? Can you uncover what motivated you to believe them?
3. Do you know anyone who supports populist leaders and politicians? What do you think they psychologically gain from these populist beliefs?
4. Do you enjoy superhero movies? What do you like about them? What kind of films do you generally like, and do you like them when you're in a particular state of mind?

8. Among Others

'Hell,' wrote the mid-twentieth-century existentialist French philosopher Jean-Paul Sartre, 'is other people';* he could have added, though, 'and so is heaven.' The truth of the matter is that humans are the most sociable beings on the planet. We think in terms of linguistic categories invented by other people; we love, hate, dream about and constantly seek the approval of others.

We became so, anthropologists tell us, way back when, about 6.5 million years ago when large tectonic movements created the savannahs of the East African Great Rift Valley. Prior to that, our ancestors lived in trees, where they were relatively protected from predators, but now, on the flatlands of the savannahs, they found themselves unprotected from and endangered by the faster, stronger and larger lions, leopards, sabre-toothed tigers and other predators.

These hominins, our ancestors, might well have gone the way of the dinosaurs and other now extinct species but for a fortunate (for us) evolutionary turn – the evolution of sociability, learning how to live in groups, cooperate and coordinate their efforts with those of other members of their collective. In turn, the complexities of human interactions led to the evolution of the so-called 'social brain', a far more developed and sophisticated thinking instrument than any other creature had. The rest is history – the human

* In his 1944 play *No Exit* (*Huis Clos*).

142

success tale in which our species came to subdue its nemeses and completely dominate Planet Earth.

Almost every aspect of human nature reflects our social orientation. The need for cognitive closure exemplifies this. In previous chapters, we have seen how the flight from uncertainty towards closure has a far-reaching influence on what and how people think. Yet its impact transcends our beliefs and attitudes. In this chapter, I will show how our craving for closure affects every personal relationship we have, the groups we belong to and our political beliefs.

Have you ever found yourself perplexed by what another person does, feels or thinks? Why would anyone believe, you might wonder, that the American 2020 presidential elections were rigged, that reptiles are taking over world governments, or that carrying out a suicide attack that kills innocents will bring the perpetrator heavenly rewards? People often dismiss such views as nonsense, perhaps attributing them to poor education, mental dysfunction, brainwashing or plain stupidity. Yet to do so is to succumb to prejudice and betrays a naivety about how people think and feel. No one has a monopoly on the truth, moral, political or otherwise. We are generally surrounded by normal, intelligent and highly educated people who can nonetheless subscribe to beliefs that sharply diverge from our own. To understand why another person thinks as they do requires empathy and perspective, the ability to put ourselves in another's place. A high need for cognitive closure can make it harder for us to do this, as it requires us to be willing to embrace uncertainty.

Empathy and perspective

Empathy is key to interpersonal relations. Political candidates at rallies and on election campaigns often profess to 'feel the pain' of their audiences. Their ability to convince people of this is often critical to their electoral success. Yet to be empathetic to others can be challenging, especially if they are very different from us. Politicians, for instance, are typically educated and 'credentialized'. They often have further college degrees, whereas their audiences might be less educated, less knowledgeable or less informed. Politicians may come from the middle class, whereas their audience might be working class. Politicians may be comfortable financially, whereas their audience might be poor and struggling. Politicians may come from a different ethnic group and be of a different religious persuasion to their audience, and so on. All these differences mean that politicians and their audiences may have had entirely different life experiences. This should all make it pretty hard for them to 'feel' what their audiences feel. It takes a special effort to transcend our own narrow circumstances to truly empathize with those who are different from us.

Yet the ability to empathize with others is key to good interpersonal relations and getting along with others, 'winning friends and influencing people', as Dale Carnegie famously put it. Where does this ability come from? Work by developmental psychologists suggests it is a natural competence that most children acquire with age as they mature and interact with others. Research shows that role-taking, that is, imagining oneself in another person's shoes, develops in middle childhood and early adolescence, so most normal adults have this capacity to some degree. As with any human ability, however, people differ. Some children never master 'role-taking' sufficiently. Children and adults who are autistic may have a limited ability to forge a 'shared reality' with others. Other children are naturally gifted in this area. Later in life this may make them effective parents, skilful psychotherapists, teachers or successful politicians.

During times of uncertainty, empathy from our leaders is of the utmost importance, and a lack of it can be crushingly disappointing. President Trump's reaction to the coronavirus pandemic is a glaring example of creating such disappointment. Amid a momentous crisis threatening hundreds of thousands of American lives, Trump bragged in his daily briefings that his TV ratings equalled the *Bachelor* finale or *Monday Night Football* programmes. In those same briefings, viewed by millions of Americans thirsting for soothing news, Trump boasted about his administration's alleged achievements in the war on drugs. This insensitivity and absence of empathy elicited sharp criticism in the US media.[1]

However, having the skill and ability to empathize isn't enough. Having perspective often requires hard work. How another person feels or what they think is, after all, a big unknown. To bridge the gap requires temporarily tolerating uncertainty while figuring out the specific circumstances of the other person. This means discerning how they differ from us and working out what we might do if we were in the other person's shoes. Having a high need for cognitive closure does not stop us from doing this, but it can make it more challenging.

Circumstances that elevate our need for closure have been found to reduce our empathy towards others. Empathy is a crucial ingredient of the human connection. The ability to identify with the emotions and experiences of someone else, to feel their joy and pain, plays a key role in all close relationships, including parenting and spousal relations. Some people are naturally endowed empathizers. They share the feelings of protagonists in films and novels and often tear up at particularly dramatic moments in the plot.

Empathy is particularly appreciated by people in extreme circumstances; someone who has attained an important accomplishment or suffered a severe setback typically wants to share their feelings with close others. Another person's failure to respond to this need often leads to disappointment and alienation. Often a failure of empathy comes from the condition in which the other party finds themselves. As laboratory studies show, these conditions can be simple or mundane, such as when we lack the energy to figure out what another person is thinking or feeling or when we are preoccupied with pressing matters of our own. As we've seen, examples include time pressure, when we feel 'under the gun' to quickly form an opinion, or being in a noisy environment where thinking becomes difficult. Another example is if we find ourselves in a troubling uncertainty that we want to escape. Why should a heightened need for closure reduce our ability to be empathetic? Very simply, it is because the craving for closure that makes people 'seize and freeze' on their own worldview reduces their ability to put themselves in another person's shoes. With the need for closure elevated, the default is to embrace our own reaction to events and assume it to be everyone's reaction. 'If they have no bread, let them eat cake,' Marie-Antoinette reputedly said in 1789. Presumably that is what *she* would have done if she ran out of bread, yet her statement is the epitome of having a poor perspective.

In a pair of clever experiments carried out by Webster-Nelson, Klein and Irvin, participants in one group were made to experience fatigue from having to undertake difficult proofreading and reading comprehension tasks.[2] We've already seen how fatigue can bring about a need for cognitive closure, as energy is needed for careful consideration. Participants in another group were given an easy reading task (inducing low levels of mental fatigue); these participants did not experience low energy or a high need for closure. Now came the important test of the empathy hypothesis. Participants were asked to engage in a social perception task: they were asked to form an impression of another person on the basis of information allegedly provided by that individual. The information given was a disappointing experience in which the person had failed in their attempt to socialize at a party. In some scenarios, the protagonist reported feeling sad and dejected. In others, they reported feeling guilty and agitated. Based on earlier personality testing, researchers knew whether each participant would be likely to experience dejection or agitation when shown the situation, so the protagonist's reaction appeared to be either similar or dissimilar to what the participant themselves would have experienced.

After reading the scenarios, participants evaluated the appropriateness of the protagonist's reaction and also answered questions about how compassionate, sympathetic, tender and warm they felt towards the protagonist. The results provided strong support for the idea that having a need for cognitive closure (elevated by mental fatigue) reduces people's capacity to empathize with others: when the protagonist's reaction was dissimilar to how the participant would have felt in the same situation, participants in the high need for closure (mental fatigue) condition judged the protagonist's reaction to be inappropriate, but the same was not true for those in the low-need-for-closure condition. In addition, they showed less empathy, compassion, sympathy and warm-heartedness towards the protagonist. In contrast, there were no differences between high- and low-need-for-closure participants (that is, fatigued and non-fatigued participants) when the protagonist's depicted reaction was similar to what they would have experienced.

These findings show that the need for cognitive closure and a desire for certainty limit people's ability to appreciate that someone else may have an entirely different reaction to them in the same situation. A lack of empathy and perspective can pose a serious obstacle to managing our relations with others. An inability to appreciate another person's point of view may lead to their derogation and vilification as wrong and unintelligent. As a possible example of this, the frightening uncertainty that the COVID-19 pandemic engendered worldwide, which probably induced the need for closure and reduced the capacity for empathy in many, could be a contributing factor in the accompanying 'pandemic' of domestic violence recorded in many countries. Data from various parts of the world lifted a veil on this unfortunate trend. In the UK, at least twenty-six women and girls were killed in instances of domestic violence in the spring of 2020.[3] Surveys carried out in the Middle East and North Africa, where few laws protect women against violence, registered an increase in gender-based violence. In Latin America, there was a spike in calls to hotlines reflecting the same. In the Chinese city of Jingzhou, the police received three times as many complaints about domestic violence as in previous years. This wave of violence did not spare high- and middle-income countries, including Australia, France, Germany,

South Africa and the United States.[4] We know that intolerance to alternative points of view soars in times of aversive uncertainty, but to what extent did it sit behind these waves of aggression?

Another compounding factor affecting closed-mindedness during the COVID-19 pandemic was an increase in alcohol consumption, a reaction to the anxiety and discomfort produced by lockdowns, restrictions of freedom, mask-wearing mandates, and so on. Nielsen surveys carried out in the spring of 2020 revealed a substantial increase in store purchases of alcohol compared to the preceding year. In March 2020, sales were 55 per cent more than in 2019, and in May they were 32 per cent more. Moreover, over the period of a year, there was a staggering 500 per cent increase in online sales of alcohol, and a Morning Consult poll revealed that 16 per cent of American adults reported drinking more during the pandemic than before.[5]

How is alcohol consumption related to closed-mindedness? Very simply, it reduces our ability to process information and induces a cognitive state known as 'alcohol myopia'[6] in which people experience a heightened need for closure. In a study that explicitly researched the connection between alcohol and the need for closure, Donna Webster had participants ingest either pure orange juice (the placebo condition), orange juice mixed with a low dose of alcohol (0.5ml ethanol/kg of body weight) or orange juice mixed with a moderate amount of alcohol (0.7ml ethanol/kg of body weight).[7] Webster then measured the individuals' need for closure and found that participants with the moderate dose of alcohol had a higher need for closure than those with a low dose, while those with no alcohol reported the lowest degree. Webster also found that participants given a moderate amount of alcohol tended to ignore unexpected information more than those given a little alcohol or none. This neglect was produced by the alcohol-induced need for closure.

In plain language, alcohol induces a kind of mental laziness and elevates people's need for closure, which reduces their ability to process information that differs from what they 'froze' upon in their intoxicated state. It's easy, therefore, to see how alcohol consumption during the pandemic may have exacerbated an existing pull towards intolerance, set as it was against a backdrop of pervasive uncertainty. (I should like to emphasize here that this does not in any way justify intolerance, domestic violence and other antisocial phenomena linked to excessive alcohol consumption. No matter the situation, a person is morally responsible for their acts.)

Another global trend during the COVID-19 pandemic was a marked increase in violent protests. In the United States, protests over the killing by police of African American men spread to over 2,000 cities and towns in all 50 states. An estimated 15 to 26 million people participated in them, making it arguably the largest instance of mass activism in US history. In many cases, the protests erupted in violence, and the looting and burning of businesses and police cars. Protests in support of the Black Lives Matter movement and against police brutality spread internationally to over sixty countries and spurred violent counterdemonstrations in defence of the police. Protests also erupted around the world in reaction to local problems: a new anti-terrorism law in the Philippines, a decision by the Communist Party of China to try Hong Kong residents in mainland China, the economic and health crisis in Israel, governmental pandemic-related restrictions in Brazil, the administration's handling of the pandemic in Poland, and so on. It is no accident that the protest movement was so intense and global. The troubling self-uncertainty that the pandemic produced in millions of people around the world fostered polarization because it encouraged individuals to embrace black-and-white thinking that demonizes political opponents and justifies violence and mayhem on behalf of a particular cause.

Participation in protests and political activism offers people certainty and the sense of worth and significance. Katarzyna Jasko, a researcher at Jagiellonian University, carried out with her colleagues a series of studies that investigated what motivates people to participate in political activism. The studies were carried out in different social contexts and with different populations, including radical left-wing supporters, members of a democratic social movement, feminist activists, environmental activists and participants and supporters of a hunger strike. It was consistently found that the more important the values of a political movement to individuals, the more personally significant they feel when participating and, consequently, the greater their willingness to make self-sacrifices on its behalf.

Intriguingly, threats to people's self-confidence can activate values that help people regain their certainty and significance. For instance, the possibility of serious illness threatens our sense of physical wellness, whereas the possibility of job loss or bankruptcy threatens our sense of economic security. Recently, my colleagues and I looked at these two threats in the context of the COVID-19 pandemic, which produced both. The threat to our health brings to mind our fragility and vulnerability. It activates our sense of dependence on others (reminiscent of our childhood) and, relatedly, our expectation/hope of kindness from others. It highlights for us the values of social concern and empathy. We found that people who saw the threat to their health as the major concern during the pandemic showed considerable social responsibility. They reported scrupulously wearing a protective mask, keeping to social distancing guidance and increasing the frequency of their online communication with family and friends. In contrast, the economic threat that COVID-19 presents reminds people of the competition that rules the marketplace. This highlights our separateness from others and our rivalry with them over limited resources. Consequently, people who are predominantly worried about their economic well-being reported a rather low sense of social responsibility during the pandemic. They described being less careful about wearing a mask and maintaining social distancing, and they tend to connect less with others online. In short, whereas the threats to our physical health and our finances both introduce self-uncertainty and lower our sense of potency and worth, they activated different values and encouraged opposite behaviours during the pandemic. People who were predominantly concerned about their health affirmed their social responsibility and restored their sense of worth and significance by trying to be 'good citizens' who care about the common good. People who were more concerned about economic and financial threats regained their significance by affirming their competitiveness and their strength against potential rivals.

Communicating

Effective communication is one of the most important interpersonal skills we can have. Whether with family and friends or in our professional endeavours, clearly expressing our needs, concerns and ideas is often key to success.

Communication is crucial to influence and persuasion. Getting people to consider and appreciate our message goes a long way towards them accepting and believing it.

Some people are known as great communicators. These are speakers who can command people's attention for hours and get their point across simply and effectively. Winston Churchill's speeches were renowned for their impact and elegance. His messages were short, pithy and to the point. Oprah Winfrey is another example of an outstanding communicator; she is known for her great ability to listen and for talking about things that matter to people. People listen to her because she gives the impression that she really cares and understands their needs and concerns.

Having perspective is essential to good communication. The effective transmission of information requires that our messages are correctly decoded. This means framing them in a way that the recipient understands. To do so, the communicator must understand their beliefs and assumptions about the topic and realize why they hold the opinions they do. If these things aren't taken into account, the message may be misconstrued, ignored and fall on deaf ears.

Effective communication requires that we understand the perspective of our listeners. Speakers must be able to figure out what the people they are addressing know and where they are coming from. This also applies to writers, for whom being understood depends to a large extent on how they frame their communications and whether they do so in consideration of readers' assumptions and mindsets. Writing coaches never tire of warning novices to avoid jargon and to frame their messages as simply as possible. Brevity and simplicity are the hallmarks of good communication. As William Faulkner remarked of Ernest Hemingway: 'He has never been known to use a word that might send a reader to the dictionary.'

Because troubling uncertainty and the need for closure that it arouses reduce our ability to have empathy and perspective, it strongly interferes with effective communication. Ironically, even though in times of uncertainty people *desire* the clearest, closure-affording messages, uncertainty hampers the transmission of ideas, and communicators may find it challenging to deliver messages that their audiences can decipher.

Considering motivation

As well as figuring out the mind frame of our listeners, or perhaps as part of the process, successful communication (and persuasion) requires that communicators recognize the listeners' motivations. Are they interested in the topic at all and, if so, how? Is there a particular thing they want to hear? Avoid hearing? All these are important issues for the communicator to consider. As Karl Popper noted: 'No rational argument will have a rational effect on a man who does not *want* to adopt a rational attitude.'[8] In other words, if the message is distasteful to the audience, they are unlikely to see its merits, however 'objectively' impressive these may seem.

Importantly, listeners' motivations with respect to a message may vary. They may be highly motivated to decode and comprehend the message and spare no effort in divining the communicator's intended meaning. This may happen when the writer is known for their wisdom or expertise and listeners are keen to learn and benefit from what they have to offer. Attentive listening also happens when people are positively disposed towards the communicator – when they like them and want to be liked by them in return.

Dale Carnegie, the author of *How to Win Friends and Influence People*, which sold over 30 million copies and continues as a bestseller more than eighty-five years after its publication, offers the following advice, aimed at satisfying the listeners' motivations and thus ensuring their open-mindedness to persuasion: 'Do not criticize, condemn or complain; be generous with praise; remember people's names; be genuinely interested in other people; do not attempt to win an argument, as "a person convinced against their will is of the same opinion still"; make people feel important.' One can readily see how all these augment people's feelings that they are significant and appreciated. It boosts their confidence and encourages them to be receptive to the message.

Other listener motivations matter in the same way. For instance, students may invest considerable effort in understanding their professor's message because the quality of their education (and their grade) depends on it. So, too, lovers of poetry or philosophy may be willing to work hard in decoding a revered author's work (for example deciphering a hermetic poem or an obscure philosophical treatise). But often listeners have neither the motivation nor the time or patience to work hard at deciphering an abstruse message. In situations of uncertainty, and under a high need for cognitive closure, they may quickly tune out overly nuanced and complex arguments and be drawn instead to clear, easy-to-understand communications, such as the black-and-white worldviews discussed in Chapter 7.

In a study that Linda Richter and I carried out some years ago, we provided participants with a set of abstract drawings and asked them to write a description of each one for themselves (the *non-social* condition) and for someone else (the *social* condition) so that they could match the descriptions to the drawings on a later occasion.[9] Half our participants had a high need for cognitive closure (as measured by our need-for-closure scale in Chapter 1) and the other half had a low need for closure. The study was carried out in two phases three to five weeks apart. In the first phase, participants wrote descriptions of thirty drawings. When our participants came back to the laboratory they were shown the same drawings and the descriptions that they or other participants had written. Their task was to match the descriptions to the figures.

Several findings of this study were revealing. First, the descriptions that participants had prepared for someone else were considerably lengthier and more detailed than those they had prepared for themselves. The descriptions they had prepared for themselves were not only much shorter and 'telegraphic', they also used idiosyncratic allusions and metaphors. Allusions and shortcuts were largely absent in the descriptions participants had prepared for someone other than them. It seems that our research subjects intuited that other people's perspectives would differ from their own and that another person would not be able to decipher their private associations as well as they could.

Overall, the descriptions they had prepared for themselves led to better identification of the abstract figures than those prepared by someone else, but the difference was much greater for individuals with a high need for closure. In other words, if someone with a low need for closure had prepared a description for someone else, it was more likely to lead to a correct identification than if someone with a high need for closure had prepared the description. The moral of the story is that we should refrain from preparing communications, lectures or speeches when we are feeling a high need for closure, prompted, for instance, by time pressure, noise, mental fatigue or gnawing uncertainty. Your ability to get 'into the shoes' of your audience, to be understood and appreciated, will be much improved if you prepare your communication in relaxed circumstances, as any pressure elevates the closure-seeking tendency.

Communication in times of uncertainty is challenged by a heightened need for cognitive closure for both the communicator and the recipient. The communicator may lack the motivation to divine the audience's perspective and may therefore frame messages in an idiosyncratic, difficult-to-understand manner – and recipients may not be able to expend the mental effort that deciphering complex or unfamiliar messages may require.

Groups and tribes

In the early decades of the twenty-first century, democracy is in retreat around the world, as autocratic regimes and dictatorial leaders spring up in countries that once seemed irrevocably committed to egalitarianism.[10] Turkey's Erdoğan, Poland's Duda, Israel's Netanyahu, the Philippines' Duterte, Brazil's Bolsonaro, India's Modi and others like them increasingly represent a return to crass nationalism and the concentration of political power in the hands of the few. The struggle between open and closed societies is several thousand years old, going back to ancient Athens, where champions of democracy like Democritus (460–370 BC) talked about the danger of the oligarchs, and Plato argued the merits of a return to a tribal system of governance headed by a patriarchal ruling class and with a stratified society governed by rigid norms and traditions that keep all citizens 'in their place'.

According to Karl Popper, in Plato's time, people's tendency to cling to their tribes and strictly observe cultural norms was due to the rampant uncertainty brought about by the opening up of society caused by population growth and the burgeoning commerce between different peoples. As Popper put it:

> This strain, this uneasiness, is the consequence of the breakdown of the closed society. It is still felt even in our day, especially in times of social change. It is the strain created by the effort which life in an open society continually demands from us – by the endeavour to be rational, to forgo at least some of our emotional social needs, to look after ourselves and to accept responsibilities.[11]

The strain that Popper talked about is the strain of aversive uncertainty, the realm of the unknown that to some people signals potential disaster.

Stressful uncertainty affects how people relate to their in-groups or 'tribes' (family, friends, members of their culture) whose 'reality' they share. It also determines how they relate to out-groups, particularly those they see as adversarial. First, under the high need for closure that uncertainty may breed, people become more 'group-centric', more emotionally connected and more dependent on their in-groups. It is, after all, through the consensual values and worldviews of the in-group that it provides certainty and closure. Humans are essentially social beings, and we constantly turn to trusted and respected others for the validation of our opinions. We typically feel uncomfortable and undermined when those whose opinion we value disagree with us.

Have you ever discovered that a film you loved, or detested, elicited a diametrically opposite reaction from a close friend? Just such a situation is explored in *Art*, a poignant play by Yasmina Reza. It tells the story of Serge and Marc, long-time friends, whose friendship is seriously strained by what we might think of as a trifling disagreement. Serge purchases for an exorbitant amount a modern painting, white on white, and can't stop adoring it, while Marc thinks his friend is the victim of a swindle and that the painting isn't worth the canvas it is painted on. Through the clever dialogue that unfolds between the characters, we learn how this disagreement about a matter of taste seriously tests their relationship, perhaps beyond repair. And though *Art* is typically billed as a comedy, it contains a deep insight into human nature and illustrates how crucial to the maintenance of closeness agreement with our close friends is, even on seemingly unimportant matters.

Now, we might think that we do not need others for the validation of *all* our views and that we typically rely on ourselves in most matters, forming our judgements independently of other people. This is, of course, true, but in large part it's *because* we implicitly assume that trusted others would agree with us! For instance, we may trust our vision and hearing, because in the past the judgement they have yielded coincided with that of other credible people (for example, our parents). Most people would agree with us that the leaves we are looking at are green, the flowers red, or that it is safe to cross a road as no traffic is coming our way.

Strikingly, classic social psychological research by Solomon Asch shows that when faced with visual perceptions that are incompatible with our own we feel confused, surprised and stressed out.[12] In Asch's experiment, research participants were asked to judge the relative length of lines. At one point, they were shown a pair of lines, A and B, in which B is longer than A. Surprisingly to one participant in the group, all the others (in fact, in collusion with the person conducting the experiment) state that A is the longer line. The purpose of the study was to determine whether in this situation, and when faced with a majority judgement that is at odds with their own visual perception, the lone true participant would yield to peer pressure. About two thirds of the participants gave a judgement that contradicted what they saw with their own eyes. But whether they conformed or not, the experience of disagreeing with others on a matter of physical reality was discombobulating to all.

Asch also found that people conform to the majority much less when their impulse is to disagree if there is even just one person who shares that impulse. Together, we can create a shared reality and so withstand peer pressure. This explains how small terrorist cells and extremist groups can be so cohesive and enduring, even though the ideology they endorse is out of step with mainstream culture and what the majority believes. Gertrude Stein had the following to say about being out of step with others and then receiving support from somebody: 'Then someone says yes to it, to something you are liking, or doing or making and then never again can you have completely such a feeling of being afraid and ashamed that you had then when you were writing or liking the thing and not anyone had said yes about the thing.'[13]

The experimental situation created by Asch was highly unusual. After all, in most matters of physical reality we assume agreement and feel no need to compare our thoughts to other people's. However, our reliance on trusted others – members of our in-group – is another matter: it is especially pronounced in matters of judgement and opinion. When it comes to values, points of view, ethics, aesthetics, politics or religion, our reliance on people whose opinion we respect is nearly absolute.

This property of human nature has an important consequence. When aversive uncertainty strikes, our acute need for closure magnifies our dependence on the consensus of our in-group. It prompts us to conform to the group's norms and cherish its 'shared reality' even more. By the same token, we seek uniformity of opinion (which provides certainty) and frown on those who express off-the-beaten-path ideas. This means that under stressful uncertainty, we favour cohesive groups whose members exhibit uniformity of opinion. Often such groups have powerful leaders whose views are (uncritically) accepted; these are groups where, as it is humorously said, 'Everyone is entitled to the boss's opinion.'

In a study that Donna Webster and I carried out in the early 1990s, we explored how members of a group react to a deviant in their midst, and how their reaction depends on these members' need for cognitive closure.[14] We approached groups of Israeli Boy and Girl Scouts and had them discuss the location of their annual summer camp. Two possible places were presented as options, a well-resourced settlement in the middle of the country and a smaller one in the middle of the desert. We knew that the Israeli Scouts were an adventurous bunch and that they much preferred the desert location over the more comfortable yet less romantic alternative, but, unbeknown to others in the group, we asked one of the members to argue for the less preferred alternative and to do so either at the beginning of the discussion, when everyone's mind was still open and their need for closure was low, or towards the end, when the pressure to reach a consensus had elevated the members' need for closure.

The reaction to the 'deviant' in the group couldn't have been more different in the two cases. When they expressed their opinion at the beginning of the session, they were pretty popular with everyone else in the group. However, when they expressed their view towards the end, their popularity plummeted precipitously. The group members' desire for consensus under the heightened need for closure led them to be impatient with the 'deviant's' disagreement and come to see it as a sign of unreasonable stubbornness.

Research reveals that in conditions of troubling uncertainty, people are drawn to autocratic groups and become annoyed and impatient with freewheeling democratic societies whose norms are relatively 'loose' and relaxed.[15] In such circumstances, people prefer leaders who provide firm guidance and express confident views, and they do not appreciate open-minded and flexible leaders whose opinions are more easily swayed by opposing opinions.[16]

Because it is the in-group, whose worldview we share, that gives us certainty, when uncertainty strikes, people run to their group 'for cover'. In other words, in times of uncertainty people feel an augmented commitment to their in-group. This may express itself in greater patriotism but also in stronger nationalism, collective narcissism, the exaltation of their country and the assertion of its superiority over others. 'My country, right or wrong,' as Carl Schurz is reported to have stated in 1872, an attitude that seems to prevail when uncertainty strikes. At such times, people often rally around the flag and are quick to blame foreign groups or nationalities for whatever ills they may be experiencing.

During the 2020 coronavirus pandemic, the US and China, for example, traded sharp barbs, charging that the other was responsible for the disaster. Senator Tom Cotton (a Republican from Arkansas) talked about the pandemic possibly emanating from a Chinese-manufactured bioweapon. President Trump and Secretary of State Pompeo referred to COVID-19 as the 'Chinese virus' and the 'Wuhan virus' respectively. On the other side, a Chinese foreign ministry spokesperson tweeted: 'It might be [the] US Army that brought the epidemic to Wuhan.'[17] Such theories and blame-castings owe their popularity to the uncertainty-borne need for cognitive closure that offers people a sense of understanding and coherence.

Summary

Our need for closure affects nearly all domains of our social relations. It determines not only how we think but also how we feel about our in-groups and their real or imagined enemies. In the realm of thinking, a heightened need for closure fosters a preference for black-and-white views and a confirmation of our prior conceptions. It motivates us to prematurely jump to conclusions on the basis of insufficient evidence, and to become confident and self-assured without good justification. It limits our interest in and capacity to understand other people's mindset and point of view, to appreciate the mood they are in or how a particular situation makes them feel. It also limits our ability to communicate with others, both as message senders (speakers or authors) and as recipients (listeners or readers). Closed-mindedness in times of uncertainty may give us a pleasing sense of assurance but it may also exact a price we might not want to pay.

Understanding how we react to uncertainty and to situations that heighten our need for closure may allow us to evaluate our inclination to succumb to its influence and avoid its unwanted effects.

In your experience

1. Do you consider yourself an empathetic person? How does this express itself with regard to those you are close to? How does it express itself in your involvement with protagonists in movies or novels?
2. Do you demand empathy from your friends and loved ones? Are they providing it for you? How do you react when they do? What about when they don't?
3. Are you a good communicator? What is the secret of your success? What challenges do you face as a communicator?
4. Are you strongly tied to your in-group? How often do you try to have contact with its members? How important to you is your group membership? Does its importance increase or decrease in times of uncertainty?

9. Self-confidence and Self-doubt

Do you consider yourself a 'strong' person? Would you like to be even stronger? I posed this question to one of my undergraduate classes in psychology and just about everyone raised their hand in affirmation. Strength is a socially valued attribute in contemporary Western cultures, applicable to all persons regardless of their gender or sexual orientation. This wasn't always the case. According to Barbara Welter, the author of *The Cult of True Womanhood: 1820–1860* (1966), an ideal nineteenth-century 'true woman' was 'frail' and too weak mentally and physically to leave her home. These days this ideal seems outmoded and ludicrous, as both women and men strive to develop their strength and pride themselves on their robustness and resilience.

Both spiritual and physical strength are widely valued in most societies, though of the two, spiritual strength, strength of character, is the more admired. 'The moral is to the physical as three is to one,' Napoleon Bonaparte once said, referring to the advantage in battle of conviction and mental resolve over brute power and material resources. Napoleon's impression was echoed in studies by Tossell and colleagues, who found in extensive research carried out over four continents that conviction and strength of beliefs – more so than physical formidability – are positively associated with the will to fight and sacrifice for others.[1]

Because it represents a source of mental strength, and because mental strength is universally valued, self-confidence is a highly prized attribute that most people vie to possess. We all want to be poised and self-assured; no one wants to be consumed by self-doubt. Popular self-help literature, by psychologists, evangelists or others, is replete with programmes and schemes that promise to build self-confidence. They aim to transform us from a diffident weakling consumed by social anxiety into a secure, unflappable adult. And according to the popular periodical *Psychology Today*, people who project confidence inspire trust, command influence and put others at ease.

I always marvel about these effects during the unnerving moments of turbulence on a flight when the plane's smooth progress is interrupted by a series of sudden drops, evoking in some passengers at least (myself included) frightful thoughts about a possible aircraft malfunction and the severe dangers this could entail. In those anxious moments the calm demeanour of the air stewards, their obvious self-confidence and their air of business as usual immediately dispels passengers' worries and quiets their apprehensions.

In Chapter 6, I referred to important research on the opposite of self-confidence, the so-called self- or personal uncertainty – the awareness of our confusion and uncertainty about our self-worth. Confronting unresolved ethical dilemmas or having doubts about our intelligence or appearance may instil misgivings about whether we actually merit and will earn others' appreciation and respect. Needless to say, this is not a pleasant feeling. Viennese psychiatrist Alfred Adler coined the term 'inferiority complex' for the sense of personal inadequacy that can dominate people's lives and push them to great efforts in order to compensate for it.

According to Adler, all humans experience feelings of inferiority and spend the rest of their lives trying to overcome them. A fully fledged inferiority complex may develop, however, when these feelings of inferiority are compounded by discouragement, disapproval or failure. Circumstances that may make us feel inferior and disempowered include not having much money, belonging to a stigmatized group and a toxic family environment in which we are subjected to constant disapproval and criticism. A condition that restricts a person's ability to function physically, mentally or socially may also be a source of our sense of inferiority.

Adler used Napoleon Bonaparte and the Greek orator Demosthenes as examples of people who were driven by their need to compensate for inborn handicaps. In Napoleon's case it was short stature and in the case of Demosthenes a stutter. For people like these, obviously extraordinarily gifted human beings, a debilitating flaw creates a jarring incongruity, a self-uncertainty that makes them put much of their energy into overcompensating for it.

In my own research on radicalization and violent extremism, I encountered several cases in which someone who had suffered a setback to their social worth went on to compensate for it by volunteering for a cause cherished by their community.[2] Among Palestinian women who became suicide bombers, some had been stigmatized because of being infertile, divorced or accused of marital infidelity, all causes of severe disgrace in traditional Palestinian society. To erase the dishonour they had suffered, they sacrificed their lives in attacks on those perceived as enemies of their people and became hailed as martyrs and heroines.

We all occasionally experience negative outcomes that lower our sense of social worth. No one is immune to rejection, failure or bad luck. These often crack the foundations of our self-assurance and introduce uncertainty about our self-worth. Research shows that people with a fragile sense of self-worth are particularly impacted by negative outcomes. The unpleasant uncertainty they experience awakens their need for self-certainty. They may then overcompensate and make themselves even more self-confident than before.

Self-uncertainty and extremism

Especially interesting is the discovery that self-uncertainty, brought about by feeling discriminated against, ignored or disrespected, makes extreme groups particularly appealing.[3] Extremism means 'putting all your eggs in one basket', concentrating on one thing only and neglecting others.[4] The more we suffer from feelings of personal uncertainty, the more we wish to be rid of them. In such conditions, we may be willing to sacrifice everything to restore our sense of self-worth. Most people are unwilling to make sacrifices; instead, they try to have it all. They may aspire to success in their career yet also value their family life and spend time with friends. That is why extremism, characterized by concentrating on one thing only, is rare. Most people tend to be moderate.

When self-doubt sets in, people turn to their groups because adherence to the group's purpose, its norms and ideals, earns them acceptance and respect. Members of moderate groups are not exclusively devoted to their group's purpose; they usually have other concerns and other groups to which they belong. Members of a tennis club, for instance, certainly care about tennis, but they care about other things as well (say literature, cooking, work) and they may be members of other groups (parent–teacher associations, corporate boards, and so on). Extreme groups, in contrast, typically focus on one thing (for example, a religious, national or social aim). Serving the group's central ideal takes precedence above all else.

Consider the statement of a Tamil Black Tiger, a member of the suicide cadre of the Liberation Tigers of Tamil Eelam (LTTE), whom my research team interviewed some years ago in Sri Lanka. The LTTE was a major terrorist organization that waged a cruel thirty-year war on the Sinhalese majority of the country in which 150,000 people lost their lives (among them heads of state, generals, journalists and senior academics). This is what our interviewee had to say about his membership in the squad: 'Family and relationships are forgotten in that place. There was no place for love . . . That means a passion and loyalty to that group, to those in charge, to those who sacrificed their lives for the group . . . Then I came to a stage where I had no love for myself. I had no value for my life. I was ready to give myself fully, even to destroy myself, in order to destroy another person.'

There is good reason why people with considerable self-doubt are attracted to extreme groups. Such groups offer a clearer way to acceptance and significance than moderate groups. Because of their single-minded devotion to their purpose, proving their commitment earns members particularly high marks from their fellow extremists. Someone who does so is therefore assured of their self-worth; they can be proud of themselves, hold their head high, their self-doubts banished.

My colleagues and I recently analysed interviews with forty German neo-Nazis, asking ourselves what had made them join the extremist movement.[5] The interviewers didn't pose the question directly, as people often have little insight into what made them do what they did.* Instead, the interviewees were asked to describe their life before joining. Unsolicited, 78 per cent mentioned grievances or problems that had caused them to experience considerable self-doubt: 61 per cent had experienced personal struggles; 61 per cent had experienced relational issues; and 25 per cent described times when their political views had been ignored or dismissed. Physical and verbal abuse within the family was mentioned frequently. One interviewee recounted:

> As long as I can remember and comprehend, my mother just hit us. For even just the smallest mistake, we got a beating. Whether it was because our room was not properly tidy or if we hadn't washed the dishes properly. There really didn't even need to be a reason. When there wasn't a reason, she just made one up . . . In the case of my brother, the beatings left behind deep emotional wounds; he wasn't able to deal with the pressure and it broke him . . . I never experienced . . . emotional love between me and my mother.[6]

Our interviewees also recalled the boost to their self-confidence they experienced on joining the extremist neo-Nazi movement. Of the interviewees, 69.4 per cent described how membership made them feel significant and important; 69.4 per cent felt they were achieving important ideological goals; and 77.8 per cent found camaraderie and

* Research by Nisbett and Wilson (1977) shows that people often rationalize choices they made for other reasons entirely. Someone might think they like a given film for its artistic qualities whereas, in fact, they do so because the film was liked by their close friends. Someone might think they purchased a car for its good repair record, whereas, in fact, they did so because of subliminal advertising.

support, that is, acceptance or respect from fellow members. One interviewee recalled his participation in a neo-Nazi event with these words: '[This] is exactly how I imagined what the New Reich would be . . . I had the feeling that I had achieved everything I wanted in my private life, I had achieved that which makes a National Socialist what he is and I was a member of the nucleus of what would become the *Neue Volksgemeinschaft* [New National Community].'[7] Another interviewee, a woman, commented on the significance she felt she had attained on reaching a leadership position: 'The advantage, as I quite soon discovered, was that I was basically safeguarded in all regards, that I could get hold of arms if I wanted to, and that I had corresponding "bodyguards" around me . . . that I had financial means at my disposal, which to earn in everyday life would take some time . . . You could demonstrate power by having a whole bunch of people backing you up.'[8]

Another interviewee commented on the atmosphere of solidarity and camaraderie that offered members a sense of significance and assurance:

> It was normal that ten comrades would stay at someone's house, or people who had just been kicked out of home would be put up by comrades . . . Or things like back then when I was given a little pocket money . . . The people who were earning money paid for the others and when you earn money somewhere, you would do the same for the members still going to school. It was also just taken as a given that people with a car would drive the younger members who didn't have a driver's license somewhere they wanted to go.[9]

In short, acceptance by the extremist group boosted members' sense of self-worth and was a major psychological factor in their joining the group and committing to its ideology.

Back to moderation

Push factors

The same feelings of self-doubt (self-uncertainty) that make membership of an extreme group attractive can also facilitate a return to moderation. Push factors repulse people from the once-attractive group; pull factors attract them back to the mainstream. Often the promise of significance and self-worth that extremism holds out can turn to bitter disappointment if the group's lofty cause and camaraderie prove to be a sham.

Our neo-Nazi interviewees often reported how the feeling that they mattered and their sense of importance that their membership had originally gratified gradually faded and wore off. Of our sample, 77.8 per cent reported disillusionment with the ideology of the extreme right. One interviewee came to view it as 'a house of cards . . . built on so many lies'. Another referred to it as 'absolute humbug . . . conspiracy theories [that] seemed like excuses to avoid having to face up to the atrocities of Nazi Germany'. Yet another stated: 'You think about . . . what you had wanted to change . . . And . . . you realize that apart from drunken brawls or crimes, you actually have nothing to show.'[10]

This change of mind and disappointment with the ideological commitment of fellow group members often occurred alongside disappointment in their friendship – the gnawing sense that the respect and acceptance that they had hoped for simply weren't there. Our thoughts are strongly affected by our motivations. If our desire for self-worth is frustrated, our gushing enthusiasm for the group's narrative is sure to be curbed as well. One interviewee who left the movement was betrayed by a comrade who lured his pregnant girlfriend away from him. His reaction was bitter disappointment with the group. As he put it: 'So much for comradeship. That is all a crock of shit, and I'm supposed to be able to trust you – loyalty and honour, and all that. Those were the things that finally finished me off with respect to the group.'[11]

Pull factors

Leaders of extreme groups typically take care to keep their members isolated from outside influences that might offer them alternative (and often less demanding) ways of attaining self-assurance and self-worth. This is often the case with cults (for example Jim Jones's Peoples Temple), which keep their members secluded and out of contact with the outside world.[12] The same is true of cadres of prospective suicide bombers, who are deliberately kept sequestered from their community.[13] Sociologists call this *renunciation*, the 'relinquishing of any relationships potentially disruptive to group cohesion, thereby heightening the relationship of individual to group'.[14] Renunciation can be accomplished by the geographical isolation of the group and by developing rules and norms that minimize group members' contacts with the outside. This is because meeting and becoming friendly with someone outside the group exposes a member to a different point of view, a different narrative. Because we typically want to agree with those we like or love, we are likely to consider a friend's perspective seriously and with an open mind. This could bring about a change of heart and lead to defection from the group altogether.

For one of our interviewees, this process started in prison. He started a fight with two of his neo-Nazi comrades, and two inmates of Turkish descent came to his aid. As he recounts: 'Then it became clear to me that two Turks had just helped me against comrades who shared my attitudes and opinions. That is something that I eventually could not come to terms with.' One thing led to another, and the crack created by this initial event kept getting wider:

> We had visit days. We went to have Turkish food. It tasted good . . . And then we came to the next topic: What are German virtues? Order, discipline, punctuality. The African said, according to that, he is completely German. 'I keep things orderly. Do you want to see my apartment? I am disciplined. I am always on time. I am there ten minutes before work starts. I am really German.' And he was right somehow. That does start to make sense after a while.[15]

Deradicalizing violent extremists

In recent years, there have been several attempts to pull violent extremists away from the movements to which they belong. In Germany, such programmes have existed for many decades; they represent German society's attempt to ensure National Socialism could never again gain ground in their country. Other such programmes, in Saudi Arabia, Singapore and Iraq, among others, have addressed Islamist extremists and attempted to disabuse them of their pernicious beliefs by offering them an alternative, peaceful route to self-significance and assurance.

It was my good fortune to be able to assess a deradicalization programme of members of the LTTE. In 2009, the Sri Lankan government initiated a decisive push to defeat the group and end the long war this organization had waged. The minister of defence in those days, later Sri Lanka's president, Gotabaya Rajapaksa, doubled the size of the Sri Lankan army and, in a tough campaign in which about 20,000 militants were killed, demolished the LTTE. Its leader, Velupillai Prabhakaran, was also killed, and the remaining 11,500 fighters surrendered to the army. Though these troops originally feared severe punishment, they were placed instead in a deradicalization programme and given access to various educational, artistic and vocational activities designed to convince them to abandon extremism and re-enter mainstream Sri Lankan society. To build the detainees' sense of confidence and self-worth, the programme placed great importance on the respectful treatment of the detainees. It allowed them freedom of movement within the (large) detention camp and freedom of religious practice (whereas the Sinhalese are predominantly Buddhist, the Tamils are Hindu). The military personnel supervising the centre were unarmed, although armed guards did watch over the camp's periphery. In addition, successful and well-respected people in the Tamil community were recruited to work with the detainees, serving as role models and inspiring them to work towards the development of professional, social and emotional skills that would allow them to reintegrate into the community.

Our team followed this process and studied it in depth. Specifically, we conducted surveys with the detainees at three time points during the programme (which lasted approximately a year). We were particularly fortunate in being able to compare a sample of detainees who received the full complement of courses and activities with a control group that, for reasons unrelated to our research, happened to receive a much more limited programme. When these two samples were compared, it turned out that those who had done the full programme were by the end of the year significantly less extreme and less supportive of violence against the Sinhalese than those in the control group. So, the programme appears to have been successful. Of even greater interest, feelings of self-worth and personal significance were markedly higher among detainees who had received the full deradicalization programme. Furthermore, this *led to* the bigger drop in support for violence that detainees exposed to the full programme exhibited.[16]

In short, the same quest for significance and the reduction of personal uncertainty that pushes people to join an extreme group can also facilitate their relinquishment of extremism and return to moderation. Once the extreme group no longer gratifies the member's need for significance, due to fissures within the group or humiliation suffered by it (for example, military defeat), members may be open to alternative ways of attaining significance, including those of mainstream society.

Significance gain

Self-uncertainty is unpleasant because it questions our self-worth. Indeed, the desire for respect and dignity is a strong motive that influences much of our behaviour. This may be fuelled not only by threats to self-worth but also by the opportunity to score a great gain in self-worth, the opportunity to become a superstar, hero or martyr. People do not only join extreme groups to repair their threatened sense of self-worth, they often do so for the glory and the glamour, for the boost to their sense of significance that membership offers. Many Islamic State (IS) recruits, for example, came from wealthy and respected families. Many were well educated, held professional degrees (for example, in medicine or engineering) and could expect respectable and profitable careers, but they abandoned it all because a greater opportunity for significance beckoned – the glory of being a glamorous fighter who kills and dies for Allah.

The anthropologist Scott Atran has spent much of his career studying what he calls 'sacred values', values of supreme importance to a group that justify the deepest sacrifices. Making such sacrifices bestows the highest worth and significance on the people ready to make them. Sacred values such as belief in God or country, the right of a nation to self-definition or sovereignty over its holy places, are non-fungible. No amount of money or other material resources can compensate for them or persuade people to betray them.

Research finds that people who care a lot about their group membership, who feel 'at one with the group', are ready to do all it takes, including killing and dying in defence of the group's sacred values.[17] This 'in-group morality', the ethical obligation to protect the group come what may, has deep evolutionary roots. Charles Darwin saw the virtues of 'morality ... patriotism, fidelity, obedience, courage, and sympathy' as products of 'natural selection'.[18] He predicted that groups populated by heroes and martyrs, better endowed with such virtues, would dominate history's unrelenting competition for survival.[19]

Heroism and martyrdom afford a tremendous sense of self-worth and self-confidence, an assurance that we matter and are significant.

An admirable feature of Atran's work is its field research into the behaviours of devoted people ready to sacrifice all for a valued cause. A striking example is his study of the 2016 Battle of Kudilah in Iraq, when coalition forces made a push to retake Mosul, the largest city controlled by IS. Close to ninety IS fighters were stacked up against several hundred coalition forces, including the Kurdish Peshmerga, the Iraqi army and Arab Sunni militia. In the fierce fighting, 50 per cent of the IS fighters lost their lives, including more than a dozen suicide attackers. Atran and his team interviewed many of the coalition fighters and measured the degree to which they felt 'fused' with their group. He also measured their commitment to their group's sacred values – 'Kurdeity' (defence of the Kurdish culture) for the Peshmerga; 'Arab-ness', the 'umma' (the community of Muslims) and 'family' for the Sunni Arabs. These are the ingredients of heroism and martyrdom. Both guarantee a supreme sense of significance and social worth.

The downside of this type of extremism can be interminable, intractable conflict. As Atran and Ginges note: 'Ample historical and cross-cultural evidence shows that when conflict is framed by competing religious and sacred values, intergroup violence may persist for decades, even centuries. Disputes over otherwise mundane phenomena (people, places, objects, events) then become existential struggles, as when land becomes "holy land". Secular issues become sacralized and non-negotiable, regardless of material rewards or punishments.'[20]

Summary

Self-uncertainty, self-doubt or feelings of inferiority affect most of us. These powerful forces motivate people to restore their sense of dignity and self-worth by affirming their commitment to values that are important to their group. It also means punishing those who flout the group's moral standards and proving your commitment by engaging in valorized action, 'putting your money where your mouth is', as it were. Great significance may come from joining extreme groups whose ambitious agenda promises glory, but this quest for self-worth may pull them back from the fringe and into the mainstream, particularly when the extreme group no longer delivers on its promise to make members feel important and worthy of respect.

In your experience

1. What, in your opinion, are your strengths? What are your weaknesses? Have you tried to address those weaknesses? If so, how? With what success?

2. Were you ever tempted to do something unusual or extreme? If you did it, under what circumstances did it happen? If you didn't, how do you explain your moderation?

3. Though terrorists and violent extremists have been known to do terrible things, can we still understand the psychological factors that prompted them to do

so? Does that in any way absolve them of responsibility for the consequences of their actions?

4. How would you prevent someone you know from joining a violent organization?

PART 3
Embracing Uncertainty

10. Accentuating the Positive

In search of the silver lining

Uncertainty is psychological. It is a subjective experience in two different ways. First, in the same situation, some people will feel uncertain while others will not. Think of the air steward who experiences little uncertainty during turbulence, while the passengers feel considerable uncertainty. Secondly, on experiencing uncertainty, some people react with dread and anxiety, while others can be positively excited by it. Like a Rorschach inkblot, uncertain situations can be seen quite differently depending on who is looking at them. For some, uncertainty brings to mind hidden dangers and evokes suppressed fears; these are the inner demons that our sense of the familiar has kept in check. For others, uncertainty suggests exciting adventures and discoveries. It hints at new possibilities that promise satisfaction, glory and significance.

Rahm Emanuel, President Barack Obama's chief of staff, famously quipped: 'You never want a serious crisis to go to waste. And what I mean by that is an opportunity to do things that you think you could not do before.' One person who lives by this dictum is the internationally renowned chef and restaurateur José Ramón Andrés Puerta, one of America's most famous and successful chefs. José Andrés, as he is generally called, boasts many accomplishments. He owns restaurants in Washington, DC, Los Angeles, Las Vegas, Orlando and New York City. He is a television personality in his native Spain.

An author and innovator, he is often credited with introducing and propagating the Spanish concept of tapas to the United States. He has also taught cooking at prestigious places such as Harvard and George Washington University. Recently, Andrés was nominated for the 2019 Nobel Peace Prize, the first chef in history to be honoured in this way. But his nomination was not because of his gastronomic inventiveness, the excellence of his cuisine or his teaching; there is as yet no Nobel Prize for cooking. Instead, the nomination recognized Andrés' work with disaster relief through his non-profit organization, World Central Kitchen.

In times of disaster, when uncertainty and chaos reign, Andrés has been serving free hot meals to millions of people in affected areas. These have included more than 3 million Puerto Ricans following the devastation caused by Hurricane Maria in 2017, more than 100,000 Bahamians who survived Hurricane Dorian in 2019, as well as victims of natural disasters in Houston, Texas, the Carolinas and California. In February 2020, when the COVID-19 pandemic struck across the globe, Andrés and his crews provided free breakfasts, lunches and dinners to the passengers and crew of the cruise ship *Diamond Princess*, which was quarantined in the port of Yokohama, Japan. And in March 2020, they did the same for the stranded passengers and crew of the *Grand Princess* off the shore of Oakland, California. Where others saw doom and gloom, Andrés identified an opportunity to rise to the occasion, and in doing so he became a great humanitarian, meriting a Nobel Prize nomination. Though he didn't win the award, his work on behalf of suffering fellow human beings is a shining example of discovering the silver lining in clouds of precariousness and chaos.

The idea that uncertain situations create an opportunity to

demonstrate courage and heroism is universal. It was this sense of opportunity and the challenge of the unknown that prompted millions in the Middle Ages to volunteer for the Crusades.[1] They did it with religious fervour, to be sure, because of the opportunity to become a heroic Christian. Similarly, the opportunity to become a hero has prompted thousands of youths to join al-Qaeda and IS and it motivated thousands of volunteers from all over the world to fight in the Spanish Civil War in the 1930s.[2] Ideology (whether religious, nationalistic or social) isn't the true reason people are ready to sacrifice their lives for a cause. The true reason is their fundamental need to be significant and appreciated by others and so have dignity and social worth.

A striking example of this is the strange story of Michael Enright. Enright is from Manchester, in England, and for decades he was a Hollywood actor. Yet in 2017, at the age of fifty-one, he volunteered to fight alongside the Kurdish militia (YPG) against IS. There was hardly a more uncertain or more dangerous situation than the one in Syria at the time. Yet despite the high likelihood of injury or death, Enright never looked back or regretted his decision.[3] To some, the choice to leave a comfortable Hollywood existence might appear bizarre and irrational. It is not. For however uncertain and filled with danger the fight against IS was, it offered Enright a golden opportunity to achieve a profound sense of significance. It allowed him to become the kind of man he yearned to be: a great idealist, defender of the innocents, a hero. Leaping into an uncertain world and risking death would, paradoxically, give him a sense of certainty about himself, his values, his purpose. This, apparently, was more important to him than comfort and convenience. Here again is a perfect example of how uncertainty, in which some people see only the potential for loss and pain, gives others, the likes of Enright, the opportunity for achievement, significance and untold glory.*

The psychology of value and expectancy

So, we all see very different things in the same uncertain situations. Some of us identify in them the potential for bad things, others the opportunity for good things. Some view the proverbial glass as half empty, others as half full. The big question is what determines these different perceptions and our optimistic or pessimistic attitudes towards uncertainty. To understand this, it is important to realize something very basic about human motivation, namely that it is composed of two elements. Psychologists call them *value* and *expectancy*.

Value refers to the desirability or undesirability of an event or outcome. In Enright's case, the question of value was how desirable to him it was to be hailed as a courageous hero, and/or how undesirable it would be to be severely wounded, captured by the enemy, or even die. *Expectancy* refers to the felt likelihood of the desirable or undesirable outcome happening. So, given the same objective situation, say travelling to Syria to join the fight against IS, someone might feel that the likelihood of gaining recognition and glory was higher than that of being injured or killed. Such a person might say that they were quite ready to take the risk of dying for a cause.

* Because, thirty years ago, he overstayed his American visa, Enright is not allowed back into the United States. He fears to go back to the UK because his collaboration with YPG might brand him as a terrorist. At the time of writing, he is marooned in the Central American country of Belize with no obvious means of subsistence.

This is probably true of the thousands of volunteers for various wars and struggles who prioritize the likelihood and desirability of glory and don't give much thought to the possibility of devastating injury or death.

It is possible to express these ideas more precisely. Viewing uncertain situations optimistically and seeing the 'silver lining' require that the combined value and expectancy of desired outcomes is seen to be greater than the combined value and expectancy of the undesired outcomes. Likewise, viewing uncertain situations pessimistically requires that the combined value and expectancy of the undesired outcomes is greater than that of the desired outcomes. For instance, consider contemplating the purchase of some shares that could rise or fall in value. An optimist may see the likelihood of a rise as higher than the likelihood of a fall and proceed to buy them. A pessimist may see the likelihood of a fall as greater and refrain from buying.

Promotion and prevention

But how do we develop these sanguine assessments of value and expectancy? Some of us naturally focus on the good things that could happen to us or that we could achieve. We dream of the fame and fortune we could attain if the stars were lined up just right and then seize opportunities to make it happen. Such people exhibit what my good friend, Columbia University professor Tory Higgins, calls the promotion focus. Other people live in fear of disaster. Rather than reaching for the stars, they are happy to be safe from the ills they dread. Tory Higgins calls this being governed by a prevention focus.[4] How do the promotion and prevention foci develop? To a large extent, it is related to the circumstances of growing up and family dynamics. The following true tale exemplifies how this could happen.

The brothers Smith

Paul and John Smith (not their real names) were sons of a highly respected and accomplished family in a large industrial city. Paul was the eldest of the family's children and John the youngest, their sister Helen being born second. Their father and their mother were both successful professionals and widely respected in their fields, the father a leading and renowned academic, the mother a great innovator in nutrition. It is not surprising, then, that the notions of excellence and success were the proverbial elephants in the room that touched everyone's lives. Intriguingly, this affected Paul and John in opposite ways.

Paul was precocious and intellectually gifted and so quickly became the focus of great expectations; that he would be the father's heir apparent and bring the family honour and renown was indelibly imprinted on his psyche. John, in contrast, was given less attention, so he was free from the (implicit) burden of maintaining the honour of the family name and serving as a poster child for its greatness. These differential family dynamics encouraged in the two brothers the development of entirely different mindsets and personalities that parallel the distinction between the promotion and prevention foci.

The pressure on Paul turned out to be more than he could bear. The sense that everyone's eyes were upon him induced in him a paralysing fear of failure, the dread of not living up to expectations, of disappointing the one person whose good opinion mattered most to him, his father. This overwhelming and chronic fear of failure translated into a prevention focus, which fostered a self-destructive pattern of behaviour. Paul got into drugs and alcohol, dropped out of a prestigious PhD programme, never held down a steady job and required financial assistance throughout his life.

John's story is different. He was no less gifted than his brother and was also raised in an environment where success and excellence were celebrated; however, set free from the weight of expectation, John became a decidedly promotion-focused person. Ambitious and hard-working, he did not hesitate in tackling challenging problems. Ultimately, he became a highly successful academic in his own right, possibly even outdoing his illustrious father in this regard.

Inducing promotion and prevention foci

Is it possible to induce in people the promotion focus, which is so helpful in confronting uncertain situations with an upbeat attitude? According to Higgins, the scientist who discovered and researched promotion and prevention foci, parenting is a major factor. Parenting that rewards the child's successes and withdraws the parent's affection in response to the child's failures induces the promotion focus, producing the emotional reactivity of a promotion-focused individual: eagerness and excitement on attaining rewards (for instance, good grades in school) and sadness and dejection at the failure to attain them.

Conversely, parenting that induces the prevention focus punishes the child for failures and stays 'neutral' or unresponsive to success. This type of parenting typically creates the emotional pattern of prevention-focused individuals, who feel great anxiety and agitation on experiencing failure and relief when avoiding it. Intriguingly, prevention-focused people are not responsive to success as such; they do not feel exuberance when it happens, only calm comfort on having avoided failure.

The secret of self-assurance: raising chutzpah

Beyond rewarding successes, parenting for promotion orientation involves an important additional element – it allows the child the independence to pursue goals on their own and outside parental supervision. This attitude conveys to the child that the parent trusts the child's ability to navigate the world on their own and allows the child to learn what those contingencies are, often by learning from their mistakes, and to develop skills and strategies in negotiating various social and physical challenges.

The Israeli author Inbal Arieli, a mother of three and a successful CEO in high-tech, argues in *Chutzpah* (2019) that the independence Israeli parents typically allow their children contributes significantly to adult Israelis' self-assurance, a recognized trait. It allows them to 'rush in where others fear to tread', and this is why Israel is a leading nation in various domains, including science and technology. Even though Israel is one of the world's smallest countries, barely the size of New Jersey and half the size of Lake Michigan, it is consistently listed at the top of international rankings in the World Intellectual Property

Organization (WIPO), the Global Innovation Index (GII) and the World Economic Forum (WEF) Global Competitiveness Report. According to the 2009 *New York Times* bestseller *Start-up Nation*, Israel has more starts-up per capita than any other country, one per 1,400 people, second only to Silicon Valley (but not to the US as a whole), and the 2019 GII reports that it has the highest number of engineers per capita, the highest gross expenditures for research and development as a percentage of gross domestic product (GDP), the highest number of scientists per million of the population, as well as the highest number of talented research and development experts in business enterprises.

According to Arieli, 'It is the unique way Israelis are brought up, within a tribe-like community and with a childhood full of challenges and risks, that is at the root of Israelis' entrepreneurial culture.'[5] She writes:

> From the moment they can raise their heads, we encourage our sons and daughters to explore the world around them, freely and without fear or constraint, which is much easier said than done! I realized when I had my first son, Yonatan, that while I couldn't expect not to worry about him, what I could do was not pass that anxiety and fear onto my son. What made the decision easier was that I had many moms around me who made the same choice. We saw our role as not just keeping our kids safe or teaching them what we knew, but also fostering in them real independence.[6]

The idea that granting children autonomy contributes to their self-assurance and creativity is consistently supported by empirical research.[7]

Arieli mentions several elements of the independence Israeli children are allowed from an early age. One is what she refers to as disorder, the lack of a constraining structure, in Hebrew, *balagan*. As she describes it, in the kindergarten,

> adults rarely interfere with the children's play . . . they offer no instruction as to how one should climb a structure or use a slide, nor do they correct children who choose to use the playground equipment in what might be considered an unconventional manner. The lack of interference is indicative of a high tolerance for unconventionality . . . Instead of following strict rules regarding social behavior and play, *balagan* fosters ambiguity, encouraging the development of skills necessary for dealing with the unpredictability of life.[8]

Scientific research supports the idea that messy environments and flexible, unstructured play are conducive to creativity. Berretta and Privette studied the effects of play on the creative thinking of 184 fourth-grade boys and girls (nine and ten years old).[9] Children were exposed to either highly structured or flexible art, drama and playground activities. It turned out that the performance of those who had chosen flexible play in a subsequent test of creative thinking was significantly better than those who had chosen structured play.

As Arieli describes it, Israeli children are trusted with responsibility in domains that are typically tightly supervised in other cultures. One example of this is their almost complete freedom in devising, designing and taking care of large bonfires at the annual holiday Lag B'Omer. Another is being allowed to play in the neighbourhood daily, completely unsupervised by adults and trusted to come home in time.

The youth movements that cultivate a culture of independence tempered by responsibility are unique to Israel. There are scores of such movements (Arieli reports fifty-five), the largest of which is the Tsofim, or Scouts, which has over 85,000 members. Whereas the mission of Boy and Girl Scouts in other countries is largely individualistic, introducing the members to the great outdoors and developing in them skills such as camping, hiking, studying wildlife, making friends and having fun, the mission of the Tsofim is strongly collectivist, stressing the importance of contributing to create a just and inclusive society.

A good friend of mine, a renowned professor in psychology at one of America's leading universities, recently told me a funny story that strikingly illustrates Israeli chutzpah. It goes like this.

He was invited to teach a summer class to a select group of students at Israel's interdisciplinary centre in Herzliya and meticulously prepared a course plan that involved the students' active participation and discussion in small groups, consistent with the best pedagogical methodology of ensuring student engagement. But when he described this plan to the students, they seemed unhappy and voiced their objections. They would much rather listen to what the professor had to say, they informed him, than discuss the course material among themselves. In response, my friend, though very much surprised (if not shocked), revised his course outline and, with the students' active participation, tailored it to their desires. According to my friend, this worked very well. The students were greatly engaged in the material and got much more out of the course than the teacher had expected, based on his experience elsewhere.

Child-rearing Israeli-style combines several elements that contribute to empowering young people and building their self-assurance, among them the autonomy granted Israeli youngsters coupled with the trust placed in them by their parents and the expectation that they will behave responsibly. Added to this, the strong sense of family and community ties afford Israeli youngsters, and the adults into whom they develop, a deep sense of a safe haven and secure base and a feeling that they are significant and matter. All this instils in them an attitude of chutzpah and an excitement about uncertainty and the adventures it promises.

Instant promotion focus?

Parenting contributes to our children becoming prevention- or promotion-focused, but what about us? Can we 'psych' ourselves to a promotion or prevention focus at will? What might it mean for us in dealing with everyday challenges? Becoming promotion-focused, for instance, might make us more ambitious about our career aspirations, becoming a better athlete or losing weight. And Higgins's research suggests it's all possible. Focusing our thoughts on the gains of success produces a momentary promotion focus, while thinking about the losses that failure would entail produces a momentary prevention focus.

Numerous experiments by Higgins and his colleagues induced these momentary prevention and promotion states. In one set of studies, undergraduate participants were asked to perform two tasks, and their success or failure on the first task determined whether the second task would be fun and enjoyable ('Wheel of Fortune' game) or dull and boring ('Unvaried

Repetition').[10] The first task required solving twenty-five easy anagrams. Participants in the promotion-focus condition were told that they would get to do the fun task if they got twenty-two or more of the anagrams right. Participants in the prevention-focus condition were told that if they solved twenty-one anagrams or fewer, they would have to carry out the dull and boring task. (Note that solving twenty-two or more out of twenty-five was defined as success, and solving twenty-one out of twenty-five or fewer was defined as failure, so the likelihood of success and failure was exactly the same in the two experimental conditions; the only difference was how these conditions were framed.) Promotion-focus framing highlighted the possibility of success, and prevention-focus framing highlighted failure. Participants performed the first task and, irrespective of their actual performance, all were told they had succeeded. The researchers then looked at the type of emotion these participants felt. Promotion-focus individuals experienced cheerfulness and exuberance, whereas prevention-focus individuals typically felt relief (that is, the absence of failure). In another experiment, Roney, Higgins and Shah presented participants in the first task with relatively difficult anagrams and told everyone that they had failed.[11] Just as the theory predicts, participants in the promotion condition felt dejected and sad, whereas those in the prevention condition felt anxious and agitated.

Though in this study the promotion and prevention orientations were induced by the experimenter, self-induction of these foci is also possible. Thinking about what it takes to succeed should put you in a promotion focus, and thinking about avoiding failure should put you in a prevention focus. Similarly, thinking about your goals puts you in a promotion frame of mind, whereas thinking about your duties, the dereliction of which would result in punishment, puts you in a prevention frame of mind.

In a creative experimental study by Liberman and colleagues, participants were instructed to think about their 'hopes and aspirations', a process that induces a promotion focus, or about their 'duties and obligations', a process that induces a prevention focus.[12] Then the participants, all students at Columbia University in New York, were asked to imagine a situation in which friends who came to visit brought them a gift: either a Columbia University mug or a Columbia University pen, each worth about five dollars. These friends also brought a gift for the participant's roommate, also either a Columbia mug or pen; if the participant received one of these objects, the roommate received the other. The question the researchers were seeking to answer was whether in this situation the participant would be willing to exchange their gift with that of their roommate. The opportunity for exchange created considerable uncertainty for the participants. Would they be happier with their roommate's gift or the gift they had received to begin with? If promotion-focus people are more likely to see potential for gain in uncertain situations, they should prefer an exchange. And if prevention-focus people see in it potential for loss, they should avoid an exchange. The findings of this experiment were consistent with this line of reasoning: 44 per cent of participants in the promotion condition opted for an exchange, compared to only 19 per cent of participants in the prevention condition.

These studies and many others prove that promotion and prevention foci can be induced situationally. This means that people can momentarily psych themselves into a promotion or prevention frame of mind by focusing on gains or losses. These studies also show that promotion-focus individuals 'accentuate the positive' in uncertain situations and see in them opportunity for improvement. In contrast, prevention-focused people 'accentuate the negative' and in uncertain situations see loss and deterioration. The fact that people can readily adopt a promotion or prevention orientation has an important implication. It suggests that our reactions to uncertainty aren't predetermined by our genes, our upbringing or the child-rearing style of our parents. It suggests that to an appreciable extent our mental reactions are in our hands and we have some control as to how we feel in uncertain situations.

Ewa Szumowska and her colleagues at the Jagiellonian University in Kraków recently conducted several studies in which participants were instructed to think either about goals they *are able* to pursue/attain under the pandemic-imposed restrictions, or about goals that they are *prevented* from pursuing because of these restrictions.[13] Participants in the control group received no goal-related instructions. The goals that people listed as possible to attain during the lockdown included: spending more time reading, developing cooking skills, home improvements, spending more time with family and gardening. The goals that people said they would have to forego because of the lockdown included: finding a new job, eating out, going to the cinema, the gym, to bars, seeing friends and family and driving their children to college. The results were telling: focusing on goal pursuits that were facilitated by the restrictions induced in participants feelings of freedom, positivity and optimism about the eventual removal of the restrictions, whereas focusing on pursuits that were thwarted by the restrictions produced a sense of constraint and pessimism.

The rise of positive psychology

Much of psychological research in the twentieth century focused on human suffering and mental pathology. Considerable effort was put into understanding depression, violence, prejudice, irrationality and bias. Far less attention was devoted to the psychology of human strengths, the factors that empower people to cope with challenges, adversity and stress – qualities such as resilience, grit and tenacity that allow people to thrive and succeed against all odds. One could say that, for most of the twentieth century, psychology has had a distinct prevention focus!

A significant break with that tradition was occasioned by a special issue of the *American Psychologist*, the flagship journal of the American Psychological Association. It appeared in 2000 under the editorship of Martin Seligman and Mihalyi Csikszentmihalyi, and it introduced a new term into psychologists' lingo: *positive psychology*. It was a watershed moment in the history of twenty-first-century psychology and launched a scientific movement that has had an enormous impact on psychological research.

Martin Seligman is one of the most eminent psychologists in the world today, the author of numerous books and articles and a former president of the American Psychological Association. Ironically, for someone who has become the progenitor and leader of the positive psychology movement, Seligman started his scientific career with research on distinctly negative phenomena. His important early discovery was what he later called 'learned helplessness'. It was accidentally found in research with dogs, in which animals deprived of the ability to escape an unpleasant situation developed a kind of neurosis and apathy. In short, they 'learned' to be helpless.[14]

In an experiment that submitted the animals to considerable discomfort, dogs were put in a situation of aversive uncertainty: at random times they received painful electric shocks which they could not avoid. In this situation, they became helpless and dejected; in response to the shocks, they simply lay down and squealed. Moreover, when later put in a situation from which they could escape, they didn't even try. Seligman saw in this paradigm a model for depression and proceeded to develop with his students the 'helplessness theory of depression', in which a person's sense of control over outcomes plays a central part. However, while control over outcomes extricates us from the clutches of depression, it does not lead to happiness as such. Interest in happiness became Seligman's new passion, which led to the positive psychology movement.

Mihalyi Csikszentmihalyi, Seligman's co-editor of the historic *American Psychologist* issue, was a world-famous pioneer in the study of happiness and creativity. He is particularly well known for his work on the experience of 'flow', the paragon of happiness, in which a person takes leave of their ego and becomes completely engrossed in the task at hand. Csikszentmihalyi's most fundamental philosophy is expressed in his statement that 'Repression is not the way to virtue. When people restrain themselves out of fear, their lives are by necessity diminished. Only through freely chosen discipline can life be enjoyed and still kept within the bounds of reason.'[15] Csikszentmihalyi was a champion of motivating people through intrinsic interest in the activity and objected to having people do things they do not enjoy just for extrinsic benefits (for example, money). His philosophy fits the popular aphorism 'Do what you like and you will not work a day in your life.'

The positive psychology movement took off with great energy and zest. It spawned research on many previously neglected psychological factors that promote happiness and satisfaction, including gratitude, forgiveness, awe, inspiration, hope, curiosity and laughter. These topics resonate particularly well with the American spirit, as expressed in the 1776 Declaration of Independence, in which the pursuit of happiness counts among people's inalienable rights. Indeed, Americans turn out to be happy people. Specifically, nine out of ten Americans report being 'very happy' or 'pretty happy'.[16] A study carried out by Shelly Gable asked research participants to list how often positive events ('A friend, romantic partner or family member complimented me') or negative events ('A friend, romantic partner or family member insulted me') occurred over the past week.[17] Participants reported positive interactions three times as often as negative interactions.

Positivity isn't restricted to Americans. In fact, measures of life satisfaction across the globe reveal that people are relatively content and satisfied with their lives. Research shows that people significantly underestimate the likelihood of negative outcomes (being diagnosed with cancer, losing their jobs or getting divorced) and overestimate their chances of being dealt positive outcomes (having gifted children, achieving more than their peers). Intriguingly, even people who live in squalid conditions and extreme poverty, such as in the slums of Kolkata, India, report being content. It appears that the capacity for contentment and the adjustment to specific circumstances has been stamped on human nature during the course of our evolution.

Seeking happiness

Positive psychology does not deny that life can have distress-ing aspects, or that there exist in the world dysfunction, pressure, trauma, malice and violence that inflict suffering on millions. Yet positive psychology offers proof that positive, life-enhancing processes shield us from those negative out-comes. In this regard, positive psychology tells us something we have always explicitly wanted to believe.

Focusing on positive values and happy states of affairs and emptying our mind of thoughts about negative out-comes and potential disasters is something that well-being gurus stress repeatedly. One of the most popular self-help books ever published has been Norman Vincent Peale's *The Power of Positive Thinking*. It has sold over 5 million copies and is in high demand to this day, seven decades after publi-cation. One of the things it suggests is focusing on success and banishing thoughts of failure. As he puts it: 'Formulate and stamp indelibly on your mind a mental picture of your-self as succeeding. Hold this picture tenaciously. Never permit it to fade . . . Never think of yourself as failing.'[18] And in a different passage he recommends, 'Definitely practice emptying your mind of fears, hates, insecurities, regrets and guilt feelings. The mere fact that you con-sciously make this effort to empty your mind tends to give relief.'[19] Peale's popular approach echoes current thinking about the value of meditation for people's mental well-being and clearing from the mind the various fears and anxieties that clutter it. These measures quiet the 'monkey mind', as modern psychology calls it.[20]

Gratitude

People's promotion and prevention foci are future-oriented; they pertain to desires they dream to fulfil and duties they feel obliged to perform. Peale's recommendation to visualize success is also about the future. But a positive attitude that gives strength in unknown situations may also come from contemplating the past and the present. In recent years, psychologists have been discovering the immense mental health benefits that come from counting our blessings and experiencing gratitude for the good things in life.

The notion that gratitude is important and beneficial has been long hailed by ethical philosophers, religious writers and contemporary writers on well-being. Eighteenth-century economist and philosopher Adam Smith held that gratitude is a cardinal civic virtue that is indispensable for societies.[21] This has been echoed in a large number of popular books on gratitude that lavish considerable praise on this concept and see it as a panacea for sundry mental health dysfunctions. One writer even promises that a grateful heart will all but assure 'whatever we are waiting for – peace of mind, contentment, grace'.[22] But can the claims of pundits and self-help gurus be trusted? Fortunately, there now exists a substantial body of systematic research by psychological scientists that offers compelling empirical evidence in response to this question.

Gratitude has been defined as 'the quality or condition of being grateful or thankful; the appreciation of and inclination to return kindness'.[23] Robert Emmons, a leader in the psychological study of gratitude, writes: 'At the cornerstone of gratitude is the notion of undeserved merit.'[24] The grateful person recognizes that they did nothing to deserve the gift or benefit. It was bestowed freely. This is reflected in the definition of gratitude as 'the willingness to recognize the unearned increments of value in one's experience', which means the gifts we have had the good luck to receive in life – talents, health, the good nature that people appreciate, the fortunate circumstances that allowed us to thrive.[25]

The positive outlook that gratitude engenders affects people's behaviour in situations suffused with uncertainty. Barbara Fredrickson, a pioneer in the experimental study of gratitude, suggests that it expands people's repertory of thoughts and actions, invites them to explore possibilities that the new situation may afford and encourages thinking 'outside the box'. Indeed, there is evidence that gratitude builds people's resources and strengthens their self-assurance, qualities that are indispensable in order to confront uncertain situations with equanimity. It does so by inviting reciprocation of the favours, gifts or acts of kindness received from other people. In turn, this begets counter-reciprocation on their part. People who are grateful to others are likely to feel loved and cared for by others. This results in the strengthening of friendships and social bonds. It bolsters our network of social support. It builds the secure base (see Chapter 3) that gives us the fortitude to face the unknown with assurance and optimism.

Even the mere expression of gratitude strengthens recipients' motivation to support and to help those expressing it. In a study carried out in a social care setting, Clark, Northrop and Barkshire looked at the frequency with which case managers visited the adolescents they were supervising in a residential treatment programme.[26] Forty-three per cent of the adolescents were visited weekly by their case managers. In the second phase, the residential units sent thank-you letters to case managers after they had visited. This resulted in a sharp increase in weekly visits, to nearly 80 per cent. In the third phase, no thank-you letters were sent, which brought down the rate of visits to about 50 per cent.

According to evolutionary scientists, the ability to experience gratitude gave humans an important survival advantage.[27] Humans who had evolved to experience gratitude reciprocated to those who had benefited them, who in turn tended to repay the favour. In this way, a positive spiral of cooperation and support developed in hunter-gatherer groups, contributing to the survival and reproduction of members who experienced gratitude and reciprocated the benefits received. There is also evidence that the ability to experience gratitude isn't uniquely human; it is also found in other species, such as chimpanzees and capuchin monkeys, which return favours and offer help and support to members of their group that helped or supported them.[28]

It turns out that experience of gratitude is to an appreciable extent under our control; we can strengthen our sense of gratitude and focus at will. Emmons and McCullough carried out an important study that demonstrates how people can make themselves feel this emotion.[29] In their experiment, students were put at random into one of three groups. In the first, students were instructed to record five major events that had most affected them during the previous week. Students in the second group recorded five hassles or stressors. Students in the third group recorded five things for which they were grateful. The results were revealing. Students who practised gratitude reported more progress towards their goals, had fewer physical complaints, engaged more frequently in physical exercise, reported higher optimism and enjoyed greater overall well-being.

An important effect of gratitude is that it counteracts and eliminates negative emotions and consequently reduces stress. Research that compared the cardiovascular activity of people who experienced either anger or gratitude revealed that appreciation reduced hypertension (as well as heart rate variability, pulse transit time and respiration rate).[30] In addition, gratitude was found to strengthen immune functioning.[31] So a grateful, appreciative person might not experience the stress and anxiety that uncertain situations evoke in others. They may not need to escape the unknown or embrace simplistic stereotypes, preconceptions and conspiracy theories. Instead, they might broaden the scope of their experience and explore the possibilities the unknown might hold.

Gratitude underlies what the psychiatrist Milton Erickson called 'generativity'. Generative adults are known to have creative and productive lives. They contribute to society, care about others and are fulfilled. Dan McAdams, a psychologist who studies how people narrate their life stories, carried out a study of generative adults. His findings revealed a strong element of gratitude. Generative adults typically recognized the early advantages they had and felt grateful for them. They also felt the need to give back to society and were attuned to the suffering of others. And, even in discussing failures and frustrations, they couched them in what McAdams calls 'redemptive sequences'. Essentially, they recognized the 'silver lining' in their trials and tribulations and how their misfortunes had ended up contributing to their development and happiness.[32]

Positive emotions

Gratitude enhances how people approach unknown situations by strengthening their social connections and their secure attachment to others. But, in addition, it may enhance people's capacity to move forward and approach challenges and reduce apprehension and the avoidance of challenges. Positive emotions (feeling happy, content and relaxed) have these effects because they make people feel safe and so increase people's creativity and exploration.[33] In contrast, negative emotions (fear or anger) increase the likelihood of people 'freezing' on familiar preconceptions and acting accordingly.

Barbara Fredrickson found that joy, for instance, creates the urge to play, push the limits and be creative.[34] It encourages us to explore the unknown without fear or anxiety and to discover what it has to offer. As with gratitude, the capacity to experience positive emotions is likely to have evolved in humans because of the advantages it conferred with respect to survival and procreation. Through play and exploration, people discover new possibilities, including new ways and means of coping with challenges.*

---

* As Fredrickson described it: 'Those of our ancestors who succumbed to the urges sparked by positive emotions – to play, explore, and so on – would have by consequence accrued more personal resources. When these same ancestors later faced inevitable threats to life and limb, their greater personal resources would have translated into greater odds of survival, and, in turn, greater odds of living long enough to reproduce. To the extent, then, that the capacity to experience positive emotions is genetically encoded, this capacity, through the process of natural selection, would have become part of our universal human nature' (Emmons and McCullough, 2004, p. 149).

Psychology and the good life

The insights and findings of positive psychology have had a major practical impact. In 2006, Harvard's Positive Psychology 1504 course, taught by Professor Tal Ben-Shahar, became the most popular Harvard course with the enrolment of over 1,400 students. The course addresses the psychology of life fulfilment and examines ways of enhancing it through empathy, friendship, love, achievement, creativity, spirituality, happiness and humour.[35]

Ben-Shahar's success was replicated resoundingly at Yale University, where Laurie Santos, a psychology professor, offered a course called 'Psychology and the Good Life' which aimed to teach students how to lead a happier, more satisfying life. Originally, 300 people enrolled in the class, but within a week this climbed to nearly 1,200, making it the most popular course in Yale's history. According to Santos, Yale students want to be happier. They want to alter harmful life habits that promote stress and the sense of endless pressure and competition. And the massive enrolment in the course has produced a change in the campus culture. As Santos put it, 'With one in four students at Yale taking it, if we see good habits, things like students showing more gratitude, procrastinating less, increasing social connections, we're actually seeing change in the school's culture.'[36]

The popularity of these positive psychology courses at Harvard and Yale is not unique. Similar courses reap great successes in scores of universities and high schools around the world, and books, courses and workshops on happiness and positivity also enjoy immense popularity with the general public. There is no doubt that positive psychology has revolutionized the way in which we think about mental health.

Summary

The popular view that uncertainty is frightening and that fear of the unknown is inevitable has been challenged by the rise of positive psychology. Research suggests that psychology's emphasis on mental problems has been lopsided – there is a vibrant positive side to the human psyche. Not everyone is prevention-oriented; some people are promotion-focused – they are excited about the positive possibilities that the future may hold. Work on gratitude and positive emotions shows how our fears and stresses can be banished and our sense of secure base augmented; we can then be liberated to enjoy exploring the unknown. Any situation, even a crisis, can be made to reveal its 'silver lining'. The positive psychology movement has explored several specific ways of enhancing people's self-assurance, their sense of agency and, above all, their optimism. I will look at these in the next chapter.

In your experience

1. Do you consider yourself a positive person? What aspects of your personal history might have affected your positivity or negativity?
2. Think about your close friends and family. Who among them seems to be generally promotion-focused, and who more prevention-focused? What

do you like or dislike about either their promotion or their prevention orientation?

3. Do you consider yourself a grateful person? Do you reflect often about your good luck and the gifts you happened to receive? Would you like to be more grateful? How might you go about becoming so?

4. What is your parenting style – or parenting philosophy (if not a parent)? Are you more of a promotion- or prevention-focused parent? What parenting style characterized your own upbringing?

11. Making Good Things Happen

Do you consider yourself an ambitious person? Do you dream of great achievements, contributions to society, widespread recognition, fame and fortune? Ambition and a promotion focus may encourage you to approach, rather than avoid, uncertain situations, but you must believe in addition that success is within reach. It is not enough to contemplate the *value* of success; one must also *expect* that success is attainable. The expectation of success augments commitment to success, in turn prompting a positive approach to uncertain situations. The expectation that things will work themselves out in the end, no matter how difficult they seem, is what is generally meant by the term 'optimism'.

There is much evidence that optimism has many important benefits, and considerable psychological research has been devoted to studying it. Essentially, optimism can be both a trait in which people differ (some people generally being more optimistic than others) and an attitude or state of mind that most people can adopt in some situations. Let's look at both in turn.

Optimism as a trait

Charles Carver, Michael Scheier and Suzanne Segerstrom have been prominent among researchers of optimism. They define it as having favourable expectations of the future that hold across different domains of life, including work, family and health.[1] But what leads to this optimistic perspective? Who is more optimistic, who is less, and why? Can we control it? Is there a way for us, as individuals, to become more optimistic?

Optimism has long been believed to be a personality characteristic that is 'relatively stable over time'.[2] Some people are 'inveterate optimists'; they see the 'silver lining' in most situations. Others are 'born pessimists'; they catastrophize uncertain situations and are quick to imagine the worst that can happen. Like most human characteristics, these tendencies are in part determined genetically.*

Explanatory style

Beyond genetics, which we cannot do much about, there are aspects of our thinking that, when ingrained, turn us into habitual optimists or pessimists. In the last half-century, research has uncovered that this is largely related to how we explain negative or positive events to ourselves. Martin Seligman, whom I mentioned earlier in relation to positive psychology, made major contributions to our understanding of optimistic and pessimistic explanations of events. It turns out that such explanatory habits have three critical

---

* A study by Shimon Saphire-Bernstein and his colleagues looked at the oxytocin gene and its role in optimistic functioning. The study compared carriers of the A allele (A/G and A/A genotypes) to carriers of the double-G allele and found that 'Carriers of the A allele of the OXTR SNP rs53576 were less optimistic, felt less personal mastery, and had lower levels of self-esteem. In addition, carriers of the A allele had higher levels of depressive symptomatology' (Saphire-Bernstein et al., 2011, p. 15120).

dimensions, Seligman's three Ps of optimism: permanence, pervasiveness and personalization.

Permanence relates to whether the cause of the positive or negative event is permanent or temporary. Imagine you failed a maths test. A permanent explanation would attribute it to your lack of talent or intelligence; after all, your degree of intelligence is stable and does not change over time. Another permanent explanation would be that mathematics is a difficult subject; this, too, is unlikely to change over time. If maths is difficult, this is unlikely to change. In contrast, a temporary explanation might ascribe the failure to a lack of preparation. Of course, the effort we put into preparing for a test is something that we can control. Next time we can work harder and do better. A temporary explanation of failure implies the possibility of future success and is therefore optimistic, whereas a permanent explanation for failure is pessimistic. Because people typically assume that our native intelligence cannot change (at least not by much), and neither can the inherent difficulty of maths problems, if we attribute our failure to our low intelligence it can, unfortunately, be predicted to happen again and again.

The opposite holds for positive events. Here a stable explanation is optimistic and an unstable one pessimistic. Suppose you took the maths test and did well. A pessimistic, temporary attribution would be that you just got lucky, and luck, as we know, is fickle, so you cannot expect to repeat your success in the future. Another temporary explanation would be that the test was particularly easy, but it cannot be expected to be as easy the next time around, so you cannot expect your success to recur. On the other hand, if you attribute your success to your talent, ability or intelligence, you can expect similar success in the future. And the same follows if you concluded that maths is an easy subject (at least for someone like you). Both these explanations portend good future outcomes and so are optimistic.

The second dimension of explanatory style is *pervasiveness*. Some people tend to globalize and catastrophize the bad things that happen to them. They feel that if things didn't go well for them in one domain, this means that they are generally inept and worthless. Imagine losing a game of tennis, having a piece of work rejected, or even being fired. Some people would be devastated by such events, acting as if any meaning had been ripped from their life and as if the event warranted despair. For these people, failure in almost any domain represents a major threat to their self-esteem. Their explanations for negative outcomes are what Seligman calls 'pervasive' or universal. Other people segment domains of endeavour and give appropriate weight to negative outcomes without generalizing them. Their explanations are limited or specific. As Seligman characterized it, 'People who make *universal* explanations for their failures give up on everything when a failure strikes in one area. People who make *specific* explanations may become helpless in that one part of their lives yet march stalwartly on in the others.'[3] If you explain failures without generalizing it to all domains, you are being optimistic. If you generalize your specific failures, you are pessimistic.

Seligman's third dimension of optimism is *personalization*. Do you explain negative outcomes by 'blaming' yourself or by attributing them to external circumstances? For instance, if you don't win a coveted prize, if you choke on a speech or have your work criticized, you might attribute it to personal failings. This is a pessimistic explanation likely to cause you distress and dejection. However, attributing the same events to external factors – for instance, to the prize committee being biased against you, to you being unwell when you gave the speech, or to the incompetence of your critics – are face-saving and therefore optimistic.

An explanatory style that attributes the causes of negative events to ourselves, viewing them as persistent and pervasive, is the hallmark of pessimistic thinking. In times of uncertainty, someone who thinks like this is likely to imagine the worst that could happen, which is likely to trigger great anxiety or fear of the unknown. In contrast, an explanatory style that ascribes negative events to external causes and views them as domain-specific rather than general, and as temporary rather than permanent, is optimistic. Someone who is accustomed to explaining outcomes in such a way is likely to be undaunted by uncertainty and inclined to explore the opportunities that it affords.*

Being and becoming an optimist

Lucky are the optimists, for they can cope with life's inevitable adversities and often prevail where others fail. Abraham Lincoln, one of America's greatest presidents, must have been an optimist to become as successful as he was despite his dismal early failures and severe personal challenges. Thomas Jr, Abraham's little brother, died days after birth. Abraham Lincoln's mother died when he was just nine years old. His beloved sister, Sarah, met her death in childbirth,

---

* Seligman (2006) devised a self-administered scale that allows you to see whether your explanatory style is optimistic or pessimistic. This is worth consulting, especially if you want to change your typical way of thinking in a positive direction.

and Lincoln's sweetheart, Ann Rutledge, whom he intended to marry, passed away not long after they had met. Later, the Lincolns' son Edward died at the age of four, and William died twelve years later at the age of eleven. Throughout his life Lincoln suffered bouts of clinical depression.[4] All those who knew him well were familiar with his 'melancholy': his episodes of weeping in public, his talk of suicide. He viewed the world as a hard and grim place in which you have to struggle constantly to survive.[5]

Yet, despite it all, Lincoln was an optimist. He had a profound faith in his strength to overcome the considerable challenges that fate had thrown his way. Indeed, it was his depression that challenged him to cope with it creatively, to dream of greatness and believe it to be attainable. Writing in the *Atlantic*, Joshua Wolf Shenk quotes Lincoln's 'irrepressible desire' to accomplish something while he lived. He wanted to connect his name with the great events of his generation, and to 'so impress himself upon them as to link his name with something that would redound to the interest of his fellow man'. This was no mere wish, Lincoln said, but what he 'desired to live for'.[6] It was this deep-seated faith in himself that fuelled his political ambitions. It accounts for the dogged persistence that ultimately made him victorious and the grand historical figure that he became. This optimistic resolve enabled Lincoln to enter the myriad uncertain situations that a political career entails and to believe himself capable of handling them to his (and America's) advantage.

Franklin D. Roosevelt (FDR) was another exceptional US president whose optimism gave him the strength to endure and prevail in times of trial. As a rising political star, he was struck with polio on 10 August 1921 and remained paralysed below the waist for the rest of his life. It is not difficult to imagine the obstacles that a disability of this magnitude could have on a politician's career. Politicians have to endure gruelling travel while campaigning, appear cheerful and ebullient in endless appearances, and voters want their candidates to exude strength and confidence. Indeed, Roosevelt took pains to conceal his suffering from the public. This would be more difficult today, with the current degree of media scrutiny. Ken Burns, who produced the highly successful documentary *The Roosevelts: An Intimate History*, suggested to a *Time* magazine reporter that 'FDR couldn't have gotten out of the Iowa caucuses because of his infirmity. CNN and Fox would have been vying for shots of him sweating and looking uncomfortable in those braces.'[7] Roosevelt's ability to carry out his work despite his infirmity attests to his incredible optimism and faith.

No one epitomized optimism more than theoretical physicist and cosmologist Stephen Hawking, who at the age of twenty-one was diagnosed with an early-onset form of motor neuron disease, more commonly known as amyotrophic lateral sclerosis (ALS) or Lou Gehrig's disease, which gradually paralyses the body. As it progressed, Hawking became unable to speak, communicating via a speech-generating apparatus, at first operated by hand and ultimately with a single cheek muscle. Despite these incapacitating disabilities, he made important scientific discoveries. Within the framework of general relativity theory, he predicted that black holes emit radiation, a notion hailed as a significant breakthrough in theoretical physics, and expounded a new theory of cosmology that integrated the general theory of relativity and quantum mechanics. For these and other achievements, Hawking gained honours bestowed only on the most successful scientists, among them being elected a Fellow of the Royal Society and receiving the Presidential Medal of Freedom in the United States. Hawking married twice and had three children in his first marriage, he travelled widely and became known worldwide; books were written about him and a film, *The Theory of Everything*, was released in 2014.

Joe Biden, the current president of the United States, has also demonstrated striking optimism in adversity. In 1972, Biden's wife Neila and daughter Naomi died in a car accident on a Christmas shopping trip; his two sons, Hunter and Beau, then aged three and four, were badly injured. Beau Biden went on to become the Attorney General of Delaware and an officer with the rank of major in the Judge Advocate General Corps and was deployed with his unit to Kosovo and later Iraq. He died of a brain tumour in 2015 at the age of forty-six. Throughout these devastating personal tragedies, Joe Biden pursued a political career. In 1973, he was elected to the US Senate as a junior senator from Delaware, although in 1987 his bid for the US presidency collapsed amid allegations of plagiarism, what Biden referred to as 'exaggerated shadow' and 'his past mistakes'. Biden pledged to be more honest and soon afterwards the American public voted him one of the most trustworthy political figures in the country.

In 1991, Biden faced controversy over his handling of the Clarence Thomas Supreme Court confirmation hearing concerning Anita Hill's allegations of sexual harassment by Thomas. In the years to follow, Biden made sure to demonstrate his commitment to women's rights: he introduced the Violence Against Women Act, signed by President Clinton, and later became the chief advocate for combating sexual assault on college campuses. In 1988, Biden underwent brain surgery to correct a leaking intracranial aneurysm and suffered a life-endangering pulmonary embolism while recuperating from the surgery. A second aneurysm was successfully operated on, but these medical setbacks kept Biden away from the Senate for seven months.

Undaunted by previous failures and health concerns, Biden announced his candidacy for president in 2007, but his campaign fell apart once again. He performed poorly in the national polls of Democratic candidates, failing to rise above single digits. He was placed fifth in the Iowa caucuses and finally withdrew from the race. Despite this, Barack Obama selected Biden as his running mate, and between 2008 and 2016 Biden served as vice-president.

Biden entered the presidential race for the third time in the 2020 elections. Although he was generally ahead of the other Democratic nominees in the national polls, his campaign had its dramatic ups and downs, and there were times when it seemed there was little hope of success. Yet, brought to the top of the ticket by the African American community, he went on to become the Democratic nominee for presidency and on 7 November that year was pronounced the winner of the presidential contest against the incumbent, Donald Trump.

Lincoln, Roosevelt, Hawking and Biden have all confronted very different personal circumstances. Roosevelt and Hawking came from well-to-do, highly educated families. The families of Lincoln and Biden were poor and struggling. Yet all four have in common an optimistic faith that, although their prospects of success seem uncertain (and, to many, dim) things will turn out well nonetheless. There are many examples of people who maintained their optimism against the odds. Walt Disney was dismissed by an editor because he lacked talent; Thomas Edison was fired from his first two jobs for being unproductive; Winston Churchill repeatedly failed exams; Oprah Winfrey was dismissed from her position as a reporter;

Marilyn Monroe was told by modelling agents that she should be a secretary; J. K. Rowling was poor, depressed, divorced and a single mother when she wrote *Harry Potter and the Philosopher's Stone*; Elvis Presley was fired by Jimmy Denny after just one performance; The Beatles were rejected by a recording company; Bill Gates dropped out of Harvard and his first business failed; and Albert Einstein didn't speak until he was four or read until he was seven.[8] It is the optimistic attitude of these people and their indomitable faith that allowed them to peer bravely into the unknown and actively discover the possibilities it offers.

Becoming an optimist

Some people, perhaps the likes of Lincoln and Hawking, are optimists by temperament. Optimism is a useful quality to possess, as it allows you to face uncertainty with courage and have faith that, however dark the present, the future is bound to be bright. This attitude can become a self-fulfilling prophecy. Optimists' persistence often pays off and they then reap the rewards of their hopefulness. But even if it does not, being an optimist carries its own rewards. It turns out that optimists enjoy better cardiovascular health, are more immune to disease and that their memory declines less with age.[9]

But what about people who aren't so lucky, and who, because of genes, early-childhood experiences or plain bad luck, have adopted a pessimistic outlook? Are they irrevocably condemned to a life of misery and suffering? Recent psychological research answers this question with a resounding no. Change is possible – even a born pessimist can learn to develop an optimistic outlook on life.

Teaching people to talk to themselves optimistically is a mainstay of cognitive therapy, an influential approach to mental problems such as phobias, depression or anxiety. Major leaders of the cognitive therapy approach, for example Albert Ellis or Aaron Beck, believe that the mental problems that cause suffering are rooted in irrational beliefs that are activated when a negative event happens or is imagined. Examples are beliefs such as 'I must be liked by every single person I meet,' which is clearly impossible, or 'I must succeed in every single task I try,' again, an expectation that is bound to be frustrated. Intriguingly, these beliefs need not be articulated explicitly or even be fully conscious; often, they are revealed in their negative consequences, when chasing the 'impossible dream' ends in failure. Don Quixote, the protagonist of Miguel de Cervantes' seventeenth-century novel, who harboured unrealistic dreams, soon became the 'Knight of the Sad Countenance'. Similarly, when people who hold irrational beliefs confront abject failure, they feel miserable as a result. This, according to theorists, is the essence of depression.

The aim of cognitive therapy is therefore the eradication of irrational beliefs. It is done through *disputation*, that is, confronting the irrational belief with evidence that it is unreasonable. For instance, if when we are rejected by a potential lover we blame ourselves for not living up to the ideal of being loved by all, we can look to examples of highly popular idols who also experienced rejection. Alternatively, we can point out that the rejection could have stemmed from the mental state or mood of the rejector rather than our own failings. Ample research evidence suggests that uprooting irrational beliefs and training people in the habit of disputation removes the tendency to get depressed and suffer dejection and misery.[10]

Disputation works because it helps pessimists learn the cognitive skills of optimists and improves their ability to approach uncertain situations with a positive attitude. Martin Seligman gives poignant examples of how such a process can work. Consider someone taking a class on a topic that excites them but who gets a low mark on a test. A pessimistic framing of this event might be that they are stupid, that others in the class probably did much better than they did and that they might as well give up because, obviously, there is no hope. A disputation of this pessimistic framing could be that they shouldn't blow a single failure out of proportion, that others in the class probably didn't do much better than they did, that it is always possible to learn from your mistakes, that completing the course will enhance their chances of getting an interesting job, and so on.

A particularly effective disputation is based on incontrovertible facts which contradict the initial pessimism. Data that other people in the course did as badly or worse on the exam than you did would be one type of evidence that counters the idea that failure reveals our own ineptness. Evidence that the mark on this exam doesn't contribute greatly to the final grade might also mitigate the initial catastrophizing. In short, carefully evaluating our pessimistic conclusion in the light of known facts may banish it from our mind and remove the dejection it causes.

To turn initial pessimism around requires practice. It means carrying out systematic exercises in order to transform the process of disputation and questioning into an ingrained habit. Seligman suggests, over a week, paying close attention to five adverse events we face, examining our beliefs and their consequences, and then trying to vigorously dispute the pessimistic beliefs. Then observe the inflow of positive energy that happens as a consequence. The adverse events could be minor everyday annoyances, nothing more dramatic: 'The mail is late; your call isn't returned; the kid pumping gas doesn't wash the windshield. In each of these, use the techniques of effective self-disputation. When you hear the negative beliefs, dispute them. Beat them into the ground.'[11] That is how you can become an optimist!

But, as with all things in life, optimism has its limits. When an optimistic outlook becomes completely divorced from reality, it can backfire and produce suffering and misery. The individual who believes it is possible to succeed in every single task or be loved by every single person is an 'optimist' of sorts, but their optimism is unrealistic and courts disaster. Ultimately, it brings about depression and helplessness, as Cervantes' 'Knight of the Sad Countenance' vividly demonstrates. So when the writing is clearly on the wall, ignoring it optimistically is ill advised. Yet an optimistic attitude is typically beneficial. It allows us to explore the unknown and discover its hidden possibilities, the 'sweetness' that the 'strong' may be concealing, just as in Samson's biblical riddle.

Parenting optimism

Childhood can often be a period of great emotional upheaval, with the child required to meet considerable social, academic and moral challenges for the first time. It is a period when they are vulnerable and exposed and in danger of sliding into pessimism and depression. Numerous circumstances can be stressful for a child: parental anxiety and nervousness about their economic situation, difficulties in their relationship, manifested in spats and acrimony, the child not doing well at school, being bullied and humiliated or excluded from their classmates' activities. Equipping children with an optimistic attitude is likely to help in such circumstances.

Seligman outlines a step-by-step method to help children avoid pessimistic thinking.[12] It involves explaining to the child that bad moods and feeling upset are caused by their thoughts about an event in their life and its causes. It is crucial to instil in the child the understanding that a pessimistic explanation – that the bad outcome is the child's fault – is just one explanation and that failing once doesn't mean you're a failure for life. Then, the adult works through several examples with the child in which the protagonist – another child – experiences adversity, explains it pessimistically and comes to feel bad about it, and guides the child carefully to form a more optimistic explanation of the setback encountered by the protagonist.

After a few sessions of this kind, the child is challenged to think of an adverse event in their own life, report the feelings it evoked in them and practise reframing them optimistically. Once the child has grasped that emotions come from ways of thinking, they are engaged in the process of disputation, and the outcome is a more hopeful and optimistic understanding of the event. This type of training, Seligman's research shows, improves a child's state of mind and imparts to them an invaluable coping skill.

Grit

Though optimism is essential, things do not always go as expected. Hardship and disappointment are part and parcel of most people's lives, and the ability to persevere despite setbacks – what Winston Churchill called 'the courage to continue' – is indispensable. Angela Duckworth, a brilliant student of Seligman, carried out definitive research on this ability, which she referred to as grit.

But what exactly is grit? Duckworth's theory identifies two ingredients: passion and perseverance. Passion is a consistent focus on one thing to the exclusion of much else. Duckworth recounts the advice the American billionaire Warren Buffett, one of the wealthiest people in the world, gave to his faithful pilot, who had dreams of a more successful career. Buffett advised: 'First you write down a list of twenty-five career goals. Second, you do some soul-searching and circle the five highest-priority goals. Just five. Third, you take a good hard look at the twenty goals you didn't circle. These you avoid at all costs. They're what distracts you; they eat away time and energy, taking your eye from the goals that matter more.'[13]

Do people follow their passions and centre their lives around a pursuit they find exciting and gratifying? Many do not. In a poll conducted by Gallup in 2014, over two thirds of the adults surveyed described not being engaged in their work, many reporting being actively disengaged. Instead of following our passion, many of us opt for a pragmatic route and follow a career path in which jobs are currently available, despite having little interest in or excitement about it. In today's materialistic world, it takes courage to risk poverty and joblessness by investing effort and resources in a passion that offers few opportunities for a respectable livelihood. Yet following a passion, something that we have a natural penchant for, gives us a shot at greatness, and if that evades us, at least a life of fulfilment. 'Never work a day in your life,' as the saying goes.

Perseverance, the second ingredient of grit, is never giving up, so when one path fails, substituting an alternative path to the same goal. Of course, jumping from one path to another at the slightest hint of failure wouldn't do; before concluding that something is unlikely to work, you must give it your all. We must never assume that success will be easy to achieve. We must be willing to devote hours, days and years, with patience and persistence. Duckworth cites dancers, musicians and telegraph operators to illustrate how long it can take to develop your skills. The dancer Martha Graham declared, 'It takes about ten years to make a mature dancer.' So does training an expert Morse operator, and 'ten thousand hours spread over ten years' is roughly what it takes to become a skilled musician.[14]

Passion and perseverance feed off each other. The stronger the passion, the more tenacious we are likely to be in its pursuit. To some extent, this also works in reverse: the more we persevere, the more we are likely to experience progress and expect success; this is likely to fan the flames of our passion. At any rate, passion and perseverance produce *grit*. Grit allows us to be undaunted by uncertainty and to explore it with zest.

While grit is a good quality to have, the question is whether it is inborn or whether it can be acquired and, if so, how. Duckworth identifies two sources of passion: *interest* and *purpose*. She recommends choosing a career in something that captures your imagination and that you enjoy. 'It may not guarantee happiness and success, but it sure helps the odds.'[15]

But how does someone develop an interest in something? Duckworth suggests that it involves a discovery (of a topic, theme or skill), the development of such an interest through exposure and the deepening of knowledge and expertise in the topic through involvement and practice. All these are important, but they stop short of explaining what makes a topic interesting to begin with, which is how a particular interest relates to a person's basic needs. My own research, backed up my personal experience, indicates that an interest or a passion for a topic develops when we feel that its pursuit will give us a sense of significance, make us feel that we matter, that we merit dignity and respect. It is the promised satisfaction of your need for recognition and social worth that fuels your passion. My own search for a career is one illustration of how this can happen.

How I became a psychologist

At the age of twenty-something, after three years of military service, I found myself at a crossroads. A new phase of my life was about to start, yet I had no idea what it should be and in which direction I should turn. I was very much looking forward to college but had no idea what to study. Rescue came from my Aunt Sophia (Zuza), the family guru. In her opinion, the writing was on the wall: I should study architecture! Why? Because I was good at drawing and found maths easy.

Not having any better ideas at the time, and having great admiration for creative architecture, I proceeded to apply to schools of architecture and was lucky enough to get into an excellent one at the University of Toronto in Canada. But although I did well academically, the architectural courses, and the design class in particular, were a struggle. I passed all my exams and secured a summer job at an architect's firm, yet I didn't feel sure that architecture was for me, or that I had it in me to become a great architect.

After considerable soul-searching, I took a fateful leap of faith. I gave up architecture and enrolled in the psychology department at the University of Toronto. I got lucky here because it turned out that this decision, too, was based on completely wrong assumptions. Serendipitously, it ended well and led to my lifelong passion: the study of human behaviour. My assumptions were wrong because I had expected to learn something mysterious and fascinating in the vein of Freudian psychoanalysis: to decipher people's dreams and become a therapist; to have the skills to ease people's suffering and cure patients of debilitating neuroses. What awaited me instead was training in the rigours of psychology grounded in neo-behaviouristic theories of learning. Instead of working with patients, I was analysing data and teaching white rats to press a lever for food. But after my initial disappointment, I discovered that scientific psychology fascinated me and that I had a knack for it. That last realization was crucial. It evoked in me the hope that I could 'make it' and succeed in a field I admired. My optimism was buoyed by the encouragement I was getting from my professors. Without their support and faith, my interest and passion for psychology would have withered on the vine. No one can be passionate for long about something they are obviously bad at.

The point is this: our overriding interest and passion for something requires that it be valued by ourselves and by the people we esteem and expected to bring us success and hence respect and significance in our own eyes and those of others. As Duckworth writes: 'Encouragement during the early years is crucial because beginners are still figuring out whether they want to commit or cut bait . . . We need small wins. We need applause. Yes, we can handle a tincture of criticism and corrective feedback. Yes, we need to practice. But not too much and not too soon.'[16] Encouragement means feedback about success; it communicates that performing an activity, be it a sport, academic study or an art form, gives us a sense of significance and dignity.

Our need for significance and esteem isn't limited to our early years or when we are choosing an interest or developing a passion. The phrase 'knowing when to quit' suggests that when the pursuit is no longer crowned with success it is time to let it go. Athletes, like basketball superstar Michael Jordan, sometimes say they stopped competing because they had nothing more to prove. This indicates that their past efforts had been aimed at proving something, namely their skill and virtuosity in an area that affirmed their significance.

Demonstrating skill and competence in an activity that is respected in our culture (for instance, sports, business, the arts or academia) is one way of gaining a sense of significance and respect. It is not the only way, however. We can gain a sense of our own significance through the realization of a societal value. Personal achievement is one such value, but there are others, for example courage, altruism, patriotism or humility. Manifest devotion to those values, especially if demonstrated by self-denial in their service, merits a considerable sense of significance and degree of admiration from a society that holds them dear. Mother Teresa, who chose to live in poverty while caring for the poor in the slums of Kolkata, gained worldwide fame for her humane work and was canonized by Pope Francis. Members of the military are often hailed as heroes for willingly putting themselves in harm's way in order to defend their nation. Examples abound.

Duckworth discusses *purpose in life* as something that can incite passion. She defines purpose as 'the intention to contribute to the well-being of others'.[17] She reports that those who demonstrate grit talk about having purpose and typically mention caring for other people, children, clients or students, or refer to devotion to a cause, country, science or society. All these serve important social values: the humanism and selflessness of caring for others, for our country, profession or society. Acting on behalf of important values means that you are a good, worthwhile person in your own eyes, and in the eyes of others in your community whose good opinion matters to you. Serving or representing values to which your society subscribes, whether it be individualistic values such as career achievement or collectivistic values such as altruism, lends you a sense of personal significance and therefore builds your self-assurance.

Summary

Some people react to uncertainty with fear and trepidation. Others confront it with hope and anticipation. The major mental qualities that determine these reactions are optimism and grit. While these are partly genetic, they can also be cultivated. Psychological research has provided important insights into the processes that underlie optimistic and/or gritty behaviours. Optimism is closely related to how we think about our past failures and successes and what we believe caused them. Attribution of failure to transient factors (bad luck or lack of effort) are optimistic in that they suggest that failure may not be inevitable and recurring. So, too, are attributions of success to stable factors such as talent and ability. The latter suggest that since your talents and abilities are stable, then so should be the successful outcomes that these bring about. People can be trained to make optimistic attributions, and psychologists have devised effective methods to this end.

Whereas optimism is essential for approaching uncertainty with a positive state of mind, obstacles and setbacks inevitably happen, so it is important for people to maintain their tenacity and commitment to their goals. Such commitment is encapsulated in the concept of grit. The two ingredients of grit are passion and persistence. These typically follow when someone finds a pursuit or occupation that they can succeed in and gain significance and social worth in doing so. The search for a significance-giving pursuit is often difficult and might take you off the path you expected to follow. Yet grit allows us to face down uncertainty and be undaunted by it. Developing it can serve you well in pursuit of your dreams.

In your experience

1. Would you describe yourself as generally optimistic or generally pessimistic? Would you like to change? How would you go about it?
2. What activities and pursuits interest you most? Are you able to devote to them the time you would like? If not, why not? Can this change? How?
3. Can you think of a friend who is particularly 'gritty' or one who lacks 'grit'? What in your opinion makes them this way?
4. What are the advantages and disadvantages of optimism? What are the advantages and disadvantages of pessimism? Do you believe it best to be a 'realist'? Is this even possible?

12. The Best is Yet to Come

The growth mindset

Fear of failure is one of the most debilitating phobias, and it causes considerable unhappiness for millions of people, preventing them from realizing their goals and living up to their aspirations. It is a common condition, affecting people across the globe. World Bank statistics indicate that in 2020, 41.2 per cent of Americans aged eighteen to sixty-four suffered from fear of failure; this figure was 48.3 per cent in the UK, 46.5 per cent in Russia, 56.8 per cent in India and 31 per cent in Germany.[1]

An important advance in seeking to address this crippling condition was Carol Dweck's concept of the *growth mindset*. She challenges the idea that internal causes of failure such as lack of ability and talent are necessarily stable. And replaces it with her growth mindset theory – the belief that our minds and brains are malleable. If so, our failures aren't inevitable. We can always change, learn and improve. There is hope!

Carol Dweck is a psychology professor at Stanford University and one of the most influential social scientists in the world today. I asked her what had inspired her to study the growth mindset and its impact. Carol's response was extensive and illuminating: 'I entered psychology just as the behaviourist era was waning and the age of cognitive social psychology was dawning. So, with the prospect of addressing human issues, I left the animal lab behind and entered the world of attribution theory. Attribution theory, in the form made popular by Bernard Weiner and others, thrilled me. No longer did I live in the stark reality of precisely programmed reinforcement contingencies, but I now lived in a more nuanced and fluid world in which people gave their own interpretations to events — a world that they constructed and interpreted and did not just register.

'What was new was the idea that two people could be in the same situation with the same things happening to them and yet ascribe different meanings to those happenings. I soon wondered what determined whether people gravitated towards one interpretation or another. Then I wondered: Were there implicit theories (or mindsets) that people held that led them to interpret their experiences in different ways and then fostered different patterns of behaviour? Could we identify these theories or mindsets? Could we link the mindsets to different behaviours? And could we change those mindsets to change behaviour? My research of the last decades suggests that the answer is yes.

'In this research, we found that people held different mindsets about the nature of human attributes, such as intelligence or personality. Some believed that a given trait (say, intelligence) was simply fixed, whereas others believed that intellectual abilities could be developed, for example, through hard work, good strategies and mentoring and help from others. How does this relate to the topic of uncertainty?

'Well, those with more of a fixed mindset about human traits, believing things are concrete and static, try to pin them down: What is my true intelligence? What is Bob's true personality? Because they believe in a fixed reality, they try to figure out what it is. And, indeed, research (by, among others, Hong, Chiu, Erdley, Levy, Stroessner, Plaks, Molden and McConnell) showed that when judging either individuals or groups, those with more of a fixed mindset made more rapid trait judgements and stuck to them more firmly in the face of counter-evidence. They seemed more reluctant to wallow in initial uncertainty or open themselves up to new uncertainty after they had made a judgement.

'When it came to the self, similar processes were in play, with one difference. People are typically hoping for positive trait judgements for themselves, not negative ones. Thus people with more of a fixed mindset often try to reduce uncertainty by opting for tasks they know they can succeed in and avoiding ones that have uncertain outcomes, whereas those with more of a growth mindset more readily take on challenges – for them, mistakes and setbacks can be learning opportunities, not condemnations of their abilities (as shown in research by Ehrlinger, Yeager, Nussbaum, Chiu, Hong, Moser and others). Those in more of a fixed mindset may even repeatedly practise problems that are easy for them, in order to feel good about their ability, rather than try harder ones that may make them feel anxious and uncertain.

'When failure seems more possible, those in more of a growth mindset tend to step up their effort and strategies in order to boost their likelihood of success. That is, they reduce uncertainty through appropriate preparation and engagement. We have also conducted "intervention" studies in which we've changed students' mindsets and, by doing so, increased their desire for challenge to the point that they were more likely to enrol in advanced maths one year later.

'However, those in a fixed mindset have a more problematic relationship with such uncertainty. Guarding against a possible negative judgement, they may employ defensive strategies, such as self-handicapping or effort withdrawal – measures that may protect their ego but, ironically, may make failure more likely (as shown in research by Nussbaum, Mangels, Rhodewalt, Moser and others). In short, those with more of a growth mindset seek and are excited by uncertainty in the form of challenges or even possible setbacks, and they tend to reduce that uncertainty through their direct, agentic [initiating, proactive] actions. However, those in more of a fixed mindset often find uncertainty more aversive or threatening – they tend to seek the certainty that easier tasks bring and often deal with uncertainty in indirect or defensive ways that may not serve them well in the longer run.

'Delving into people's mindsets has provided a source of endless fascination. In the course of this work, I have repeatedly gone down what looked like dark alleys and found brightly lit boulevards. In the course of this work, I have made uncertainty a close, even cherished, friend.'

In her book *Mindset*, Dweck goes back to an early time in her career when she studied how children cope with failure. She did so by having children solve puzzles that by design grew more and more difficult. To her astonishment, some kids loved the difficult puzzles and were thrilled to attempt them. Based on these observations and subsequent research, Dweck developed her theory of 'mindset': the 'fixed' mindset and the 'growth' mindset. The former assumes that all our abilities and talents are unchanging, so our intelligence or IQ is attributed from birth; likewise, whether we are either lazy or industrious, moral or immoral, trustworthy or not. The presumed stability of our attributes allows us to assess and measure them, but never to change them.

The growth mindset, however, assumes that human attributes, including intelligence, morality, tenacity or willpower, are malleable or in flux. Like a muscle that can be strengthened through exercise, they too can grow and develop. Whereas someone with a fixed mindset regards each task as a test that reveals their true attributes, someone with a growth mindset regards each task as an opportunity to learn and improve. Someone with a fixed mindset reacts to failure with deep disappointment; they feel humiliated and diminished by it, sinking into depression and indulging in ruminations that keep the upset alive. Someone with a growth mindset, on the other hand, learns from failure, pinpoints its causes and identifies which part of their performance needs more work. Far from being defeated by failure, the growth-minded person enters an active learning mode and appreciates the opportunity to improve.

Just think what fixed and growth mindsets mean when confronting an unknown, uncertain situation. The 'fixated' individual might fear the possibility of falling short and refrain from taking risks, attempting to escape the situation altogether. The growth-minded individual might do the opposite; not fearing failure, they explore the possibilities the situation offers of progress and success.

In our society at least, the fixed mindset is the dominant mode of understanding reality. We label people as intelligent or unintelligent, talented or untalented, creative or uncreative, athletic or unathletic. These labels determine how we treat people and relate to them. In hiring for sports teams, businesses and academia, for example, we typically go for 'talent', 'brilliance', 'intelligence' and other labels that assume people's fixed characteristics. We largely ignore the possibility of growth and development. We underestimate the blood, sweat and tears behind any kind of worthwhile achievement. The emphasis on labels makes people do all they can to *seem* talented and brilliant. They worry about appearances and avoid risking failure. They are defensive about their possible shortcomings and loath to admit their mistakes and learn from them. This results in a conservative approach that avoids uncertainty and misses potential.

Dweck's *Mindset* contains many examples of the detrimental aspects of a fixed mindset. One is the Enron Corporation,* hailed by *Fortune* magazine as America's Most Innovative Company for six consecutive years (between 1996 and 2001). The downfall of Enron was, however, even more spectacular than its rise. Whereas in August 2000 its shares were worth over $90.75, in December 2001 they sank to just $0.26. As Dweck explains, Enron created a corporate culture that worshipped talent and motivated its employees to appear extremely competent, which led its executives to make risky and ethically questionable decisions. It was this inability of Enron executives to admit to their mistakes, and instead of

---

* Enron was an energy-trading and utility company based in Houston, Texas, that perpetrated one of the biggest accounting frauds in history.

taking remedial action their decision to pile cover-up on top of cover-up, that caused the company's demise.

Individualistic American culture has created the 'super-star' system in which people strive to be extraordinary 'winners' and everyone fears appearing a 'loser'. Willy Loman, the pathetic anti-hero of Arthur Miller's *Death of a Salesman*, commits suicide when he feels like a failure. American CEOs are hailed as cultural superheroes, their salaries reaching astronomic levels. In 2017, the average annual salary of a CEO in the 350 top US companies reached $14.25 million, almost twice as much as CEO salaries in other industrialized countries. Being a 'winner', a 'genius', a 'superstar', is a status we dream to attain and dread to lose.

In contemporary Western societies, fame and celebrity are of supreme value. Attaining them is the ultimate goal for many people. In their mind it is proof that they are superior beings, better than ordinary Joes, in a class all of their own. In 1961 the author Daniel Boorstin defined celebrity as 'a person who is known for his well-knownness'. The British journalist Malcolm Muggeridge had this to say on the topic: 'Today one is famous for being famous. People who come up to one in the street or in public places to claim recognition nearly always say: "I've seen you on the telly!" '[2] And in 2009, Amy Argetsinger, a *Washington Post* journalist, called well-known people whose fame has not been earned by any successful career accomplishments 'famesque'.

The fixed mindset has immense implications for people's sociopolitical worldviews. It encourages a stratified view of society in which people are assumed to merit, by accident of birth or their inborn talents, different positions in the social hierarchy; this creates deep inequalities. Karl Popper in *Open Society and Its Enemies* (1945) criticized Plato's defence of a society divided into classes. In Plato's social philosophy, according to Popper, 'The problem of avoiding class war is solved, not by abolishing classes, but by giving the ruling class a superiority which cannot be challenged . . . The workers, tradesmen . . . are only human cattle whose sole function is to provide for the material needs of the ruling class.' In such a closed society, 'True happiness . . . is achieved only by justice, i.e. by keeping one's place. The ruler must find happiness in ruling, the warrior in warring, and, we may infer, the slave in slaving.'[3]

The fixed mindset, according to which some people are better or more deserving than others, has been common throughout history. It underlies the logic of monarchies and the trappings of aristocracy. It spawned caste systems in South Asian countries, eugenic theories about racial superiorities and inferiorities, and the concept of 'class' in contemporary Western societies. The growth mindset, in contrast, embodies the spirit of democracy and social justice. From ancient Greece onward (despite Plato), it underlies the social movements for equality, the presumption enshrined in the US Declaration of Independence that all men and women are created equal. It is also at the heart of the American dream, whereby with effort and hard work anyone can reach for greatness.

It is striking to realize how pervasive the fixed mindset is in our culture. For instance, Mensa was founded in 1946, intended to create an 'aristocracy of the intellect'. To do so it set the condition for membership as an IQ of above 130 points. Interestingly, Mensa members, counting close to 65,000 worldwide, do not necessarily boast great achievements or make considerable contributions to society. Peter Sturgeon, who called the first Mensa meeting in the US in

Brooklyn in 1940, said, 'We are not geniuses.'[4] Indeed, the growth mindset theory suggests that having superior intelligence is not enough, and that resting on your intellectual laurels will not deliver success. Rather, it is effort, persistence and the ability to learn from our failures, which the growth mindset enables, that are the key ingredients.

The fixed mindset is widespread in the world of sport. There the myth reigns that 'natural talent' is the stuff that sports heroes are made of – despite ample evidence that the secret lies instead in training, tenacity and hard work. These attributes are encouraged by the growth mindset, which refuses to yield to the gloomy present and hails the possibility of improvement. In *Mindset,* Dweck rolls out story after story of talented athletes who failed to remain on top and hard-working athletes who had great success. Whereas outsiders, including coaches and sport commentators, never tire of singing the praise of the athlete's 'gifts', 'innate sports IQ' and other aspects of athletic 'genius', athletes themselves often tell of struggle, persistence and sacrifice. Athletes who lack this kind of tenacity often fail and, even if their ability takes them to the top, they do not stay there long. Examples are the boxer Mike Tyson and the tennis players Martina Hingis and John McEnroe; these athletes believed that their special talent made them invincible, yet when they failed or lost, their frustration was too much to bear and they fell apart.

True sports giants, though sometimes lacking in natural ability, have something more important: strength of character and the belief that present handicaps are temporary; they are just obstacles to be overcome by training and persistence. In this class belong such all-time heroes as Michael Jordan, who was dropped from his high-school team and passed over by his chosen college (North Carolina State), and Babe Ruth, who at the start of his career wasn't a particularly good hitter.

Writing in *The New Yorker*, Malcolm Gladwell aptly observed that people typically value natural ability over dogged effort.[5] We are all aware of the derogatory sense of the epithet 'trying too hard', and the admiration inherent in the 'genius' label. What explains this? Two things, mainly. One is people's excitement about the unusual, the special, the outstanding. Stories about geniuses are more exciting, interesting and attention-grabbing than those about ordinary people striving, so people like to tell and listen to such stories and to interpret unusual events (both desired and undesired) in exceptional terms. The other reason is that the fixed mindset offers order and predictability; as in Plato's perfect world, people can be expected to act in accordance with their essences. When we crave certainty and closure and this comes to pass, this is pleasing and reassuring. In contrast, the growth mindset ushers in uncertainty and flux. If people can change, there is no knowing what will become of them. To someone with a high need for closure, this is disquieting and anxiety-evoking.

Falling in and out of love

An intriguing application of Dweck's mindset theory is in the area of romantic relations. In popular culture, 'falling in love' often means finding the perfect person, a human who can do no wrong. They are assumed to be the soulmate, the yin to our yang, or vice versa. This glorification of another person is almost always unrealistic; it is strongly distorted by our overriding motivation to love and be loved. The problem with such limerence (as this limitless adoration is called) is that sooner or later we discover that the over-idealized object of our infatuation isn't as godlike as we had originally assumed. Instead, they are mere mortals with their share of potentially annoying idiosyncrasies. To someone with a fixed mindset the realization that their chosen one isn't the paragon of perfection will most likely be deeply disappointing. It could even prompt them to break up with them and begin the search for another unattainable ideal. Someone with a growth mindset, however, isn't likely to put all their stock in their partner's apparent traits. They would rather take a chance on exploring the potential of the relationship and embarking on a journey of mutual discovery.

The growth mindset is of particular value in the context of rejection: a common, near-inevitable counterpart of romance. Someone with a fixed mindset is likely to experience 'heartbreak' when they are rejected. Like the young Werther in Goethe's 1774 novel, they may be driven to suicide, assuming that the rejection means they are for ever 'unlovable'. Unlike Werther, however, not everyone directs the frustration against themselves. Aggression towards the person responsible for the humiliation is more common. Researchers estimate that between 15 to 30 per cent of divorces entail a great degree of conflict. They can be highly acrimonious and protracted affairs, often lasting for years, in which former spouses harm each other verbally, if not physically.

People with a growth mindset react to break-ups very differently. 'For them, it was about understanding, forgiving and moving on. Although they were often deeply hurt by what happened, they wanted to learn from it'[6] and to emerge from the difficult situation with a sense of deeper self-understanding.

Self-handicapping

An especially troubling consequence of the fixed mindset and the belief in natural genius is the phenomenon of self-handicapping – engaging in self-destructive behaviours to protect our 'claim to fame'. Once a person is pronounced smart, intelligent, creative or athletic, they may not want to risk losing that label and hence their fixed way of seeing things. In situations in which our abilities are tested (for example, a college exam), we may set up external conditions that all but assure our failure. This deflects the explanation for failure away from us and defends our previous standing. For instance, someone who as a child was considered especially intellectually gifted might avoid situations where their intelligence is put to the test, for example, in a quiz, a trivia contest or a maths tournament. In order not to lose to their 'reputation', they may use drugs or alcohol, protecting their standing, though assuring their poor performance, by creating a compelling explanation for their failure.

In a landmark study on self-handicapping, Edward Jones and Steve Berglas asked research participants to undertake a problem-solving task.[7] Half the participants received easy problems to solve and the other half difficult ones. Regardless of how the participants performed, they were all told they had succeeded. Before attempting an additional problem-solving task, participants were given a choice between a 'performance-enhancing' and a 'performance-impairing' drug. It was found that participants who had received the difficult problem and who felt their success was due to chance and unlikely to be repeated were more likely to choose the performance-impairing drug, to protect themselves from the anticipated loss of esteem due to failing in the task.

Further research on self-handicapping has uncovered several interesting things. First, people differ in their use of it. Some people are 'inveterate' self-handicappers, whereas others do not use this mechanism at all. There's even a scale – the self-handicapping scale (SHS) – that reliably measures this. People who score highly on the SHS invest less effort and practice in tasks that are important to their self-esteem. They also give excuses, such as temporary malaise, fatigue or intoxication, and create external obstacles prior to engaging in the task, for instance waiting until it is too late to start preparing for a test or taking on a challenge that most people would fail in (hence their own failure does not appear to reflect their own low ability). Second, a lot of self-handicapping behaviour takes place unconsciously: someone might get drunk the night before an important test or a sports competition, or they might stay up late and not get enough sleep, or neglect to revise or train by doing other things that suddenly seem incredibly important. All these occur without our explicit awareness that our choices, actions or inaction are geared to protect our ego when the outcome of the competition or the exam seems uncertain. So, in times of uncertainty, when our reputation hangs in the balance, fear of failure prompts some people to engage in self-handicapping; they deliberately fail but make sure their prestige is shielded by an excuse of their own making.

But perhaps the most interesting thing about self-handicapping is that it follows on from a fixed mindset.

People with a growth mindset aren't as committed to their current status or prestige as they are to improvement, learning and development. Consequently, they do not fear the unknown and view it as an opportunity for advancement. Self-handicapping is opposed to these objectives and therefore people with a growth mindset are unlikely to engage in it. Research by Frederick Rhodewalt found that high self-handicappers believe that traits such as intelligence or morality are immutable.[8] In other words, they have a fixed mindset. They therefore avoid uncertain situations and choose only ones in which they will look good and can demonstrate their fixed ability. In contrast, low self-handicappers have a growth mindset; they are not afraid to fail because they believe they can learn and improve.

Self-handicapping and explanatory style

Remember the optimistic explanatory style put forward by Seligman (Chapter 11)? It includes attributing failures to external factors and successes to internal factors such as talent or ability. The tennis great John McEnroe, for example, was known for excusing his losses by attributing them to bad umpires, the weather, being upset or distracted – all factors external to his ability or talent, which were left out of the equation and thus protected.

Research suggests that such externalization of failure can have a positive effect on someone's subsequent performance. Martin Seligman and his team of co-authors gave negative feedback to swimmers on their first performance (poor times) and recorded the explanations they gave for their failure. It was found that the swimmers who attributed their (alleged) poor performance to low ability or lack of talent did worse in their next performance, whereas swimmers who excused their performance by making external excuses did as well as before. This shows the positive effect of protecting the ego with an 'optimistic' explanatory style.

There is a significant psychological difference, however, between an optimistic explanatory style and self-handicapping. Explanatory style occurs *after the event*, that is, after the successful or unsuccessful outcome. In contrast, self-handicapping comes *before* the performance and is designed to protect the ego in anticipation of a possible failure. Moreover, self-handicapping typically involves creating conditions that will serve as excuses for the expected failure (for example, imbibing alcohol before a performance or missing training or revision sessions). Unfortunately, such actions are likely to impede performance, so self-handicapping is highly counterproductive; it means 'shooting yourself in the foot' or sabotaging your own efforts.

From the standpoint of Dweck's mindset theory, both optimistic explanatory style and self-handicapping reflect a mindset bent on protecting our fixed endowments (talent or ability) from being damaged by failure. A growth mindset, however, isn't threatened by failure; instead, it regards it as a temporary phase on the route to improvement that comes from learning from our mistakes.

Developing the growth mindset: on the audacity of hope

Dweck's message extends a ray of hope to those with a fixed mindset. These are people who feel that their essence is defined by a current failure or rejection. However, those who feel 'successful' may also immunize themselves against the risk of denting their reputation, preferring to self-handicap than face uncertainty. As Winston Churchill so aptly put it, 'Success is not final, failure is not fatal: it is the courage to continue that counts.' It is this 'courage to continue' that Dweck's approach effectively instils in her writings, lectures and workshops.

In short, learning and development are the road to success. According to Dweck, the human brain is like a muscle: it can be developed. Neither our current standing, whether inferior or superior, nor our current outcomes, whether success or failure, matter all that much, given the potential for change and, more emphatically, for improvement. This hope-giving idea is then translated into possible fixed- and growth-mindset reactions to a variety of hypothetical failures or setbacks. They include a wide array of situations, including rejection by your university of choice, anxiety about performing well in a high-level competition, being passed over for promotion and the dissolution of a marriage. The distinction between the fixed and the growth mindsets is applicable to many areas of life where success matters. Dweck acknowledges that embracing the growth mindset might not be easy. It means abandoning the comfort of fixed or secure knowledge. It means facing a deep uncertainty that for some might feel dark and scary.*

---

* In an autobiographical note, Dweck writes (2006, p. 219): 'When I was exchanging my fixed mindset for a growth one, I was acutely aware of how unsettled I felt . . . As a fixed mindsetter, I kept track each day of my successes. At the end of a good day, I could look at the results . . . and feel good about myself. But as I adopted a growth mindset and stopped keeping track, some nights I would still check my mental counters and find them at zero. It made me insecure not to be able to tot up my victories.'

The growth mindset is the belief in possibility. It is rooted in the idea that our fate isn't sealed by immutable destiny but rather is malleable and open-ended. No matter how dire the circumstances, the unfathomable game of life typically conceals 'moves' that, if only we were able to utilize them, would extricate us from the clutches of entrapment and put us on the path to success. We need faith, however, in our ability to make those discoveries, the optimism that things will be good at the end and, if they aren't good yet, this isn't the end. And we also need the perseverance to keep going, and the patience and grit to see things through.

The tyranny of testing

Scientists such as Martin Seligman, Carol Dweck and Angela Duckworth have advanced our understanding of how to empower people so that they can confront uncertainty with confidence. Like most of us, these scientists accepted the general notions of success prevalent in our culture, which in the educational domain at least are defined in terms of good grades at school, admission to a prestigious college, graduating with honours, and so on. These markers of academic success derive from the various assessments carried out by the educational institutions. Such assessments have come under poignant criticism for the way in which they label people and place them in fixed categories.

Kenneth Gergen, a leading psychological theorist, and Scherto Gill, an eminent education scholar, recently articulated the considerable problems of the current philosophy of assessment which creates fixed categories of people: some are pronounced intelligent or gifted; others are depicted as dumb or mediocre. Much like Dweck, who railed against these fixed categories, Gergen and Gill decry these consequences, but rather than coaching people on how to transcend the pigeonholes into which they are placed, they view the issue as systemic. They critique 'the tyranny of the assessment tradition [that includes] practices of examining, grading, and high-stakes testing of students'.[9] These tests, the authors argue, not only do not reliably predict future success but also create stress and misery for millions of students, who come to regard their educational experience as a kind of nightmare.

The problem is that testing has become the end of education, rather than a means of identifying areas for improvement. Instead of contributing to the student's development as an intellectually curious, ethical and socially competent human being, the present system of education means narrowly 'teaching to the test'. This produces standardized educational 'products' – the people who have gone through this system – that are then infused into the economy, and the major question people then have is whether their investment in education was ultimately worth it in terms of the salary they earn or the position they have attained. As Gergen and Gill put it: 'Whether the educational process enhances creative potential, curiosity, moral sensitivity, aesthetic appreciation, a sense of justice, openess to others who differ, or capacities to collaborate with peers is of minor significance.'[10]

A great deal has been said about the low validity of educational assessment in predicting future success. All it essentially measures is test performance. It is uninformative about a student's potential, creativity and intelligence. The reasons are obvious and well known. Test performance is affected by the culture that the student has soaked up at home. Kids who benefit from a home environment filled with intellectual stimulation, kids who grow up in a home culture where reading and intellectual discussion are common and whose parents support their academic pursuits and tutor them as needed are at a great advantage when it comes to test taking in comparison to kids whose home environment lacks those features. Students whose home culture highlights academic achievements come to value them as a source of significance and social worth. Consequently, they are more motivated to study hard at school than students whose home culture is less concerned with academic values.

Test performance is also affected by students' mental and physical condition. This too is very much dependent on conditions at home. A child who has benefited from healthy nutrition and who is rested and mentally at ease is at a considerable advantage in comparison to a child who comes to the test situation tired, hungry and tense, perhaps due to conflict, violence or abuse suffered at home.

Finally, the attitude to studying that prevails in any given classroom is based on the values of the more popular students, who serve as opinion leaders. These determine how hard any one student will strive to excel in academic tasks. A child in a classroom where popularity depends primarily on looks, athletic ability or ostentatious affluence, and where good students are considered lowly nerds, 'brown-nosers' who 'kiss up' to the teachers, may be ambivalent about school success and not work as hard to obtain good grades. In short, the ample differences that determine students' degree of preparedness for academic tests belie the assumption that test results and the associated grades reflect students' inherent aptitude and potential. Obviously, they do not.

The 'cookie cutter' approach is only part of the price of the 'certainty' about people's potential that standardized testing promises to deliver. Even more disturbing is what this does to students. Research suggests that whatever intellectual curiosity and excitement about exploring the world kids may have are mostly gone by the time they graduate. Tod Wodicka describes this colourfully in his novel *All Shall Be Well; And All Shall Be Well; And All Manner of Things Shall Be Well* (2007):

> 'Will this be in the examination, Mr Hecker?' was the limit of my students' interest in any given subject. If it was going to be in the test they took notes, if it was not going to be in the test they did not take notes. Their silent, depth less stares were unnerving. I told myself that they were not stupid – for how could the final attainment of thousands of years of human progress be stupid?

The assessment regime exacts a heavy toll on students' mental health. Approximately 1,100 US students commit suicide each year.[11] As reported in *Atlantic* magazine on 9 October 2015, the incidence of depression in the US among students aged between fourteen and seventeen increased by 60 per cent between 2009 and 2017, and among twelve- to thirteen-year-olds by 50 per cent. In a survey conducted with students of these ages at private schools, about half reported feeling stressed all the time.[12] Almost invariably the reasons were schoolwork, grades and college and university admissions that are inextricably connected to grades. The stress leads many students to self-harm to the point of committing suicide.[13]

No less concerning is the (unintended) consequence that testing has for students' social relations in the classroom and beyond. The grades differentiate students and identify some as more worthy. Through the academic standards that schools emphasize, grades discriminate between students and establish a hierarchy of value. At the top are the 'good students', the recipients of good grades, whereas at the bottom are the 'bad students', who are made to feel dumb and worthless in the school setting. So, early in life, some children are stamped with the label of 'loser' and others with that of 'winner'. Those who come to self-define as losers may misidentify with education altogether. They may drop out and seek alternative ways of gaining a sense of significance, perhaps in lines of work that require less immersion in the educational system. Labels given to them in school can come to define them for years to come, if not for life. The hierarchy of worth that the assignment of grades creates also introduces toxicity into the classroom. Mutually hostile cliques may develop, the 'bullies' taking out their frustration on the 'nerds', for instance. As a result, these groups come to abhor the school experience and dream about avenging their humiliation.[14] Teachers can find themselves caught between the 'warring' camps and often feel impelled to take sides. Typically, they defend the 'good students' against the 'troublemakers', which exacerbates the latter's feelings of hurt. The hierarchies created by the current modes of educational assessment are carried over into adulthood and contribute to economic inequalities.[15] The downstream consequence is that millions feel forgotten and left behind.[16] This promotes the rise of populism and the fraying of contemporary societies.

Envisioning alternative assessment

Given the serious problems with the current culture of educational assessment, the question inevitably arises about what can be done about it. Giving up on assessment is not an option. People, after all, need to make life and career choices that are informed by knowledge of their special talents, aptitudes and inclinations. Gergen and Gill propose a relational approach that would see assessment as a process that not only evaluates educational achievements but also promotes human development. To do so, schools needs to cultivate students' capacity to let go of their rigid beliefs, tolerate uncertainty and open themselves up to new ideas.

Relational assessment would de-emphasize summative assessment, which marks what has already been achieved; instead, it would emphasize the constant enrichment of learning. This would be accomplished by both teachers and students working together, by identifying possibilities rather than firmly 'knowing'. This process avoids allocating grades and making fixed summaries of a student's potential. It eliminates the threat that testing and evaluation entail these days, and allows learning to encourage growth and intellectual development.

In line with this idea, the type of collaboration of students and teachers championed by Gergen and Gill aims to enhance, enrich and make more enjoyable the process of learning, a process which should promote sustained engagement. The student should feel respected and cared for. They should feel that the teacher is genuinely interested in them acquiring a skill or mastering a subject. Comparison and competition with other students should be minimized, and the student should be encouraged to measure their progress against the baseline they have set for themselves.

Gergen and Gill focus attention on students' need for a sense of significance and highlight the critical role of the social network (which includes the teacher and fellow students) in addressing that need. Ensuring that the student feels appreciated, listened to and that they have influence on others in the classroom keeps them engaged in the learning process and enables them to benefit from it in multiple ways. This approach promises to foster students' social and intellectual growth and is therefore preferable to the motivation-stultifying strategy of current assessment practices. Although it sacrifices the certainty and clarity of summative assessment and is in some ways complex and multifaceted, it may be a more productive way to approach education.

Summary

A lot of recent research in the field of psychology has addressed issues of permanence and change, tapping into the corresponding themes of certainty and uncertainty. This work has highlighted the psychological costs of pessimism, which is promoted by the belief that failure is permanent. Some approaches, such as Seligman's (see Chapter 11), promote optimistic practices based on ways of thinking: attributing failures to transient causes and success to stable causes. Others, for example Dweck's, stress the basic malleability of human attributes and the ever-present potential for improvement. Whereas both Seligman and Dweck have based their interventions on people's attributions and beliefs about fixity and change, Duckworth's approach (see Chapter 11) stresses the importance of motivation for dealing with life's challenges and developing grit. Finally, Gergen and Gill raise the issues of certainty and uncertainty to the systemic level. They condemn the prevalent approach to children's education that creates the destructive fixity of dividing people into 'winners' and 'losers'. Such a hierarchy undermines genuine learning and creates resentments and tensions that upset the workings of society and mar social relations.

In your own experience

1. What is your general attitude towards failure? Are you afraid of it? How much so? What do you typically do about it?
2. Is your mindset closer to the fixed one described by Dweck, or do you believe that growth in things such as talent and ability (including smarts and intelligence) is possible?
3. Describe the feelings you experience before a test or a competition. Are you anxious about it? Are you excited? Would you prefer tests to be eliminated?
4. Do you ever feel that you are self-handicapping in order to prevent a shameful failure? Do you realize the costs of self-handicapping to those who practise it? What alternative attitude could you adopt to avoid having to pay these costs?

13. The Allure of Detachment and Mystery

Have you ever had the feeling that you worry too much? That there is more to life than work and your career? That you yearn to get away from the 'rat race' but do not have the nerve to quit? If you occasionally entertain these thoughts, you are not alone. Millions of people like you are increasingly turning to Eastern philosophy in search of the balance our rushed lives seem to lack.

Whereas the Western mode of dealing with uncertainty is to 'attack' it through optimism, growth mindset or grit, the Eastern way draws its inspiration from the concept of Buddhist acceptance and emotional detachment. This influential attitude to life's inevitable uncertainties begins with Buddha's story and his deep interest in alleviating human suffering.

Buddha's own life journey was a headlong leap into uncertainty, buoyed, apparently, by his strong sense of self, which stemmed from his noble upbringing. He was born as Siddhartha Gautama around 567 BC to a wealthy and powerful family. Surrounded by princely luxury, he was taught by the most sophisticated brahmins and trained in 'aristocratic' sports such as archery, swordsmanship, wrestling, swimming and running. He married Gopa, with whom he had a son. Yet despite all this, despite having everything a young man might desire, he was restless and dissatisfied.

He rode beyond the palace walls in his chariot. There, in the streets of Kapilavastu, he was stunned to encounter human suffering. He saw a sick man, an old man and a corpse en route to the site of its ritual burning. He was troubled to learn from his charioteer that these were not isolated instances – the fate of all humans is, after all, to get ill, get old and die. The very idea of such suffering was foreign to Siddhartha. Never before had it entered his mind that suffering existed.

Intrigued and unsettled, he decided to leave his former life and embark on a journey of discovery, aiming to learn about suffering and how it could be conquered. He silently parted from his sleeping wife and son, cut his hair and donned the robes of an ascetic. Ahead lay the vast unknown, uncertainties to be explored, illumination to be attained. In a tangled jungle fraught with danger of all kinds the Buddha's famed search for enlightenment commenced. The rest is history. These days, an estimated 535 million people worldwide practise Buddhism, between 8 and 10 per cent of the world's population.

Young Siddhartha's natural and intrepid acceptance of uncertainty is reflected in the Buddhist attitude to the unknown, which differs radically from the Western perspective. The Western, activist way of coping with uncertainty involves creating a sense that all will be well in the end, that with proper training and learning we can convert uncertainty into a desirable outcome. In contrast, the Buddhist approach preaches the *acceptance* of uncertainty. It holds that uncertainty can yield both good and bad outcomes and that suffering is part and parcel of being human – suffering simply *is*. It exists and cannot be eliminated, but we can control our attitude towards it.

Buddhism admonishes us to brace ourselves for possible surprises, whether pleasant or unpleasant. Because impermanence reigns, anything can happen. And whatever happens may not last. To recall Winston Churchill's words, 'success isn't final' and 'failure isn't fatal'. And because of this, attachment to things (say, people or possessions) and great emotional investment in potential outcomes such as coveting success and dreading failure is unreasonable and counterproductive.

Desire and aversion, which are the two poles of attachment and investment, are Buddhism's two cardinal poisons of the mind, responsible for much human suffering. It is because of desire, for example, that people suffer from perfectionism, pride, low self-esteem, self-loathing, jealousy and grief. The popular Buddhist author K. Sri Dhammananda expresses this poignantly: 'Wise people must not be enslaved by craving for pleasure . . . satisfaction and new desires chase one another in an unending succession, like waves on a sea. This continual arising and search for the satisfaction of desires is the basis that constitutes mundane, human life and gives one a constant sense of frustration.'[1] For the Tibetan Buddhist author Yongey Mingyur, chasing the satisfaction of desires is

> a type of addiction, a never-ending search for a lasting 'high' that is just out of reach . . . [this is] linked to the production of dopamine, a chemical in the brain that generates . . . sensations of pleasure . . . Over time our brains and our bodies are motivated to repeat the activities that stimulate the production of dopamine . . . We literally get hooked on anticipation.[2]

Research by Kent Berridge, a leading neuroscientist at the University of Michigan, suggests that the hormone dopamine is critically involved in 'wanting', that is, experiencing desire. Dopamine is released in the brain when people engage in sex, consume food or use cocaine. In this sense, dopamine is strongly linked to all sorts of addictions. We crave activities that result in dopamine production. Our desires are never satisfied for long, and the more we are addicted to 'wanting', the more time we devote to chasing our never-ending desires. According to Buddhism, our enslavement to desire of various sorts is at the root of all human suffering.

If indulging our desires is inconsistent with Buddhism, how then should we go about fulfilling our essential needs and quelling the 'desires' these evoke? The Buddhist answer to this question is enshrined in the concept of the Middle Way. It means avoiding the extremes of indulgence on the one hand, and asceticism (denying our needs through self-immolation) on the other. These concepts are akin to what my colleagues and I have called 'moderation',[3] the opposite of extremism. Extremism focuses exclusively on a given need, whether it's a biological need such as hunger or a psychological need (say, the desire for dignity and esteem), in a way that neglects other needs (for example, health or safety). In contrast, moderation is the balanced, well-rounded satisfaction of all our basic needs. Extremism produces emotional spikes and dips, fostering mental states that waver between exuberance and agony. Moderation produces quiet contentment, the ideal emotional state for a Buddhist.

The Buddhist practice of meditation allows us to loosen the grip on our mind of various fears and desires. It affords liberation from that 'monkey on our back', as the Buddhist metaphor has it. Meditation involves noticing our thoughts and feelings (realizing that we are anxious, fearful or ecstatic) rather than focusing on their content ('I have failed the exam,' 'I will lose my job'). Meditation distracts us from the acute emotional experience via observation. The resulting detachment dulls the intensity of the emotional experience and allows us to move on to other matters.

Impermanence

According to Buddhism, the deep wisdom that brings contentment requires realizing the impermanence of things and recognizing that both satisfaction and frustration are fleeting states that will vanish sooner or later and give way to other feelings. A central idea here is detachment from outcomes. This means refraining from investing too much hope in the attainment of our goals, from assigning too much importance to the satisfaction of our desires or devoting too much anxious rumination to our possible failure to satisfy them. In essence, Buddhist detachment is liberation from caring too much.

This notion is encapsulated in an entertaining anecdote about the detached acceptance of uncertainty that characterizes Zen Buddhism. A little boy gets a horse on his fourteenth birthday, and all the villagers applaud, saying, 'How wonderful for him, what a great gift!' But the Zen master says, 'We shall see.' Two years later, the boy falls off the horse and breaks his leg, and all the villagers say, 'Oh, how terrible. What will the boy do?' Yet the Zen master says, 'We shall see . . .' Then there is a war and all the young men go off to fight, but the boy can't go because of his broken leg. And the villagers all say, 'How lucky for the boy, how wonderful.' And the Zen master, of course, reacts with: 'We shall see.'

The Buddhist insight into the fleeting nature of emotional experiences is supported by recent scientific research. People's happiness on obtaining a coveted outcome, and their misery on failure to obtain it, vanish over time, just as Buddhism predicts. Buddhist gurus are also right about something else. Not only does our happiness or unhappiness last but a brief moment, but because they arise from unforeseen circumstances we cannot predict them very well.

Weddings or the birth of a child are often cast as very happy events, the happiest moments of your life, yet they may turn out to be highly stressful and not at all 'happy'. Family members might fuss incessantly about being treated appropriately at the wedding celebration. The couple might be consumed with anxiety about the logistics of catering for their guests. One or both might be fighting off a cold. All these may contribute to the sense of pressure and result in an experience quite different from what is generally portrayed. In a striking demonstration of this phenomenon, Philip Brickman and his associates compared the experiences of twenty-two lottery winners with twenty-two members of a control group who were non-winners and twenty-nine victims of catastrophic accidents that had left them paraplegic or quadriplegic.[4] The experimenters asked members of all three groups about the pleasure they derived from things such as chatting with a friend, watching TV, eating breakfast, laughing at a joke or receiving a compliment. On analysing the results, the researchers found to their surprise that the accident victims derived slightly more happiness from these everyday events than the lottery winners. This was unexpected because you might think that accident victims would generally be dejected and unhappy. Even more surprising was the finding that the lottery winners reported being only slightly happier than people with paraplegia or quadriplegia – 4 out of 5 versus 2.96 out of 5. The control group scored on average 3.82 out of 5, not significantly less than the lottery winners. Surprisingly, too, the accident victims scored above the midpoint of the scale, which suggests that in the long term having won the lottery didn't bring people enduring happiness, nor did a catastrophic accident make people lastingly unhappy, just as the Buddhist gurus predicted.

Social psychologists Timothy Wilson, a professor at the University of Virginia, and Daniel Gilbert, a professor at Harvard, carried out trailblazing research on people's ability to predict the emotions they would feel in specific circumstances. Their resounding conclusion was that such ability, known professionally as 'affective forecasting', is quite meagre. The fleeting nature of our feelings, whether positive or negative, intuited by Buddhist thinkers millennia ago, is in a large part responsible for these forecasting mistakes. In research carried out by Daniel Gilbert and his colleagues, it was found that though a positive tenure decision makes assistant professors much happier than a negative one, years later those who were denied tenure are as happy as those who were granted it.[5]

People's inability to forecast the future is quite widespread. Sports fans overestimate how happy they will be if their team win the competition and how long their happiness will last.[6] Students overestimate their negative emotional reaction to interacting with a student from a different racial group.[7] And women predict that they will experience anger in response to sexually harassing questions posed to them in an interview, whereas in fact they experience fear.[8]

In short, the future is uncertain, and we can't generalize from how we feel in the present or from how we think we would feel to how we will actually feel. The context may be different from how we imagined, so we may be wrong about the intensity of or even the kind of reactions we have. Plus, the rate at which our situations change is faster than we often imagine, so we are not very good at predicting the duration of our emotional response.

While Gilbert and Wilson's research is revelatory, their collaborative journey is no less fascinating. Recently, I asked them how it came about. It turns out their meeting was a matter of chance, and its outcomes, now of historic importance, were ones they would never have predicted. Here is the story.

They met in 1991, when both were on sabbatical in Palo Alto, California. They quickly became friends and thought it might be fun to collaborate on a project, so they spent several months discussing how people deal with unwanted information. Tim had been working on the topic of 'mental contamination'* and Dan had been working on the topic of 'Spinozan belief systems',† so this was the natural intersection of their interests. They talked and scribbled and devised a theory, which they published several years later to the apparent interest of precisely no one.[9]

When their sabbaticals ended, they parted ways, not expecting to work together again. A few weeks after returning home, Dan went to lunch with a friend and told him about some difficult developments in his personal life. His friend asked how he was coping and Dan said that, much to his surprise, he felt just fine. His friend asked whether he

* According to Wilson and Brekke (1994), mental contamination is the process whereby someone makes an unwanted judgement, has an unwanted emotion or acts in a detrimental way because of an unconscious cognitive bias, such as by buying a product having been unconsciously influenced by an advertisement.
† Dan Gilbert's (1991) work on Spinozan belief systems suggested that the acceptance of information is automatic and part of comprehending the information, whereas rejection of information requires effortful and critical examination of the information.

thought he could have predicted that reaction a year earlier. It was a light-bulb moment. Can people predict what will make them happy? If not, then why not? And why hasn't anyone ever asked that question – or answered it?

After lunch, Dan hurried back to his office and called Tim to talk about this. Tim was intrigued and had some good ideas. He offered to run a preliminary study, just to see if people made mistakes when predicting their emotional responses to future events. A few weeks later he called Dan to report that the data was uninterpretable. But the two kept talking about the idea and eventually tried another study. Which was successful. As was the study after that. In a relatively short time, they had enough data to write a paper on a new topic which they decided to call 'affective forecasting'.[10] They never suspected that this paper would be cited nearly 2,000 times in the decades that followed and lead to an explosion of research on affective forecasting that would span disciplines, from law to medicine to behavioural economics. Because they'd enjoyed working together so much, they decided to carry on. A quarter of a century later, they've published nearly sixty papers together, six of which have been published in *Science*.

Theirs is probably one of the longest and most successful collaborations in the history of social psychology and so people often ask them about its parameters – about the rules and roles and mutual agreements that govern it. But they've never discussed it. Indeed, they never *decided* to work together for a lifetime; they just started one day and somehow never stopped. They attribute the success of their partnership to a few things.

First, like most partners, they have different talents; but unlike most partners, they recognize and deeply appreciate the things that the other one does much more, so the work they produce together is better than the work either would have produced alone, and that single fact has kept them coming back for more.

Second, a life in science is a steady string of failures interrupted by the occasional small victory. Having a partner with whom to share the constant disappointments and rare triumphs makes the former more bearable and the latter more enjoyable. It is good to have someone who hates Reviewer #2 every bit as much as you do.

Third, a lifetime of thinking together and writing together is a bonding experience that has made Tim and Dan close friends. There's never been a cross word between them, they've never had an argument and they both believe they got the better deal. The security of their friendship has allowed each of them to take risks – to risk failing, to risk being stupid or wrong, to risk trying something crazy and going way out on a limb and maybe irritating others by doing so – because they both know that, no matter what happens, they will always have each other's back.

So that's Tim and Dan's story. You can try to guess which of them wrote the first draft of it, which then crossed half of it out and which then put half of it back in, but your chances probably aren't much better than fifty:fifty. And when Tim and Dan look at this essay a year from now, they won't remember who did what. And maybe that's their secret.

The story of Tim and Dan's collaboration is relevant to the topic of uncertainty in a number of ways. First, there is the serendipity of their meeting, which illustrates how important luck can be in determining events and their outcomes. Second, their story shows how important friendship and social support are in confronting the supreme uncertainty that hovers over frontiers of knowledge, the epitome of the unknown. As we saw in Chapter 3, a sense of secure attachment, made up of a *safe haven* to which we can run for cover and a *secure base* from which we can launch our explorations, is essential to exploring the mysteries of nature and unearthing its secrets. The profound trust that Dan and Tim had in each other's commitment provided this. Third, the substance of their discoveries is particularly important. Even though Buddhists and others have highlighted the flux and impermanence that characterize life, Gilbert and Wilson's research pins this down and, through imaginative empirical research, demonstrates its implications. Life is unpredictable and our momentary feelings depend on chance circumstances. As a consequence, our ability to project ourselves into the future is limited. How we feel at the present is a poor guide to knowing how we will feel in the future and how long we will feel that way. Recognizing this may help us to reduce the volatility of our emotions and mitigate our concerns and anxieties. No matter how you feel or fear, it will pass.

Uncertainty reigns

From the Buddhist perspective, uncertainty is the rule, not the exception. In recognition of this, the Buddhist attitude is one of detachment. It means not feeling too euphoric about your successes and not feeling too upset about your failures. The Western activist attitude to life, and its portrayal as intense struggle, is often juxtaposed with the Buddhist attitude of acceptance and letting go. Yet notable Western thinkers over the years have had insights that call Buddhism to mind. We can think not only of Heraclitus' notion of continuous change and Churchill's musings on the transience of success and failure, but also of the Romantic poet John Keats, who wrote to his brothers in 1817 that 'negative capability . . . that is, when man is capable of being in uncertainties, mysteries, doubts, without any irritable [impatient] reaching after fact and reason' impedes creative thought, and of Rudyard Kipling's celebrated poem 'If', which praises equanimity in the face of failure and success alike. Similarly to the spirit of Buddhism, Kipling views human maturity as independence from desires and emotional detachment. 'If you can meet with Triumph and Disaster/And treat those two impostors just the same,' then 'you'll be a Man, my son!' The poem extols a 'cool' attitude to events as the optimal orientation to whatever ups and downs await us on life's journey.

The Buddhist acceptance of uncertainty has two advantages. The first is relative immunity against life's vicissitudes and upheavals that comes from detachment. The second is the inner freedom and peace of mind that emotional indifference to our successes or failures may bring. It is this sense of liberty that allows us to be open-minded about inevitable change and accommodate our reactions to emerging circumstances. These are apparent in the Buddhist influence on contemporary schools of psychotherapy. These include Mindfulness-Based Stress Reduction (MBSR), Mindfulness-Based Cognitive Therapy (MBCT), Dialectical Behaviour Therapy (DBT), and Acceptance and Commitment Therapy

(ACT), all of which incorporate Buddhist practices of meditation and mindfulness and aim to equip people to deal with the ephemeral and uncertain nature of life.

Furthermore, research suggests that the practice of mindful meditation affects the way our brain functions. Reports show that mindfulness results in a decreased activation of the amygdala, the brain structure that controls our responses to emotional events. This supports the idea that our emotional investment in both positive and negative outcomes is reduced through meditation.

Some findings suggest that although meditation initially increases responsiveness to emotionally charged images in the areas of the cortex responsible for cognitive control, experienced meditators show reduced activity in those areas. Apparently, meditation novices, in trying to overcome their habitual response to emotional situations, show greater activation of the relevant brain areas, while experienced meditators have become accustomed to subduing their emotional response and so no longer need to exercise deliberate cognitive control over their feelings. Research on the impact of mindful meditation on brain structures and processes is a growing and promising field of neuroscience. Its findings are likely to cast new light on the way our brains can be better prepared to deal with uncertainty.

The appeal of mystery

The Buddhist model is what Tory Higgins (see Chapter 10) might call *prevention-focused*. After all, the aim of Siddhartha's exploration was to reduce suffering; it was to bring people back from the realm of agony rather than lead them to the realm of ecstasy. As we have seen, this can be achieved by reducing excessive emotional investment in dreams and nightmares alike. Limiting our desires and curbing our fears may deliver a sense of quiet contentment, not entirely unlike the idea of 'feeling much better after giving up hope', as a humorous inscription on T-shirts and coffee mugs has it.

Other approaches to uncertainty accentuate its positive aspects and highlight its potential for exuberance and creativity due to the captivating mystery that accompanies it. The therapist Estelle Frankel describes various mystical traditions such as the Jewish Kabbalah, Zen Buddhism, ancient myths, and the poets and philosophers who across the centuries have extolled the unparalleled experience of awe that uncertainty can engender and its potential for enlightenment and epiphany. Certainty is constraining and fixating; it boxes us into categories or stereotypes, limiting our freedom and subduing our potential. In reference to certainty, Nietzsche remarked that, 'Convictions are more dangerous enemies of truth than lies.'[11] In his view, a liar is at least aware of speaking untruths, whereas the person with conviction is blissfully unaware of possibly being wrong. Conviction, according to this view, is a trap that limits our ability to gain insight – a Procrustean bed that forces stereotypic constraints on the mind and impoverishes understanding. As Gertrude Stein once told a reporter: 'I cannot afford to be clear, because if I was I would risk destroying my own thought.'[12]

Diverse schools of mysticism have held that true faith surpasses understanding. True faith is therefore shrouded in uncertainty – intellectually speaking. In this sense, liturgy and the reification of God (for example, in the form of paintings or statues) misses the essence of religiosity that is faith and mistakes idolatry for devotions. The biblical story of the golden calf makes this very point. In this fable, the Israelites, after having encountered a living god whose nature they are unable to comprehend, proceed to build a golden calf, a familiar and popular idol in ancient Egypt. As Frankel puts it: 'We humans are prone to such regressions. In moments of anxiety or uncertainty, we tend to seek comfort in old patterns and familiar habits, like the addict who reaches for his substance when faced with stress or uncertainty.'[13]

The mystics recognize that uncertainty may be hard to bear, even agonizing, but out of the agony may come a person's finest hour. The darkness may turn to light and a person can rise to previously unimagined heights of insight and authenticity.

Depth psychology

Exploration of the unknown is an essential aspect of depth psychology (the psychology of the unconscious), which includes classical psychoanalysis. It is by delving into the repressed, currently unconscious memories of past trauma and conflict that healing can take place. Insight often depends on intuition, and intuition requires letting go of a coherent, clear and rational way of looking at things. It demands giving up control and letting the mind wander freely, as if in a dream.

Sigmund Freud admonished therapists to adopt an attitude of 'evenly hovering' attention, unfocused on any particular aspect of how the patient is presenting.[14] He recommended 'making no effort to concentrate the attention on anything in particular, and in maintaining in regard to all that one hears the same measure of calm, quiet attentiveness.'[15] Similarly, Wilfred Bion, a mystic psychoanalyst, influenced profoundly by the Jewish Kabbalah, recommended that his followers

eschew reliance on theory and technique.[16] According to this
view, both are 'blinders' that stand in the way of insight.[17]
Bion suggested his followers set them aside in order to be
more acutely aware of the reality confronting the therapist.[18]

In the face of uncertainty and confusion about a patient,
Bion warned, looking to a theory for guidance may mean
that you miss something important. As he put it:

> when you have a particularly dark spot, turn on to it a shaft
> of piercing darkness. Rid yourself of your analytic theories.
> Rid yourself of what you picked up about the patient; get
> rid of it. Bring to bear on this dark spot a shaft of piercing
> darkness . . . If you want to see a very faint light, the more
> light you shut out the better, the bigger the chance of seeing
> the faint glimmer.[19]

As Francesca Bion, Wilfred's wife, expressed it: 'He
believed that "*La réponse est le malheur de la question*" ["the
answer is the misfortune of the question"]. His interest was
in thought and contemplation rather than in arriving at a
firm conclusion.'[20]

The idea that preconceptions and systematic coherence may
obscure true insight and stand in the way of creativity is reminiscent of the mind clearing in Buddhist-inspired meditation. It
also appears in the musings of artists, writers and scholars
about the sources of their inspiration. The nineteenth-century
French mathematician Henri Poincaré described how moments
of 'sudden illumination' arrive serendipitously:

> One evening, contrary to my custom, I drank black coffee and
> could not sleep. Ideas rose in crowds; I felt them collide until
> pairs interlocked, so to speak, making a stable combination. It
> seems, in such cases, that one is present at his own unconscious

work, made partially perceptible to the over-excited conscious-ness, yet without having changed its nature. Then we vaguely comprehend what distinguishes the two mechanisms or, if you wish, the working methods of the two egos.[21]

In a similar vein, Albert Einstein remarked: 'A new idea comes suddenly and in a rather intuitive way. That means it is not reached by conscious logical conclusions. But thinking it through afterwards, you can always discover the reasons which have led you unconsciously to your guess.'[22]

So letting go of a mental focus, refraining from dwelling on definite ideas and allowing our associations and observa-tions to flow freely often bring to mind unusual possibilities you might have missed otherwise. This is supported by empir-ical research carried out by the Italian researchers Chirumbolo and colleagues, who reported a significant negative relation-ship between the need for cognitive closure and creativity.[23] As we saw in Chapter 2, the need for closure encourages the embracement of clear-cut ideas and an intolerance of uncer-tainty, which, as great thinkers of the past have intuited, and contemporary research shows, suppresses creativity.

The mystery of chronic pain

One uncertainty that affects millions of people all over the world is chronic pain. In Western societies, many people suf-fer from this at some point in their lives, so much so that persistent pain of unclear origin has been considered a pub-lic health crisis.[24] Pain typically signals that something is wrong with the bodily system and that action is needed to take care of the problem. Yet there is uncertainty about the nature of the problem and, until that is dispelled (through a doctor's authoritative diagnosis), people may have their own ideas about the cause. With chronic pain, which can be impossible to diagnose, the cause or cure may never be found, and uncertainties and doubts around it may spin out of control, causing people anxiety that magnifies their pain and compounds it with mental anguish. 'Is it cancer?', 'What if it's too late?', 'Perhaps I am dying?' and 'I can't bear not knowing' are some of the catastrophic thoughts that come into the mind of someone whose pain is relentless. Research attests that the greater people's intolerance of uncertainty, the greater the intensity of the pain they experience.[25]

In recent years, the US government has recognized the severity and ubiquity of problems arising from chronic pain. The first decade of the twenty-first century was designated by US Congress as the Decade of Pain Control and Research, and a number of bills supporting improvements in pain care in the departments of Veterans Affairs and Defense health-care facilities were signed into law. In parallel, psychology has developed several approaches and procedures designed to deal with the uncertainty-driven anxiety that can accompany chronic pain. Essentially, these consist of countering the negative thoughts and/or diverting attention away from the pain stimulus in order to reduce the intensity of the experience. For instance, mindful meditation, relaxation training and hypnotherapy promote deep breathing and focus attention on the present, inviting detachment from an exclusive preoccupation with the pain. Fear-avoidance therapies reduce people's anxieties about moving in certain ways that could exacerbate the pain, and cognitive behavioural therapies counter the catastrophic thoughts that chronic pain can induce, replacing them with facts and realistic assessments, which in many cases suggest that, while unpleasant in and of itself, the pain is not a symptom of a more serious underlying problem.

Accepting life's transitions

Life is change, and change by definition is a journey into uncharted territory, and hence into uncertainty. Life transitions inevitably happen, in part because of the process of maturation and ageing and in part because of the unanticipated events that take us by surprise, such as accidents, divorce, the death of a loved one, emigration to a new country or losing a job.

The uncertainty produced by such life transitions often means the loss of self-assurance. Our previous methods of coping may no longer apply, and we may feel less competent in the new situation, hence less worthy and significant. In addition, some life transitions entail real and irrevocable losses of competencies, such as those triggered by illness and ageing, which may compound the problem. Ageing, for instance, probably means the decline of physical strength, stamina and energy and a deterioration of our cognitive abilities (for example, memory), sexual prowess and good looks. In a Western culture that worships youthfulness, these losses can be psychologically painful and humiliating.

Adjustment to life transitions is particularly difficult for those with a high need for closure and an aversion to uncertainty. Such people generally feel uncomfortable with change; they cling to the past and are reluctant to let go of prior situations, competencies and relationships. In the case of ageing, for instance, this can motivate their efforts to stay in their former psychological space by trying to preserve their youthful appearance through cosmetic and surgical means, dieting and exercise. Such strategies may work for a while and postpone the inevitable, yet ultimately the change is bound to come, and it will find the uncertainty-intolerant 'deniers' woefully unprepared.

People with a low need for closure, in contrast, are more attuned to change and better able to explore the options it offers ahead of time, that is, before the changed situation is upon them. Such people may anticipate change and plan for it. In the case of ageing and/or retirement they may develop new interests and passions, compile a 'bucket list' of things they want to accomplish and develop new social networks, usually with people in a similar situation, who will support and applaud their endeavours and not judge them by stand-ards of worth and significance that are no longer attainable.

I recently witnessed some good friends during a particu-larly challenging life transition: the wife had been diagnosed with terminal cancer and given six months to live. The diag-nosis came as a complete surprise, totally confounding the couple's life plans and expectations. Yet rather than dwelling on the tragic aspects of this situation – that their long life together was coming to an end, or the terror of death and loss – they quickly decided to work out what they were still able to do to maximize the quality of their last months together and do what they most enjoyed to the very last. Their response brought home to me how important it is, even in the face of a frightening life transition, to accept change and do our very best to exploit the possibilities that it affords.

Summary

Unlike the activist Western perspective that aims to increase our sense of control and empowerment, instilling in us the courage to explore uncertainty and maximize success, the Buddhist perspective stresses the impermanence of things and recommends detachment from worldly outcomes (success and failure). The Western attitude looks for a 'happy ending', whereas the Buddhist one eschews the very notion of an 'ending' and highlights instead the constancy of flux and impermanence. Glimpses of Buddhist insight appear in Western thought as well, and the notion that creativity and exploration flourish in the absence of constraining preconceptions has been voiced by leading Western psychotherapists and scientists alike. Living with uncertainty applies to such seemingly purely physical phenomena as chronic pain. Detachment from the sensation and focusing attention on the here and now attenuates the suffering and dulls the pain.

In your experience

1. How do you react to change? Do you accept it? Do you resist it?
2. Are you a fatalist? How important to you is having control over what happens?
3. Are you a creative person? If so, can you recall situations when new ideas came into your mind?
4. How do you typically react to physical pain? How do you react to feeling unwell? Does feeling unwell arouse your anxiety? Do you see a connection here to the uncertainty that feeling unwell entails?

14. Living with Differences

The problem of otherness

According to some interpretations, the biblical story of the Tower of Babel (Genesis 11:1–9) is offered as an explanation (origin myth) for linguistic and cultural differences among the people who inhabit our planet.[1] In the story people attempt to build a tower that reaches to heaven, and to punish their arrogance God scatters them across the earth. For, as the Lord said, 'If as one people all sharing a common language they have begun to do this, then nothing they plan to do will be beyond them.'[2]

Cultural diversity has benefited humanity in myriad ways. It has immensely enriched our pool of ideas in the domains of art, gastronomy, fashion, architecture and medicine, among others. But it has also introduced 'otherness'. Many millennia ago, our ancestors, way back on the savannah, formed cooperating groups to defend themselves against animal predators, yet they continued to face one source of mortal danger – other groups of humans that fiercely competed with them for food, water, land and other resources. This contributed to the evolution of something that has plagued humanity to this very day: fear of, and aversion to, otherness. In many ways, this instinctive tendency continues to threaten our existence on this planet, leading to near-incessant wars but also to prejudice, discrimination and cruelty towards other human beings. Now, in the twenty-first century, human ingenuity, science and technology have brought the people of the world into closer contact with each other. And the great challenge is to turn this to our advantage, to learn to live with our differences and not to let them tear us apart; in short, to develop a 'common language' so that, paraphrasing the Bible, 'nothing we plan will be beyond us'. This chapter explores ways in which we can learn to live with differences.

Immigration

More than at any point in history, these days we are likely to encounter people who differ from us in their culture, background, ethnicity or religion. A major driver of this is an unprecedented wave of immigration and a stream of refugees in search of a better, safer or more prosperous future.

According to the 2019 report of the International Migration Stock of the Population Division of the United Nations, the number of international migrants has reached 272 million – 3.5 per cent of the world population in that year. Global warming is likely to amplify these numbers. There is ample evidence that it has increased precipitation levels and given rise to extreme weather events all over the planet.[3] The growing frequency of hurricanes, fires, droughts, cyclones, severe windstorms and heatwaves is having disastrous environmental consequences, including depleted biodiversity, loss of life and lasting adverse health impacts of extreme weather.[4] These are all expected to swell the volume of immigration worldwide. People whose homes have been destroyed by hurricanes and wildfires are often forced to relocate, as are those whose livelihoods (for example agriculture and livestock) have been derailed. Data shows an increase in migration flows due to climate change, and future forecasts are nothing short of alarming.[5] It is predicted that up to a billion people world-wide will have to flee their homes due to climate change by 2050.[6] The World Bank projects that almost 4 million people from Central America and Mexico alone could become climate migrants by the same date.[7] Needless to say, swelling numbers of migrants pose serious challenges to the political, educational and economic systems of host countries across the globe.

Denizens of host countries often view immigration through an economic lens and fear the competition they feel immigrants might bring. These fears are likely to have little basis in fact. A recent analysis by Esposito, Collignon, and Scicchitano finds that immigration into Europe reduces, not increases (!), unemployment in the countries surveyed, both in the short and the long term.[8] The threat that immigration poses is largely psychological. It stems from discomfort with otherness, the perceived strangeness of the norms, values and customs of the immigrants. The fear is that these will undermine the cultural stability and the peace of mind of locals in the host communities, ushering in confusion and uncertainty. This challenges people's faith that their tried-and-tested ways of doing things are superior and unique.

Technology

Beyond immigration, our experience of diversity is driven by technological developments which have vastly expanded the volume of air travel and enabled electronic communication that knows no borders. As a consequence, considerable diversity has been injected into previously homogeneous communities. In my travels to Italy in the 1990s, the social landscape I saw was almost exclusively Italian (shops, markets, restaurants, people), but by the end of the first decade of the twenty-first century you could walk for miles in central Rome (the *centro storico*) and see lots of diverse shops, markets, restaurants and people, mostly Asian. A similar increase in diversity has also occurred in other European cities. Whereas in the past, these places exhibited homogeneity of language, ethnicity and culture, today they display a remarkable heterogeneity.

The growth of the airline industry has allowed millions of people to travel with ease to all four corners of the planet. In 2019, for instance, the number of international trips was nearly a billion and a half. Tourism now represents 10.4 per cent of GDP globally (and 45 per cent of the GDP in emergent economies). Meanwhile, in cyberspace, the mind-boggling developments in computer-based technologies, software and the internet has produced what Thomas L. Friedman has called Globalization 3.0. It 'has made us all next-door neighbors' and 'is more and more driven . . . by a much more diverse – non-Western, non-white – group of individuals. Globalization 3.0 makes it possible for so many more people to plug in and play, and you are going to see every color of the human rainbow take part.'[9]

Our experience of diversity, through tourism, immigration and technology, is now a fact of life and it is likely to increase exponentially in years to come. Yet the uncertainty that diversity introduces may be stressful and troublesome to many. True, even in a homogeneous society, people differ from each other. Each one of us is unique and wishes to be accepted, respected and loved for the special person we are. Nonetheless, we share a common culture, common values, language, customs and history. In a homogeneous society, our differences as individuals are counterbalanced by this shared culture. An influx of strangers whose reality is drastically different from our own tips the balance between what we share and what sets us apart in favour of the latter. Hence the uncertainty, confusion and anxiety.

Dealing with differences

Reducing diversity

One approach to this problem of otherness has been to suppress diversity and force different groups of entrants into a common mould. This characterized the melting-pot approach to immigration taken by countries such as the US and Israel. Within one or two generations, newcomers to the United States were expected to be thoroughly Americanized. They were to speak no other language but English. They were expected to have few ties to their ancestral land. The norm was so strong that they would play, watch and enthuse about American sports and, like everyone else, chase the American dream of fame and fortune.

Celebrating diversity

In recent years, the concept of the melting pot has come under attack for rejecting diversity, instead placing value on assimilation and belittling the value of other cultures. The reaction to this concept took the form of the currently prevalent ideal of multiculturalism, which champions the idea that people's cultural roots are important. Yet pursuing multiculturalism, though laudable in the abstract, has had several unintended consequences. Some have decried its moral relativism – the notion that all cultures have equal moral value. It is easier to grasp this point of view when we consider specific practices that are at sharp odds with Western values. Even a staunch multiculturalist might baulk at serving dog meat in restaurants, at cockfights held in the street, at female circumcision or the marriage of twelve-year-old girls to older men. Many who support multiculturalism in the abstract might recoil from endorsing cultural customs that flagrantly offend Western ethical and aesthetic sensibilities.

A related issue is that multiculturalism coexists uneasily with national cohesion, which assumes that there is a consensus about values and norms. This issue has elicited considerable controversy and heated debate. The Canadian sociologist Reginald Bibby discusses the problem in *Mosaic Madness*. As he puts it: 'Canada has been encouraging the expression of viewpoints without simultaneously insisting on the importance of evaluating the merits of those viewpoints . . . Our expectation has been that fragments of the mosaic will somehow add up to a healthy and cohesive society. It is not clear why we should expect such an outcome.' He goes on: 'We triumphantly discarded the idea that there are better and best choices in favor of worshipping choice as an end in itself.'[10] A study conducted by the University of Victoria suggests that ethnic enclaves increase many Canadians' sense of alienation from Canada as a nation. The study also finds that immigrants into Canada find living in enclaves easier than integrating into mainstream Canadian culture.

In 1984, the historian Geoffrey Blainey wrote, with regard to Australia, another country founded on immigration, like Canada and the US, that multiculturalism threatens to transform the country into a 'cluster of tribes', to create division and undermine national cohesion. Moreover, Blainey contended, it raises the spectre of double allegiances, and 'could in the long term also endanger Australia's military security because it sets up enclaves which in a crisis could appeal to their own homelands for help'.[11]

The Netherlands legal philosopher Paul Cliteur voiced, in *The Philosophy of Human Rights* (1999), an impassioned critique of multiculturalism based on the unacceptability of cultural relativism – the acceptance that every culture's values are legitimate, and the implicit legitimation of practices and prejudices that are abhorrent from the Western perspective, among them infanticide, torture, slavery and homophobia. To make the point, Cliteur caustically equates multiculturalism with acceptance of such anathema as Auschwitz, Pol Pot and the Ku Klux Klan. In short, 'anything does not go', culturally speaking. We have to exercise a moral choice, Cliteur insists.

Multiculturalism has come under strong criticism in the UK as well. Leo McKinstry, a British journalist, has called it a 'profoundly disturbing social experiment' that thwarts national integration 'when ethnic groups are encouraged to cling to customs, practices, even languages from their homeland'. Ed West, author of *The Diversity Illusion* (2013), argued that the British political establishment has welcomed and encouraged multiculturalism for reasons of political correctness, without thinking the policy through sufficiently. He contends that the arguments that morally justify multiculturalism, namely that people of the same group need their own cultural identity, apply equally to the White majority in Britain. The former Archbishop of York, John Sentamu, stated in 2005 that 'Multiculturalism has seemed to imply, wrongly for me: let other cultures be allowed to express themselves but do not let the majority culture at all tell us its glories, its struggles, its joys, its pains.' And former prime minister Tony Blair made the case for Britain's 'essential values'; upholding them, he felt, is a 'duty' for all Britons. As he put it: 'Belief in democracy, the rule of law, tolerance, equal treatment for all, respect for this country and its shared heritage – then that is where we come together, it is what we hold in common.'

Similar criticisms of multiculturalism have been voiced in the United States, namely that it undermines national cohesion and social integration while promoting society's breakdown into separate ethnic enclaves (known as Balkanization). Among others, Samuel Huntington, famous for his theory about the Clash of Civilizations, contended that multiculturalism is essentially anti-Western. He argued that multiculturalism assaults 'the identification of the United States with Western civilization, denies the existence of a common American culture, and promotes racial, ethnic, and other subnational cultural identities and groupings'.[12]

Harvard political scientist Robert D. Putnam carried out a large longitudinal study on the relationship between diversity and social trust. His findings are disturbing. A survey of 26,200 people in forty American communities suggests that the more diverse a given community, the greater the decline in trust and in reliance on societal institutions. As Putnam put it: '[People] don't trust the local mayor, they don't trust the local paper, they don't trust other people and they don't trust institutions.'[13]

Nonetheless, people need knowledge in order to make decisions and act in pursuit of their goals. This means that they need to trust at least some sources. When trust in society at large declines, people turn to a narrower circle – their family, friends, charismatic leaders. This can lead, critics of multiculturalism have alleged, to the fractionalization of society along various fault lines.

Diversity malaise

The uncertainty that diversity introduces can be burdensome and anxiety-evoking. As we saw in Chapter 2, uncertainty elevates people's need for cognitive closure and fuels anti-diversity sentiments and the politics of xenophobia. These trends aren't new or unique to the here and now. They derive from the threats that uncertainty can produce in people who already feel fragile and vulnerable.

Politicians have typically been quick to exploit people's apprehension towards otherness and use it to gain power and influence. In 1789, Stanislas Marie Adélaïde, the comte de Clermont-Tonnerre, a French nobleman and a liberal politician at the time of the French Revolution, stated the case against otherness in reference to the Jews:

> The Jews should be denied everything as a nation, but granted everything as individuals; they must disown their judges, they must have only ours; they must be refused legal protection for the maintenance of the supposed laws of their Jewish corporation; they must constitute neither a state, nor a political corps, nor an order; they must individually become citizens; if they do not want this, they must inform us and we shall then be compelled to expel them. The existence of a nation within a nation is unacceptable to our country.[14]

Nearly two and a half centuries later, on 2 October 2020, French president Emmanuel Macron announced that the government would present a bill in December to strengthen a 1905 law that officially separated Church and state in France, stating:

> We must tackle Islamist separatism. A conscious, theorized, political-religious project is materializing through repeated deviations from the Republic's values, which is often reflected by the formation of a counter-society, as shown by children being taken out of school, the development of separate community, sporting and cultural activities serving as a pretext for teaching principles which aren't in accordance with the Republic's laws. It is indoctrination and, through this, the negation of our principles, gender equality and human dignity.[15]

In reaction to waves of immigration and the 2015 'refugee crisis',* far-right anti-immigration parties have been soaring in popularity across Europe. By 2017, in Western European nations, on average, 11 per cent of votes were cast for anti-immigration parties. According to some estimates, by 2035, the percentage of the vote for anti-immigration parties is likely to rise to at least 15 per cent.[16] In Germany, the anti-immigration Alternative für Deutschland party (Alternative for Germany) gained ninety-four seats in the Bundestag in the 2017 federal elections, becoming the main opposition party in Germany. It was the first time since the end of the Second World War that a party with a neo-Nazi agenda had gained seats in the German parliament.

Far-right parties paint immigrants in highly negative stereotypic terms. Muslim immigrants are depicted as rapists,

---

* When 1.3 million refugees, mostly from Syria, arrived in Europe to escape the ravages of war.

terrorists or misogynists. Jews are viewed as power-hungry cosmopolitans who plot world domination. Immigrants are presented as contaminating the national purity of European states and/or subjugating their rightful populations to global rule by evil international elites. That otherness painted in this way can induce a troubling uncertainty in people is supported by empirical research. A study by Orehek, Fishman and colleagues published in 2010 investigated how the Dutch reacted psychologically to strangers in their midst.[17] Strikingly, it was found that the greater the proportion of Muslims in a participant's neighbourhood, the greater their need for certainty and cognitive closure; this, in turn, was correlated with negative perceptions and attitudes towards Muslims.

Given global population growth, the violent clashes that rage in various parts of the world and the negative impact of climate change on the availability of crucial resources (food and water) for millions of people, the volume of immigration is likely to increase in the future. If aversion to difference and fear of the other are inevitable, it is likely that we are heading towards increased tension, conflict and the polarization of societies. But is it a foregone conclusion? Can't people subdue their fear of strangers and learn to live with those who are different from them? Social psychologists have been looking at this possibility for a long time and have experimented with interventions aimed at de-emphasizing the differences among people and setting conditions for cooperation and harmony among diverse groups.

Accentuating commonality

In the summer of 1953, social psychologists Muzafer and Carolyn Sherif carried out a landmark field experiment on conflict and conflict resolution.[18] They invited twenty-two young boys to spend time at a summer camp in Robers Cave Park in south-eastern Oklahoma. At first the boys were all housed together in a big bunkhouse, then, after a few days, they were split into two groups and assigned to two cabins at a distance from one another that meant they could no longer see or hear the other group. The cabins had their own separate areas for various activities (swimming and boating) and the researchers posed as camp personnel in order to carry out systematic observations of the boys' behaviour. In the 'friction phase', the two groups were made to compete against each other for prizes. This process created animosity and tension between the groups, so much so that 93 per cent of the boys' friendships were within their own group. In the concluding 'integration stage', the two groups participated in joint tasks on which they needed to cooperate. The important finding here was that engagement in common projects appreciably reduced the tension between the groups. The take-home message is that focusing on a common goal overshadows differences and promotes good feeling. It is consistent with the folk wisdom that confronting common enemies solidifies group cohesion and promotes a sense of unity among members.

These insights are supported by further research. A study carried out by Morgan, Wisneski and Skitka found that after the 9/11 attack a large portion of the American population felt a stronger sense of unity and patriotism.[19] Other studies found that common enemies enhance friendship among group members and that people tend to bond particularly strongly over a shared dislike.[20] As the sociologist William Sumner wrote in 1906: 'The relation of comradeship and peace in the we-group and that of hostility and war towards other-groups are correlative to each other. The exigencies of war with outsiders are what make peace inside.'[21]

Divisiveness under threat

But is this invariably the case? Common experience in the COVID-19 pandemic places a question mark over this belief. Despite knowing that the virus is a common enemy and that it can attack Americans irrespective of race, gender, social class or ethnicity, social tensions in the US that exist between members of the Black Lives Matter movement and those of far-right militias such as the Proud Boys or Oath Keepers soared during the pandemic. It appears that the common threat made Americans more divided and polarized than before. So when does a common goal or enemy unify people and when does it drive people apart? Extensive research on the issue suggests that a common task can increase cohesion among group members. However, when no organized group exists, when people disagree on whether the threat is common, or whether it actually exists (as was the case in the US during the 2020 pandemic), rather than coming together, society may fall apart along the fault lines, divisions and subgroups within it.

The contact hypothesis

One intriguing idea in social psychology about reducing people's aversion to 'strangeness' and the prejudice and discrimination that it may evoke is the *contact hypothesis*. It states that our animosity towards others is because they are unfamiliar. The logical response to this is simple. If unfamiliarity breeds tension, reducing it should lower it.

In 1954, *The Nature of Prejudice* by renowned psychologist Gordon Allport was published. It was highly influential and presented perhaps the most widely known form of the contact hypothesis. It stated that contact with people from a different ethnic, racial or cultural group, under the right conditions, could constitute a particularly useful intervention for the reduction of prejudice. According to Allport, properly managed contact could reduce the stereotyping, prejudice and discrimination that commonly occur between rival groups and thus promote better intergroup relations. Through such contact, people will notice each other's basic humanity, the common nature they all share, and this should reduce their fear of each other and promote cooperation and harmony. Over the years, social psychologists have carried out extensive research on the contact hypothesis, summarized in the influential meta-analysis of 515 studies on this topic by Pettigrew and Tropp.[22] They concluded that contact typically reduces prejudice because it makes clear to people their fundamental similarity, their common core as humans.

The CEDAR programme

But what about the differences around the common core? As critics of multiculturalism have pointed out, these can be substantial and profound. They include differences in beliefs about the world, values and practices. Some cultural customs that are sacrosanct in one society may violate the deeply held beliefs of the members of another society. Can people learn to live with such differences? The hope that they can formed the basis of an intriguing initiative by a number of American social scientists under the acronym CEDAR (Communities Engaging with Difference and Religion).[23]

The CEDAR programme recognizes that many nations today are on the horns of a dilemma. Many of their citizens understand the moral value of diversity and the acceptance of otherness, but others fear that these might undermine their nation's shared reality and warn against the fragmentation diversity might produce. What can be done to enable people to live and function together despite, and in light of, their differences?

CEDAR accepts the existence of differences. What's more, it assumes that they are of great psychological importance to people. People care deeply about their principles, customs and values; they will not yield easily to the melting-pot perspective. CEDAR founders Seligman, Wasserfall and Montgomery claim that liberal democracies have typically denied the importance of differences, as in the melting-pot approach.[24] Just like the eighteenth-century comte de Clermont-Tonnerre, today's liberal societies distinguish between a public sphere focused on what different members of society have in common and a private sphere where they differ. This private sphere is seen as out of bounds for others; it is viewed as 'nobody's business' and so is ignored and unexplored. Seligman and his co-founders do not see this as tolerance but rather as a denial of the important differences between communities. The private sphere invites the alienation of these communities from each other's uniqueness, the things that really matter and determine who they are. Such alienation could contribute to the emergence of separate cultural enclaves that threaten social cohesion.

In contrast, the CEDAR approach advocates acquainting diverse groups with their cultural differences. This is accomplished through the creation of shared experiences and reflection on those experiences. This aims to develop new capacities to live with differences, rather than avoiding the subject. The CEDAR approach is therefore fundamentally different from multiculturalism. Whereas multiculturalism risks contributing to the fragmentation of society and the creation of separate ethno-cultural enclaves, CEDAR emphasizes that common experiences are inherent in 'living *with*' differences.

The CEDAR method is to put academics in different areas of social science in touch with community leaders, activists and others to take 'the insights of anthropology and social science out of the classroom and into the world'. In practice, CEDAR creates microcosms that mix people 'to explore just what it means to live in [a] community and still be members of different communities'.[25] Over the more than a decade that CEDAR has been operative, it has brought together people from over fifty countries for a (one-time) meeting of two weeks for people from different cultural backgrounds.

A typical CEDAR workshop immerses participants in a

shared intellectual and emotional experience. These encounters are carried out in a safe space and include daily lectures, facilitation work in small groups and joint site visits. These provide the backdrop against which participants share their experiences and explore (and come to understand and appreciate) their different ways of living. As the authors state: 'Individually, participants attest to a deep personal transformation of their taken-for-granted ways of thinking; collectively, they achieve a new awareness of what can be done, evidenced by the emergence of what are effectively new spaces and modes of interaction.'[26]

So far the CEDAR initiative has been a limited experimental effort carried out with small budgets and on a correspondingly restricted scale, but its successes, attested to by the participants, should encourage governments, NGOs and institutions to widen the scope of the programme to reach ever-widening circles of participants. If in the twenty-first century differences are inexorable, learning how to live with them without denying or trivializing them could be a way of accommodating uncertainty and embracing it.

Summary

Ever-growing diversity in today's interconnected world challenges societies to understand and address the possible consequences of people's experience of otherness. Our aim should be to minimize its adverse impact on people's lives and explore its potential. Diversity introduces uncertainty about what we can expect from those who are different to us, and reactions to diversity mimic in some sense our reaction to uncertainty. Flight from diversity is achieved by stressing our commonality of purpose or by suppressing differences altogether, as in the melting-pot approach to immigration. The multiculturalist strategy celebrates differences and ignores the divisive impact they may have on national cohesion. Finally, the contact hypothesis and the CEDAR programme emphasize the constructive exploration of differences under safe conditions where the imagined threat of the other is minimized. Such an approach may not only teach people to live with differences but also to benefit from them.

In your experience

1. How much contact have you had with people from a different culture? In these encounters, do you typically focus on what you and those others have in common or on your differences? Have you ever tried to learn about aspects of your friends' or acquaintances' cultures that differ from yours?
2. Do you think that our instinctive fear of otherness can be overcome? Based on what you have learned in this chapter, how would you go about it?
3. How, in your opinion, is uncertainty related to people's fear of otherness? Is a need for closure relevant to this? How?
4. In your opinion, do all kinds of uncertainty enhance people's fear of otherness? If not, which kinds do not, and why?

Conclusion:
Avoiding and Approaching Uncertainty

'I stay on in doubt with yes and no
dividing all my heart to hope and fear'
– Dante, *Inferno*, Canto VIII[1]

I began writing this book when the COVID-19 pandemic was in its early stages, and much of the book was completed in its shadow. As I embark on this summing-up, the grip of this horrendous plague is slowly loosening. In part due to 'COVID fatigue', things are gradually returning to normal. In the neighbourhood where I live, you see more people in the streets, most no longer wearing protective face masks. Restaurants are filling up with groups and couples, schools and universities are open, theatres and museums are planning new shows and exhibitions.

Yet, experts tell us, pronouncing the COVID virus fully defeated is grossly premature. Major uncertainties about it remain. How effective are the boosters, and for how long? How potent and reliable are the treatments? Could more lethal variants of the virus re-emerge? We are still on a learning curve about much of it, still very much in the dark. And as I write these lines, another grave source of precariousness, the war in Ukraine, the first on European soil since 1945, is upsetting most people's expectations and feeding insecurities. It palpably illustrates the general truths that 'life is change' and 'the future isn't ours to see'.

How then can we relate to the uncertainties that life keeps throwing our way? What lessons do the preceding pages offer about how to deal with the inevitable unpredictability that surrounds us?

Uncertainty and you

The first and perhaps the most fundamental lesson to be drawn concerns your self-awareness in relation to uncertainty. Knowing how you typically react to the unknown, how strong your need for closure is, how you feel in unpredictable circumstances and realizing the consequences of your possible reactions will allow you to adjust and compensate for inclinations that ultimately may result in outcomes you would rather avoid. Knowing that you are too bent on closure and predictability may motivate you to dial it down a little. Knowing that you are too much of a risk-taker and sensation-seeker may move you to curb your enthusiasm for novelty and uncertainty and settle down somewhat.

Uncertainty as a blank slate

It will also help if you realize that uncertainty as such is neither necessarily good nor necessarily bad. Uncertainty simply is, and your reactions to it are of your own making. Like a blank screen, or a Rorschach inkblot, uncertainty becomes what you project on to it: your fears, your hopes and your aspirations. Moreover, using the psychological insights described in this book, you could learn ways of modifying those reactions, developing optimism, a growth mindset and grit that will boost your confidence and allow you to con-front uncertainty fearlessly.

The trade-offs of openness and closure

Another important lesson is to realize that both excessive closed-mindedness and excessive open-mindedness have distinct downsides, with moderation often emerging as the winner. Cognitive closure, for all its disadvantages, isn't 'all bad'. A high need for closure promotes clarity and decisive-ness, whereas a low need for closure can instil paralysis by (over)analysis, and immerse us in endless confusion, ambigu-ity and indecision. A high need for closure promotes stable commitment, whether to an idea, a group or a relationship; it inspires loyalty to your country or your family and so pro-motes and protects things most people value. Commitment, after all, serves as the cornerstone of any human endeavour; hardly anything can be achieved without it. Similarly, open-mindedness, while generally appreciated, isn't 'all good', as excessive chasing of novelty and uncertainty may reduce the potential to build anything lasting or worthwhile. In short, in navigating one's relations with uncertainty, the 'golden mean' is often the answer.

Moderation and detachment

Excessive avoidance of or seeking after uncertainty stems from attaching too much importance to possible outcomes, driving a dread of failure and an insatiable craving for suc-cess. Rather than protecting ourselves against failure with convention and tradition, or seeking success in wholly uncharted territories, the Buddhist approach recommends dialling down one's magnitude of caring altogether and injecting a degree of stoicism into our reactions to life events. Emotional detachment from the inevitable ups and downs that life dishes out helps to promote peace of mind. Nothing matters very much, proclaims this approach. It is 'all small stuff', as Richard Carlson put it; and Ecclesiastes, millennia ago, famously proclaimed: 'Meaningless! Meaningless! . . . Everything is meaningless.' Curbing one's desires, caring less about successes and failures, taking oneself less seriously, practising a level of detachment from one's pursuits, can promote healthy moderation and avoid the extremes of reacting to uncertainty, acting as a brake on an unreasonable dread of the unknown and on the ceaseless chasing of novelty and adventure.

Love and uncertainty

Research demonstrates the crucial importance of loving relations in forming an optimal orientation towards uncertainty. Having a secure base of love and trust enables you to explore novelty with confidence, without being 'paralysed' by fear of failure and disaster. At the same time, appreciating the importance of the safe haven that love offers keeps us from flying too far off course on the wings of adventure and ending up 'lost in the sea' of uncertainty and confusion. In an important sense, The Beatles' counsel 'All you need is love' hits the nail on the head, at least as far as your relationship with uncertainty is concerned. Cultivating your secure base in human relationships and investing in it could prove crucial to your sense of well-being in times of turmoil and change.

Living with differences

A final lesson, but hardly the least important, is about accepting the uncertainty introduced by others, especially people who differ from you in their culture, their thinking and behaviour, their beliefs and their values. Accepting these differences without judging them, understanding without necessarily agreeing, granting others the right to their views and customs, however much they diverge from yours, is, in today's increasingly interconnected world, a major imperative and a major challenge. Addressing this challenge with a constructive spirit would constitute a giant step towards welcoming uncertainty and making it your friend rather than your foe.

Notes

Introduction: Escaping and Embracing Uncertainty

1 R. N. Carleton (2016). 'Fear of the unknown: one fear to rule them all?' *Journal of Anxiety Disorders*, 41, 5–21, p. 5.
2 https://www.goodreads.com/quotes/246514-we-fear-that-which-we-cannot-see
3 https://www.laphamsquarterly.org/fear/weird-tales
4 https://www.unognewsroom.org/story/en/275/who-press-conference-covid-19-and-mental-health-care

Chapter 1: Measuring Your Need for Closure

1 A. W. Kruglanski (1990). 'Motivations for judging and knowing: implications for causal attribution', in E. T. Higgins and R. M. Sorrentino (eds.), *Handbook of Motivation and Cognition: Foundations of Social Behavior*, Vol. 2. New York: The Guilford Press, pp. 333–68, p. 337.
2 D. M. Webster and A. W. Kruglanski (1994). 'Individual differences in need for cognitive closure'. *Journal of Personality and Social Psychology*, 67(6), 1049.

Chapter 2: The Price of Premature Closure

1 R. L. Dickinson and L. Beam (1931). *A Thousand Marriages*. Baltimore: Williams and Wilkins.

2 D. M. Webster (1993). 'Motivated augmentation and reduction of the overattribution bias'. *Journal of Personality and Social Psychology*, 65(2), 261–71.

3 C. M. Steele and R. A. Josephs (1990). 'Alcohol myopia: its prized and dangerous effects'. *American Psychologist*, 45(8), 921–33.

4 https://www.nber.org/papers/w25785

5 W. James (1890). *The Consciousness of Self.*

6 D. Campbell (1988). 'The author responds: Popper and selection theory', *Social Epistemology*, (2)4, 371–7.

7 V. E. Frankl (2006). *Man's Search for Meaning: An Introduction to Logotherapy*. Boston: Beacon Press, pp. 65–6.

Chapter 3: Who Needs Certainty?

1 B. K. Cheon et al. (2015). 'Genetic contributions to need for closure, implicit racial bias, and social ideologies: the role of 5-HTTLPR and COMT Val158Met'. Unpublished data. Nanyang Technological University.

2 B. K. Cheon et al. (2014). 'Gene × environment interaction on intergroup bias: the role of *5-HTTLPR* and perceived outgroup threat'. *Social Cognitive and Affective Neuroscience*, 9(9).

3 A. Roets et al. (2015). 'The motivated gatekeeper of our minds: new directions in need for closure theory and research', in J. M. Olson and M. P. Zanna (eds.), *Advances in Experimental Social Psychology*, Vol. 52. Academic Press, pp. 221–83.

4 V. Viola et al. (2014). 'Routes of motivation: stable psychological dispositions are associated with dynamic changes in cortico-cortical functional connectivity'. *PLOS One*, 9(6), e98010.

5 Bob Woodward, Sunday, 23 June 1996, p. A1, 20.

6 J. Hayden (2001). *Covering Clinton*. New York: Praeger, p. 47.

7 D. Frum (2000). *The Right Man*. New York: Random House, p. 20.

8 Ibid., p. 92.

9 B. York. 'Bush loyalty test'. *National Review*, 30 Dec. 2008. Retrieved from https://www.nationalreview.com/2008/12/bush-loyalty-test-byron-york/

10 J. Klein (2003). *The Natural: The Misunderstood Presidency of Bill Clinton*. New York: Broadway Books.

11 Associated Press. 'Clinton: Obama is "naive" on foreign policy'. *NBC News*, 24 July 2007. Retrieved from https://www.nbcnews.com/id/wbna19933710

12 M. D. Salter (1940). 'An evaluation of adjustment based upon the concept of security'. University of Toronto Press. University of Toronto Studies Child Development Series No. 18, p. 45.

13 J. Bowlby (1951). 'Maternal care and mental health'. *Bulletin of the World Health Organization*, 3(3), 357–533, p. 361.

14 https://www.hrw.org/news/2018/06/05/us-bashes-un-critiquing-trump-family-separation-policy?gclid=CjoKCQjwmuiTBhDoARIsAPiv6L-J_XJnF2fZPhQCXYqY-iExY_Toncp_-tlZ8hp6NUiWdgQDc2pD1fcaAjXmEALw_wcB

15 T. Armus (2020). 'The parents of 545 children separated at the border still haven't been found'. https://www.texastribune.org/2020/10/21/donald-trump-immigration-parents-children-separated/

16 B. Mejia (2020). 'Physicians group releases report on psychological effects of family separation'. Retrieved 14 March 2021 from https://www.latimes.com/california/story/2020-02-25/family-separation-trauma

17 M. Liu (2017). 'War and children'. *American Journal of Psychiatry Residents' Journal*, 12(7), 3–5. doi: 10.1176/appi.ajp-rj.2017.120702.

18 D. Drehle (2021). 'What 500,000 Covid-19 deaths means'. Retrieved 14 March 2021 from https://www.washingtonpost. com/opinions/what-500000-covid-19-deaths-means/2021/ 02/19/8492c9b0-72e1-11eb-b8a9-b9467510f0fe_story.html

19 https://www.historytoday.com/archive/feature/ mourning-prince-albert

20 P. A. Boelen and J. van den Bout (2010). 'Anxious and depressive avoidance and symptoms of prolonged grief, depression, and post-traumatic stress disorder'. *Psychologica Belgica*, 50(1–2), 49–67.

21 L. I. M. Lenferink et al. (2017). 'Prolonged grief, depression, and posttraumatic stress in disaster-bereaved individuals: latent class analysis'. *European Journal of Psychotraumatology*, 8(1), 1298311.

22 P. R. Shaver and C. M. Tancredy (2001). 'Emotion, attachment, and bereavement: a conceptual commentary', in M. S. Stroebe et al. (eds.), *Handbook of Bereavement Research: Consequences, Coping, and Care*. American Psychological Association, pp. 63–88.

23 D. Fahmy (2020). 'Americans are far more religious than adults in other wealthy nations'. Retrieved from https://www.pewre search.org/fact-tank/2018/07/31/americans-are-far-more-religious-than-adults-in-other-wealthy-nations/; D. Fahmy (2020). 'With religion-related rulings on the horizon, U.S. Christians see Supreme Court favorably'. https://www.pewre search.org/fact-tank/2020/03/03/with-religion-related-rulings-on-the-horizon-u-s-christians-see-supreme-court-favorably/

24 P. C. Hill and K. I. Pargament (2003). 'Advances in the conceptualization and measurement of religion and spirituality: implications for physical and mental health research'. *American Psychologist*, 58, 64–74.

25 D. W. Foy, K. D. Drescher and P. J. Watson (n.d.). 'Religious and spiritual factors in resilience'. *Resilience and Mental Health*,

90–102; S. Shuster (n.d.). 'The populists'. *TIME Magazine.* Retrieved from https://time.com/time-person-of-the-year-populism/

26 V. Saroglou (2002). 'Beyond dogmatism: the need for closure as related to religion'. *Mental Health, Religion and Culture,* 5(2), 183–94.

27 J. W. Grant (1998). *The Church in the Canadian Era.* Vancouver: Regent College Publishing, p. 160.

28 R. Padgett and D. O. Jorgenson (1982). 'Superstition and economic threat: Germany, 1918–1940'. *Personality and Social Psychology Bulletin,* 8(4), 736–41; S. M. Sales (1972). 'Economic threat as a determinant of conversion rates in authoritarian and nonauthoritarian churches'. *Journal of Personality and Social Psychology,* 23(3), 420. https://wartimecanada.ca/essay/worshipping/religion-during-second-world-war

29 C. S. Wang, J. A. Whitson and T. Menon (2012). 'Culture, control, and illusory pattern perception'. *Social Psychological and Personality Science,* 3(5), 630–38.

30 K. H. Greenaway, W. R. Louis and M. J. Hornsey (2013). 'Loss of control increases belief in precognition and belief in precognition increases control'. *PLOS One,* 8(8), e71327.

Chapter 4: Adult Attachment

1 N. L. Collins et al. (2006). 'Working models of attachment and attribution processes in intimate relationships'. *Personality and Social Psychology Bulletin,* 32, 201–19.

2 N. L. Collins (1996). 'Working models of attachment: implications for explanation, emotion, and behavior'. *Journal of Personality and Social Psychology,* 71(4), 810–32; N. L. Collins and S. J. Read (1990). 'Adult attachment, working models, and relationship

quality in dating couples'. *Journal of Personality and Social Psychology*, 58(4), 644–63.

3 M. Mikulincer (1997). 'Adult attachment style and information processing: individual differences in curiosity and cognitive closure'. *Journal of Personality and Social Psychology*, 72(5), 1217.

4 J. S. Mill (1843). *A System of Logic*. London: John W. Parker, Vol. 2, p. 534.

5 B. C. Feeney and M. Van Vleet (2010). 'Growing through attachment: the interplay of attachment and exploration in adulthood'. *Journal of Social and Personal Relationships*, 27(2), 226–34.

6 M. Mikulincer and P. R. Shaver (2001). 'Attachment theory and intergroup bias: evidence that priming the secure base schema attenuates negative reactions to out-groups'. *Journal of Personality and Social Psychology*, 81(1), 97–115.

7 M. Mikulincer, P. R. Shaver and E. Rom (2011). 'The effects of implicit and explicit security priming on creative problem solving'. *Cognition and Emotion*, 25(3), 519–31.

Chapter 5: Cultures of Certainty and Uncertainty

1 D. N. Levine (1985). *The Flight from Ambiguity*. Chicago: University of Chicago Press.

2 W. Empson (1947). *Seven Types of Ambiguity*, 2nd edn. London: Chatto and Windus, p. 68.

3 W. Strauss and N. Howe (1991). *Generations*. New York: William Morrow and Company; W. Strauss and N. Howe (2000). *Millennials Rising*. New York: Vintage Books; J. M. Twenge (2006). *Generation Me*. New York: Free Press.

4 C. T. Tadmor et al. (2012). 'Multicultural experiences reduce intergroup bias through epistemic unfreezing'. *Journal of*

Personality and Social Psychology, 103(5), 750–72. https://doi.org/10.1037/a0029719

5 A. K.-Y. Leung and C.-Y. Chiu (2010). 'Multicultural experience, idea receptiveness, and creativity'. *Journal of Cross-Cultural Psychology*, 41(5–6), 723–41.

Chapter 6: The Power of the Situation

1 W. Mischel and Y. Shoda (1995). 'A cognitive-affective system theory of personality: reconceptualizing situations, dispositions, dynamics, and invariance in personality structure'. *Psychological Review*, 102(2), 246–68.

2 K. van den Bos (2001). 'Uncertainty management: the influence of uncertainty salience on reactions to perceived procedural fairness'. *Journal of Personality and Social Psychology*, 80(6), 931.

3 K. van den Bos, J. van Ameijde and H. van Gorp (2006). 'On the psychology of religion: the role of personal uncertainty in religious worldview defense'. *Basic and Applied Social Psychology*, 28, 333–41.

4 G. Hofstede (2001). *Culture's Consequences*, 2nd edn. California: Sage Publications.

5 I. McGregor and D. C. Marigold (2003). 'Defensive zeal and the uncertain self: what makes you so sure?', *Journal of Personality and Social Psychology*, 85(5), 838–52.

6 G. L. Cohen et al. (2007). 'Bridging the partisan divide: self-affirmation reduces ideological closed-mindedness and inflexibility in negotiation'. *Journal of Personality and Social Psychology*, 93(3), 415.

7 D. A. Sherman, L. D. Nelson and C. M. Steele (2000). 'Do messages about health risks threaten the self? Increasing the

acceptance of threatening health messages via self-affirmation'. *Personality and Social Psychology Bulletin*, 26(9), 1046–58.

8 J. Greenberg, T. Pyszczynski and S. Solomon (1986). 'The causes and consequences of a need for self-esteem: a terror management theory', in R. F. Baumeister (ed.), *Public Self and Private Self.* Springer Series in Social Psychology. New York: Springer.

9 A. J. Lambert et al. (2014). 'Towards a greater understanding of the emotional dynamics of the mortality salience manipulation: revisiting the "affect-free" claim of terror management research'. *Journal of Personality and Social Psychology*, 106(5), 655–78.

10 A. Rosenblatt et al. (1989). 'Evidence for terror management theory: I. the effects of mortality salience on reactions to those who violate or uphold cultural value'. *Journal of Personality and Social Psychology*, 57(4), 681–90.

11 A. W. Kruglanski, M. Gelfand and R. Gunaratna (2012). 'Terrorism as means to an end: how political violence bestows significance', in P. R. Shaver and M. Mikulincer (eds.), *Meaning, Mortality, and Choice: The Social Psychology of Existential Concerns.* American Psychological Association, pp. 203–12. https://doi.org/10.1037/13748-011

12 E. Orehek and A. W. Kruglanski (2018). 'Personal failure makes society seem fonder: an inquiry into the roots of social interdependence'. *PLOS One*, 13(8).

13 D. Cohen et al. (2017). 'Defining social class across time and between groups'. *Personality and Social Psychology Bulletin*, 43(11), 1530–45.

Chapter 7: The Pitfalls of Black-and-White Thinking

1 J. S. Mill (1859). *Essay on Liberty*. London: John W. Parker and Son, p. 34.

2 I. Berlin (1969). *Four Essays on Liberty*. London: Oxford University Press.

3 J. Haidt (2012). *The Righteous Mind: Why Good People are Divided by Politics and Religion*. London: Allen Lane.

4 C. G. Lord, L. Ross and M. R. Lepper (1979). 'Biased assimilation and attitude polarization: the effects of prior theories on subsequently considered evidence'. *Journal of Personality and Social Psychology*, 37(11), 2098–109.

5 S. Kiss (2012). 'On TV Westerns of the 1950s and '60s'. *New York Public Library*. Retrieved from https://www.nypl.org/blog/2012/12/01/tv-westerns-1950s-and-60s

6 https://www.bbc.com/culture/article/20141106-why-are-russians-always-bad-guys; https://www.journals.uchicago.edu/doi/10.1086/711300

7 A. W. Kruglanski et al. (2020). 'Terrorism in time of the pandemic: exploiting mayhem'. *Global Security: Health, Science and Policy*, 5(1), 121–32.

8 M. Marchlewska, A. Cichocka and M. Kossowska (2017). 'Addicted to answers: need for cognitive closure and the endorsement of conspiracy beliefs'. *European Journal of Social Psychology*, 48(2), 109–117.

9 D. Groh (1987). 'The temptation of conspiracy theory, or: Why do bad things happen to good people?', in C. F. Graumann and S. Moscovici (eds.), *Changing Conceptions of Conspiracy*. New York: Springer, pp. 1–37, p. 16.

10 Ibid., p. 19.

11 N. Smith (2017). 'Populist attacks on elites are a dead end'.

Bloomberg. Retrieved from https://www.bloomberg.com/
opinion/articles/2017-05-03/populist-attacks-on-elites-are-
a-dead-end

12 S. Shuster (n.d.). 'The populists'. *TIME Magazine*. Retrieved
from https://time.com/time-person-of-the-year-populism/;
A. Argandoña (2017). 'Why populism is rising and how to
combat it'. *Forbes*. Retrieved from https://www.forbes.com/
sites/iese/2017/01/24/why-populism-is-rising-and-how-to-
combat-it/?sh=27fe74831d44

13 S. Amaro (2017). 'CFOs worldwide are concerned populism is
hurting the world's economy'. CNBC. Retrieved from https://
www.cnbc.com/2017/03/15/cfos-worldwide-are-concerned-
trumps-policies-will-lead-to-a-trade-war-with-china.html

14 R. F. Inglehart and P. Norris (2016). 'Trump, Brexit, and the
rise of populism: economic have-nots and cultural backlash'.
HKS Working Paper No. RWP16-026. Accessible at https://
papers.ssrn.com/sol3/papers.cfm?abstract_id=2818659

15 T. Piketty (2014). *Capital in the Twenty-first Century*. Cambridge,
MA: Harvard University Press.

Chapter 8: Among Others

1 I. Schwartz (2020). 'CNN's John King: Trump "shameless" for
using coronavirus briefing to talk about war on drugs'. *Real Clear
Politics*. Retrieved from https://www.realclearpolitics.com/
video/2020/04/01/cnns_john_king_trump_shameless_
for_using_coronavirus_briefing_to_talk_about_war_on_
drugs.html; M. Gerson (2020). 'We've officially witnessed the
total failure of empathy in presidential leadership'. *Washington
Post*. Retrieved from https://www.washingtonpost.com/

opinions/america-needs-empathetic-leadership-now-more-than-ever/2020/04/02/1f6935f2-750c-11ea-87da-77a8136c1a6d_story.html

2 D. M. Webster-Nelson, C. F. Klein and J. E. Irvin (2003). 'Motivational antecedents of empathy: inhibiting effects of fatigue'. *Basic and Applied Social Psychology*, 25, 37–50.

3 J. Bradley. 'As domestic abuse rises, UK failings leave victims in peril'. *New York Times*, 2 July 2020. Retrieved from https://www.nytimes.com/interactive/2020/07/02/world/europe/uk-coronavirus-domestic-abuse.html

4 C. Bettinger-Lopez and A. Bro (2020). 'A double pandemic: domestic violence in the age of COVID-19'. *Council on Foreign Relations.* Retrieved from https://www.cfr.org/in-brief/double-pandemic-domestic-violence-age-covid-19

5 E. Michael (2020). 'Alcohol consumption during COVID-19 pandemic: what PCPs need to know'. *Healio News*. Retrieved from https://www.healio.com/news/primary-care/20200416/alcohol-consumption-during-covid19-pandemic-what-pcps-need-to-know; T. Christensen (2020). 'COVID-19 pandemic brings new concerns about excessive drinking'. *American Heart Association*. Retrieved from https://www.heart.org/en/news/2020/07/01/covid-19-pandemic-brings-new-concerns-about-excessive-drinking

6 C. M. Steele and R. A. Josephs (1990). 'Alcohol myopia: its prized and dangerous effects'. *American Psychologist*, 45(8), 921–33.

7 D. M. Webster (1993). 'Motivated augmentation and reduction of the overattribution bias'. *Journal of Personality and Social Psychology*, 65(2), 261–71.

8 K. Popper (1945). *The Open Society and Its Enemies*. Oxfordshire: Routledge, pp. 230–231.

9 L. Richter and A. W. Kruglanski (1997). 'The accuracy of social perception and cognition: situationally contingent and process-based'. *Swiss Journal of Psychology*, 56, 62–81.

10 C:\Users\embelanger\Library\Containers\com.apple.mail\ Data\Library\MailDownloads\C7EF0457-23BD-4C7D-A897- 98FE3BA78545\Freedom; *Freedom House* (2019). 'Democracy in Retreat'. Retrieved from https://freedomhouse.org/report/ freedom-world/2019/democracy-retreat; J. Reykowski (2021). 'Right-wing conservative radicalism as a pursuit of a cultural hegemony'. *Nauka*, 2.

11 K. R. Popper (1966). *The Open Society and Its Enemies*, revised edition. New York: Routledge and Kegan Paul, Vol. 1.

12 S. E. Asch (1961). 'Effects of group pressure upon the modification and distortion of judgments', in M. Henle (ed.), *Documents of Gestalt Psychology*. Berkeley and Los Angeles: University of California Press, pp. 222–36.

13 G. Stein (n.d.), quotation. *Good Reads*. Retrieved from https:// www.goodreads.com/author/quotes/9325.Gertrude_Stein? page=2

14 A. W. Kruglanski and D. M. Webster (1991). 'Group members' reactions to opinion deviates and conformists at varying degrees of proximity to decision deadline and of environmental noise'. *Journal of Personality and Social Psychology*, 61(2), 212–25.

15 J. T. Jost et al. (2003). 'Political conservatism as motivated social cognition'. *Psychological Bulletin*, 129(3), 339–75.

16 E. Orehek et al. (2010). 'Need for closure and the social response to terrorism'. *Basic and Applied Social Psychology*, 32(4), 279–90.

17 D. Ignatius. 'How did Covid-19 begin? Its initial origin story is shaky'. *Washington Post*, 2 April 2020. Retrieved from https:// www.washingtonpost.com/opinions/global-opinions/how-

did-covid-19-begin-its-initial-origin-story-is-shaky/2020/
04/02/1475d488-7521-11ea-87da-77a8136c1a6d_story.html

Chapter 9: Self-confidence and Self-doubt

1 C. C. Tossell et al. (2022). 'Spiritual over physical formidability determines willingness to fight and sacrifice through loyalty in cross-cultural populations'. *Proceedings of the National Academy of Sciences*, 119(6), e2113076119.
2 A. W. Kruglanski and D. M. Webster (1991). 'Group members' reactions to opinion deviates and conformists at varying degrees of proximity to decision deadline and of environmental noise'. *Journal of Personality and Social Psychology*, 61(2), 212–25.
3 M. A. Hogg (2012). 'Self-uncertainty, social identity, and the solace of extremism', in M. A. Hogg and D. L. Blaylock (eds.), *The Claremont Symposium on Applied Social Psychology: Extremism and the Psychology of Uncertainty*. Malden, MA: Wiley-Blackwell, pp. 19–35.
4 A. W. Kruglanski et al. (2021). 'On the psychology of extremism: how motivational imbalance breeds intemperance'. *Psychological Review*, 128(2), 264–89; A. W. Kruglanski, E. Szumowska and C. Kopetz (2021). 'The call of the wild: how extremism happens'. *Current Directions in Psychological Science*, 30(2), 181–5.
5 A. W. Kruglanski, D. Webber and D. Koehler (2019). *The Radical's Journey: How German Neo-Nazis Voyaged to the Edge and Back*. New York: Oxford University Press.
6 Ibid., p. 107.
7 Ibid., p. 135.
8 Ibid.
9 Ibid., p. 134.

10 Ibid., pp. 164, 165, 167.

11 Ibid., p. 174.

12 D. Chiu (2020). 'Jonestown: 13 things you should know about cult massacre'. *Rolling Stone*. Retrieved from https://www.roll ingstone.com/culture/culture-features/jonestown-13-things-you-should-know-about-cult-massacre-121974/

13 A. Merari (2010). *Driven to Death: Psychological and Social Aspects of Suicide Terrorism*. New York: Oxford University Press.

14 R. M. Kanter (1968). 'Commitment and social organization: a study of commitment mechanisms in utopian communities'. *American Sociological Review*, 33(4), 499–517. https://www.jstor.org/stable/2092438, p. 507.

15 Kruglanski, Webber and Koehler (2019), pp. 168–9.

16 D. Webber et al. (2018). 'Deradicalizing detained terrorists'. *Political Psychology*, 39(3), 539–56.

17 S. Atran (2010). *Talking to the Enemy: Violent Extremism, Sacred Values, and What it Means to be Human*. London: Penguin; S. Atran (2016). 'The devoted actor: unconditional commitment and intractable conflict across cultures'. *Current Anthropology*, 57(S13), S192–S203; Á. Gómez et al. (2017). 'The devoted actor's will to fight and the spiritual dimension of human conflict'. *Nature Human Behaviour*, Vol. 1, pp. 673–9. https://doi.org/10.1038/s41562-017-0193-3; W. B. Swann Jr et al. (2010). 'Identity fusion and self-sacrifice: arousal as a catalyst of pro-group fighting, dying, and helping behavior'. *Journal of Personality and Social Psychology*, 99(5), 824–41.

18 C. Darwin (1871). *The Descent of Man, and Selection in Relation to Sex*. London: John Murray, pp. 163–5.

19 Ibid., p. 16.

20 S. Atran and J. Ginges (2012). 'Religious and sacred imperatives in human conflict'. *Science*, 336(6038), 855–7. doi: 10.1126/science.1216902, p. 857.

Chapter 10: Accentuating the Positive

1 A. Jotischky (2004). *Crusading and the Crusader States*. London: Pearson Education, pp. 1913–36.

2 V. B. Johnston (1968). *Legions of Babel: The International Brigades in the Spanish Civil War*. University Park, PA: Pennsylvania State University Press.

3 M. Roig-Franzia. 'A British actor left Hollywood to fight ISIS. Now he's marooned in Belize. It's quite a story'. *Washington Post*, 15 Oct. 2019. Retrieved from https://www.washington post.com/lifestyle/2019/10/15/british-actor-left-holly wood-fight-isis-now-hes-marooned-belize-its-quite-story/

4 E. T. Higgins (1998). 'Promotion and prevention: regulatory focus as a motivational principle', in M. P. Zanna (ed.), *Advances in Experimental Social Psychology*, Vol. 30. Cambridge, MA: Academic Press, pp. 1–46.

5 I. Arieli (2019). *Chutzpah: Why Israel is a Hub of Innovation and Entrepreneurship*. London: HarperCollins, p. 6.

6 Ibid., p. 7.

7 For example, A. S. Dreyer and M. B. Wells (1966). 'Parental values, parental control, and creativity in young children'. *Journal of Marriage and the Family*, 28(1), 83–8; D. M. Jankowska and J. Gralewski (2020). 'The familial context of children's creativity: parenting styles and the climate for creativity in parent–child relationship'. *Creativity Studies*, (15)1, 1–24; J. Gralewski and D. M. Jankowska (2020). 'Do parenting styles matter? Perceived dimensions of parenting styles, creative abilities and creative self-beliefs in adolescents'. *Thinking Skills and Creativity*, 38, article 100709; B. C. Miller and D. Gerard (1979). 'Family influences on the development of creativity in children: an integrative review'. *Family Coordinator*, 28(3), 295–312.

8 Arieli (2019), pp. 24–5.

9 S. Berretta and G. Privette (1990). 'Influence of play on creative thinking'. *Perceptual and Motor Skills*, 71(2), 659–66.

10 C. J. Roney, E. T. Higgins and J. Shah (1995). 'Goals and framing: how outcome focus influences motivation and emotion'. *Personality and Social Psychology Bulletin*, 21(11), 1151–60.

11 Ibid.

12 N. Liberman et al. (1999). 'Promotion and prevention choices between stability and change'. *Journal of Personality and Social Psychology*, 77(6), 1135.

13 E. Szumowska et al. (2020). Unpublished data. Jagiellonian University.

14 M. E. Seligman (1972). 'Learned helplessness'. *Annual Review of Medicine*, 23(1), 407–12.

15 M. Csikszentmihalyi (1998). *Finding Flow: The Psychology of Engagement with Everyday Life*. London: Hachette.

16 D. G. Myers (2000). 'The funds, friends, and faith of happy people'. *American Psychologist*, 55(1), 56.

17 S. L. Gable. (2000). 'Appetitive and aversive social motivation'. Unpublished doctoral dissertation, University of Rochester, Rochester, NY.

18 N. V. Peale (1980). *The Power of Positive Thinking*. New York: Random House, p. 12.

19 Ibid., p. 17.

20 R. Puff. 'Quieting the monkey mind with meditation'. *Psychology Today*, 19 Oct. 2011. Retrieved from https://www.psychologytoday.com/us/blog/meditation-modern-life/201110/quieting-the-monkey-mind-meditation

21 A. Smith (1759). *The Theory of Moral Sentiments*. London: Penguin.

22 S. B. Breathnach (1996). *The Simple Abundance Journal of Gratitude*. London: Little, Brown.

23 *New Shorter Oxford English Dictionary* (1993), Vol.1, p. 1135.

24 R. A. Emmons and M. E. McCullough (eds.) (2004). *The Psychology of Gratitude*. Oxford: Oxford University Press, p. 5.

25 P. A. Bertocci and R. M. Millard (1963). *Personality and the Good: Psychological and Ethical Perspectives*. New York: McKay, p. 389.

26 H. B. Clark, J. T. Northrop and C. T. Barkshire (1988). 'The effects of contingent thank-you notes on case managers' visiting residential clients'. *Education and Treatment of Children*, 11(1), 45–51.

27 R. L. Trivers (1971). 'The evolution of reciprocal altruism'. *Quarterly Review of Biology*, 46(1), 35–57.

28 F. B. de Waal (1997). 'The chimpanzee's service economy: food for grooming'. *Evolution and Human Behavior*, 18(6), 375–86; F. B. de Waal and M. L. Berger (2000). 'Payment for labour in monkeys'. *Nature*, 404(6778), 563.

29 R. A. Emmons and M. E. McCullough (2003). 'Counting blessings versus burdens: an experimental investigation of gratitude and subjective well-being in daily life'. *Journal of Personality and Social Psychology*, 84(2), 377–89.

30 R. McCraty et al. (1995). 'The effects of emotions on short-term power spectrum analysis of heart rate variability'. *American Journal of Cardiology*, 76(14), 1089–93.

31 R. McCraty (2003). 'The energetic heart: bioelectromagnetic interactions within and between people'. *Neuropsychotherapist*, 6(1), 22–43.

32 D. P. McAdams (2013). *The Redemptive Self: Stories Americans Live By*, revised and expanded edition. New York: Oxford University Press.

33 For example, M. A. Davis (2009). 'Understanding the relationship between mood and creativity: a meta-analysis'. *Organizational Behaviour and Human Decision Processes*, 108(1), 25–38.

34 B. L. Fredrickson and C. A. Branigan (2001). 'Positive emotions', in T. J. Mayne and G. A. Bonanno (eds.), *Emotion:*

Current Issues and Future Developments. New York: Guilford Press, pp. 123–51.

35 P. Russo-Netzer and T. Ben-Shahar (2011). ' "Learning from success": a close look at a popular positive psychology course'. *Journal of Positive Psychology*, 6(6), 468–76.

36 D. Shimer. 'Yale's most popular class ever: happiness'. *The New York Times*, 26 Jan. 2018. Retrieved from https://www.nytimes.com/2018/01/26/nyregion/at-yale-class-on-happiness-draws-huge-crowd-laurie-santos.html?login=email&auth=login-email.

Chapter 11: Making Good Things Happen

1 C. S. Carver, M. F. Scheier and S. C. Segerstrom (2010). 'Optimism'. *Clinical Psychology Review*, 30(7), 879–89, p. 879.

2 Ibid., p. 886.

3 M. E. Seligman (2006). *Learned Optimism: How to Change Your Mind and Your Life*. New York: Vintage Books, p. 46.

4 J. W. Shenk (2005). 'Lincoln's great depression'. *Atlantic Monthly*, 296(3), 52.

5 Ibid.

6 Ibid.

7 J. Kluger (2014). 'FDR's polio: the steel in his soul'. *TIME*. Retrieved from https://time.com/3340831/polio-fdr-roosevelt-burns/.

8 J. Brown (2011). '50 famously successful people who failed at first'. *Addicted2Success*. Retrieved from https://addicted2success.com/motivation/50-famously-successful-people-who-failed-at-first/

9 E. F. Hittner et al. (2020). 'Positive affect is associated with less memory decline: evidence from a 9-year longitudinal study'. *Psychological Science*, 31(11), 1386–95.

10 S. G. Hofmann et al. (2012). 'The efficacy of cognitive behavioral therapy: a review of meta-analyses'. *Cognitive Therapy and Research*, 36(5), 427–40.

11 Seligman (2006), pp. 223, 225.

12 Ibid.

13 A. Duckworth (2016). *Grit: The Power of Passion and Perseverance*. New York: Scribner, p. 66.

14 Ibid., p. 120.

15 Ibid., p. 99.

16 Ibid., pp. 107, 108.

17 Ibid., p. 143.

Chapter 12: The Best is Yet to Come

1 https://tcdata360.worldbank.org/indicators/aps.fofail?country=BRA&indicator=3108&viz=line_chart&years=2001,2020

2 M. Muggeridge (1967). *Muggeridge through the Microphone: BBC Radio and Television*. London: British Broadcasting Corporation, p. 7.

3 K. R. Popper (1966). *The Open Society and Its Enemies*, revised edition. New York: Routledge and Kegan Paul, Vol. 1, pp. 46–7, 169.

4 K. Bartlett (1985). 'Mensans go for the mix: the club is smart but its members are not all chic and fashionable'. *Los Angeles Times*. Retrieved from https://www.latimes.com/archives/la-xpm-1985-09-15-mn-23351-story.html

5 M. Gladwell. 'The talent myth'. *The New Yorker*, 22 July 2002, pp. 28–33.

6 A. Booth and P. R. Amato (2001). 'Parental predivorce relations and offspring postdivorce well being'. *Journal of Marriage and Family*, 63(1), 197–212, p. 140.

7 S. Berglas and E. E. Jones (1978). 'Drug choice as a self-handicapping strategy in response to noncontingent success'. *Journal of Personality and Social Psychology*, 36(4), 405.

8 F. Rhodewalt (1994). 'Conceptions of ability, achievement goals, and individual differences in self-handicapping behavior: on the application of implicit theories'. *Journal of Personality*, 62(1), 67–85.

9 K. J. Gergen and S. R. Gill (2020). *Beyond the Tyranny of Testing: Relational Evaluation in Education*. New York: Oxford University Press, p. 2.

10 Ibid., p. 6.

11 https://www.activeminds.org/programs/send-silence-packing/

12 N. R. Leonard et al. (2015). 'A multi-method exploratory study of stress, coping, and substance use among high school youth in private schools'. *Frontiers in Psychology*, 6, 1028.

13 D. Harley (2016). 'Student raises funds to prevent suicide'. *The Grizzly*, 40(12), 1–2.

14 For example, K. Farr (2018). 'Adolescent rampage school shootings: responses to failing masculinity performances by already-troubled boys'. *Gender Issues*, 35(2), 73–97.

15 T. Piketty (2018). 'Brahmin left vs merchant right: rising inequality and the changing structure of political conflict'. WID.world Working Paper, 2018/7.

16 A. Case and A. Deaton (2020). *Deaths of Despair and the Future of Capitalism*. Princeton: Princeton University Press.

Chapter 13: The Allure of Detachment and Mystery

1 K. Sri Dhammananda (2003). *Everything is Changeable*, p. 36.

2 Y. Mingyur (2010). *Joyful Wisdom*. London: Bantam, p. 53.

3 A. W. Kruglanski et al. (2021). 'On the psychology of extremism: how motivational imbalance breeds intemperance'. *Psychological Review*, 128(2), 264.

4 P. Brickman, D. Coates and R. Janoff-Bulman (1978). 'Lottery winners and accident victims: is happiness relative?', *Journal of Personality and Social Psychology*, 36(8), 917.

5 D. T. Gilbert et al. (1998). 'Immune neglect: a source of durability bias in affective forecasting'. *Journal of Personality and Social Psychology*, 75(3), 617.

6 T. D. Wilson et al. (2000). 'Focalism: a source of durability bias in affective forecasting'. *Journal of Personality and Social Psychology*, 78, 821–36.

7 R. K. Mallett, T. D. Wilson and D. T. Gilbert (2008). 'Expect the unexpected: failure to anticipate similarities leads to an intergroup forecasting error'. *Journal of Personality and Social Psychology*, 94(2), 265–77.

8 J. A. Woodzicka and M. LaFrance (2001). 'Real versus imagined gender harassment'. *Journal of Social Issues*, 57, 15–30.

9 T. D. Wilson, D. T. Gilbert and T. P. Wheatley (1998). 'Protecting our minds: the role of lay beliefs', in V. Y. Yzerbyt, G. Lories and B. Dardenne (eds.), *Metacognition: Cognitive and Social Dimensions*. California: Sage Publications, pp. 171–201.

10 D. T. Gilbert et al. (1998). 'Immune neglect: a source of durability bias in affective forecasting'. *Journal of Personality and Social Psychology*, 75(3), 617.

11 F. Nietzsche (1996). *Human, All Too Human: A Book for Free Spirits*, trans. R. J. Hollingdale. Cambridge: Cambridge University Press, p. 179.

12 J. R. Mellow (1974). *Charmed Circle: Gertrude Stein and Company*. London: Phaidon Press.

13 E. Frankel (2017). *The Wisdom of Not Knowing: Discovering a Life of Wonder by Embracing Uncertainty*. Colorado: Shambhala Publications, p. 82.

14 S. Freud (1950). *Collected Papers*. (5 vols.).

15 Ibid., 1912/1950, p. 324.

16 M. Eigen (2012). *Kabbalah and Psychoanalysis*. New York: Routledge.

17 J. S. Grotstein (2007). 'On: projective identification'. *International Journal of Psychoanalysis*, 88(5), 1289–90.

18 J. Aguayo (2014). 'Bion's "Notes on memory and desire" – its initial clinical reception in the United States: a note on archival material'. *International Journal of Psychoanalysis*, 95(5), 889–910.

19 W. R. Bion, J. Aguayo and B.D. Malin (2019). *Wilfred Bion: Los Angeles Seminars and Supervision*. London: Routledge.

20 Ibid.

21 M. Popova. 'Inclining the mind toward "sudden illumination": French polymath Henri Poincaré on how creativity works'. *Marginalian*. Retrieved from https://www.brainpickings.org/2013/08/15/henri-poincare-on-how-creativity-works/

22 Cited in J. Stachel (2002). *Einstein from 'B' to 'Z'*. Boston: Birkhäuser, p. 89.

23 A. Chirumbolo et al. (2004). 'Effects of need for closure on creativity in small group interactions'. *European Journal of Personality*, 18(4), 265–78.

24 R. D. Kerns, J. Sellinger and B. R. Goodin (2011). 'Psychological treatment of chronic pain'. *Annual Review of Clinical Psychology*, 7, 411–34.

25 For example, D. Donthula et al. 'Does intolerance of uncertainty affect the magnitude of limitations or pain intensity?', *Clinical Orthopaedics and Related Research*, 478(2), 381; S. F. Fischerauer et al. (2018). 'Pain anxiety differentially mediates the

association of pain intensity with function depending on level of intolerance of uncertainty'. *Journal of Psychiatric Research*, 97, 30–37.

Chapter 14: Living with Differences

1 T. Hiebert (2007). 'The Tower of Babel and the origin of the world's cultures', *Journal of Biblical Literature*, 126(1), 29–58.

2 Genesis 11: 6. NET Bible. Retrieved 3 March 2022.

3 National Academies of Sciences, Engineering and Medicine (2016). *Attribution of Extreme Weather Events in the Context of Climate Change*. Washington, DC: National Academies Press.

4 L. M. Bouwer (2019). 'Observed and projected impacts from extreme weather events: implications for loss and damage', in R. Mehler el al. (eds.), *Loss and Damage from Climate Change*. Cham, Switzerland: Springer, pp. 63–82.

5 A. Lustgarten. 'The great climate migration has begun'. *New York Times Magazine*, 23 July 2020. Retrieved from https://www.nytimes.com/interactive/2020/07/23/magazine/climate-migration.html

6 IOM (2017). 'Migration, climate change and the environment: a complex nexus'. Geneva: International Organization for Migration.

7 World Bank Group. 'Groundswell: preparing for internal climate migration policy note #3: internal climate migration in Latin America' 16 Mar. 2018. Retrieved from https://documents1.worldbank.org/curated/en/983921522304806221/pdf/124724-BRI-PUBLIC- NEWSERIES-Groundswell-note-PN3.pdf.

8 P. Esposito, S. Collignon and S. Scicchitano (2020). 'The effect of immigration on unemployment in Europe: does the core-periphery dualism matter?', *Economic Modelling*, 84, 249–58.

9 T. L. Friedman. 'It's a flat world, after all'. *The New York Times*, 3 Apr. 2005.

10 R. W. Bibby (1990). *Mosaic Madness*. Toronto: Stoddart, pp. 10, 14.

11 G. Blainey (1984). *All for Australia*. Methuen Haynes.

12 S. P. Huntington (1975). 'The United States', in M. Crozier, S. P. Huntington and J. Watanuki, *The Crisis of Democracy: Report on the Governability of Democracies to the Trilateral Commission*. New York: New York University Press, pp. 76–7.

13 Quoted in M. Valpy (2007). 'Seismic tremors: religion and the law', in J. G. Stein et al., *Uneasy Partners: Multiculturalism and Rights in Canada*. Ontario: Wilfrid Laurier University Press, p. 123.

14 J. R. Berkovitz (1989). *The Shaping of Jewish Identity in Nineteenth-century France*. Detroit: Wayne State University Press, p. 71.

15 E. Macron. 'Fight against separatism – the Republic in action'. *France Diplomacy*, 2 Oct. 2020.

16 N. Breznau (2018). 'Anti-immigrant parties and Western European society: analyzing the role of immigration and forecasting voting'. Mannheim Centre for European Social Research.

17 E. Orehek et al. (2010). 'Need for closure and the social response to terrorism'. *Basic and Applied Social Psychology*, 32(4), 279–90.

18 M. and C. W. Sherif (1953). *Groups in Harmony and Tension: An Integration of Studies on Intergroup Relations*. New York: Harper.

19 G. S. Morgan, D. C. Wisneski and L. J. Skitka (2011). 'The expulsion from Disneyland: the social psychological impact of 9/11'. *American Psychologist*, 66(6), 447.

20 J. K. Bosson et al. (2006). 'Interpersonal chemistry through negativity: bonding by sharing negative attitudes about others'. *Personal Relationships*, 13(2), 135–50.

21 W. G. Sumner (1906). *Folkways: A Study of the Sociological Importance of Usages, Manners, Customs, Mores, and Morals*. Boston: Gin and Company, p. 12.

22 T. F. Pettigrew and L. R. Tropp (2006). 'A meta-analytic test of intergroup contact theory'. *Journal of Personality and Social Psychology*, 90(5), 751.

23 A. B. Seligman, R. R. Wasserfall and D. W. Montgomery (2015). *Living with Difference: How to Build Community in a Divided World.* Oakland, CA: University of California Press.

24 Ibid.

25 Ibid., p. 10.

26 Ibid., p. 11.

Conclusion: Avoiding and Approaching Uncertainty

1 John Ciardi's translation (2009). London: Signet.

Bibliography

Adorno, T. W. et al. (1950). *The Authoritarian Personality*. New York: Harper and Row, Inc.

Aguayo, J. (2014). 'Bion's "Notes on memory and desire" – its initial clinical reception in the United States: a note on archival material'. *International Journal of Psychoanalysis*, 95(5), 889–910.

Allport, G. W. (1954). 'The nature of prejudice'. Cambridge, MA: Addison.

Altemeyer, B. (1988). *Enemies of Freedom: Understanding Right-wing Authoritarianism*. San Francisco: Jossey-Bass.

Amaro, S. (2017). 'CFOs worldwide are concerned populism is hurting the world's economy'. CNBC. Retrieved from https://www.cnbc.com/2017/03/15/cfos-worldwide-are-concerned-trumps-policies-will-lead-to-a-trade-war-with-china.html

Argandoña, A. (2017). 'Why populism is rising and how to combat it'. *Forbes*. Retrieved from https://www.forbes.com/sites/iese/2017/01/24/why-populism-is-rising-and-how-to-combat-it/?sh=27fe74831d44

Arieli, I. (2019). *Chutzpah: Why Israel is a Hub of Innovation and Entrepreneurship*. New York: HarperCollins.

Armus, T. (2020). 'The parents of 545 children separated at the border still haven't been found'. https://www.texastribune.org/2020/10/21/donald-trump-immigration-parents-children-separated/

Asch, S. E. (1961). 'Effects of group pressure upon the modification and distortion of judgments', in M. Henle (ed.), *Documents of Gestalt Psychology*. Berkeley and Los Angeles: University of California Press, pp. 222–36.

Associated Press. 'Clinton: Obama is "naive" on foreign policy'. NBC News, 24 July 2007. Retrieved from https://www.nbcnews.com/id/wbna19933710

Atran, S. (2016). 'The devoted actor: unconditional commitment and intractable conflict across cultures'. *Current Anthropology*, 57(S13), S192–S203. https://www.journals.uchicago.edu/doi/full/10.1086/685495

Atran, S. (2010). *Talking to the Enemy: Violent Extremism, Sacred Values, and What It Means to be Human*. London: Penguin.

Atran, S., and Ginges, J. (2012). 'Religious and sacred imperatives in human conflict'. *Science*, 336(6038), 855–7. doi: 10.1126/science.1216902.

Bartlett, K. (1985). 'Mensans go for the mix: the club is smart but its members are not all chic and fashionable'. *Los Angeles Times*. Retrieved from https://www.latimes.com/archives/laxpm-1985-09-15-mn-23351-story.html

BBC News (2006). '"Conform to our society", says PM'. BBC News.

Benmelech, E., and Klor, E. F. (2020). 'What explains the flow of foreign fighters to ISIS?', *Terrorism and Political Violence*, 32(7), 1458–81.

Berglas, S., and Jones, E. E. (1978). 'Drug choice as a self-handicapping strategy in response to noncontingent success'. *Journal of Personality and Social Psychology*, 36(4), 405.

Berkovitz, J. R. (1989). *The Shaping of Jewish Identity in Nineteenth-century France*. Detroit: Wayne State University Press.

Berlin, I. (1969). *Four Essays on Liberty. London: Oxford University Press.*

Berretta, S., and Privette, G. (1990). 'Influence of play on creative thinking'. *Perceptual and Motor Skills*, 71(2), 659–66.

Bertocci, P. A., and Millard, R. M. (1963). *Personality and the Good: Psychological and Ethical Perspectives*. New York: McKay.

Bettinger-Lopez, C., and Bro, A. (2020). 'A double pandemic: domestic violence in the age of COVID-19'. *Council on Foreign Relations.* Retrieved from https://www.cfr.org/in-brief/double-pandemic-domestic-violence-age-covid-19

Bibby, R. W. (1990). *Mosaic Madness.* Toronto: Stoddart.

Bion, W. R. (1967). 'Notes on memory and desire', in R. Langs (ed.), *Classics in Psychoanalytic Technique.* New York and London: Jason Aronson Inc., pp. 259–60.

Blainey, G. (1984). *All for Australia.* North Ryde: Methuen Haynes.

Boelen, P. A., and van den Bout, J. (2010). 'Anxious and depressive avoidance and symptoms of prolonged grief, depression, and post-traumatic stress disorder'. *Psychologica Belgica,* 50(1–2), 49–67. https://doi.org/10.5334/pb-50-1-2-49

Boorstein, D. J. (1961). *The Image: A Guide to Pseudo-Events in North America.* New York: Vintage Books.

Booth, A., and Amato, P. R. (2001). 'Parental predivorce relations and offspring postdivorce well being'. *Journal of Marriage and Family,* 63(1), 197–212.

Bosson, J. K., et al. (2006). 'Interpersonal chemistry through negativity: bonding by sharing negative attitudes about others'. *Personal Relationships,* 13(2), 135–50.

Bouwer, L. M. (2019). 'Observed and projected impacts from extreme weather events: implications for loss and damage', in R. Mechler et al. (eds.), *Loss and Damage from Climate Change.* Cham, Switzerland: Springer, pp. 63–82.

Bowlby, J. (1951). 'Maternal care and mental health'. *Bulletin of the World Health Organization,* 3(3), 357–533.

Bradley, J. 'As domestic abuse rises, UK failings leave victims in peril', *New York Times,* 2 July 2020. Retrieved from https://www.nytimes.com/interactive/2020/07/02/world/europe/uk-coronavirus-domestic-abuse.html

Breathnach, S. B. (1996). *The Simple Abundance Journal of Gratitude.* London: Little, Brown.

Breznau, N. (2018). 'Anti-immigrant parties and Western European society: analyzing the role of immigration and forecasting voting'. Mannheim Centre for European Social Research.

Brickman, P., Coates, D., and Janoff-Bulman, R. (1978). 'Lottery winners and accident victims: is happiness relative?', *Journal of Personality and Social Psychology*, 36(8).

Brown, J. (2011). '50 famously successful people who failed at first'. *Addicted2Success.* Retrieved from https://addicted2success.com/motivation/50-famously-successful-people-who-failed-at-first/.

Brown, R. (1965). *Social Psychology.* New York: The Free Press.

Campbell, D. (1988). 'The author responds: Popper and selection theory', *Social Epistemology*, (2)4, 371–7. doi: 10.1080/02691728808578506.

Carleton, R. N. (2016). 'Fear of the unknown: one fear to rule them all?', *Journal of Anxiety Disorders*, 41, 5–21.

Carlson, R. (2017). *Don't Sweat the Small Stuff – and It's All Small Stuff: Simple Ways to Keep the Little Things from Taking Over Your Life.* New York: Hachette.

Carnegie, D. (1936). *How to Win Friends and Influence People.* New York: Simon & Schuster.

Carver, C. S., Scheier, M. F., and Segerstrom, S. C. (2010). 'Optimism'. *Clinical Psychology Review*, 30(7), 879–89.

Case, A., and Deaton, A. (2020). *Deaths of Despair and the Future of Capitalism.* Princeton: Princeton University Press.

Chapman University (2017). 'America's Top Fears 2017'. Retrieved from https://blogs.chapman.edu/wilkinson/2017/10/11/americas-top-fears-2017/

Cheon, B. K., et al. (2014). 'Gene × environment interaction on intergroup bias: the role of 5-HTTLPR and perceived outgroup threat'. *Social Cognitive and Affective Neuroscience*, 9(9).

Cheon, B. K., et al. (2015). 'Genetic contributions to need for closure, implicit racial bias, and social ideologies: the role of 5-HTTLPR and COMT Val158Met'. Unpublished data. Nanyang Technological University.

Chirumbolo, A., et al. (2004). 'Effects of need for closure on creativity in small group interactions'. *European Journal of Personality*, 18(4), 265–78.

Chiu, D. (2020). 'Jonestown: 13 things you should know about cult massacre'. *Rolling Stone*. Retrieved from https://www.rollingstone. com/culture/culture-features/jonestown-13-things-you-should-know-about-cult-massacre-121974/

Christensen, T. (2020). 'COVID-19 pandemic brings new concerns about excessive drinking'. *American Heart Association*. Retrieved from https://www.heart.org/en/news/2020/07/01/covid-19-pandemic-brings-new-concerns-about-excessive-drinking

Clark, H. B., Northrop, J. T., and Barkshire, C. T. (1988). 'The effects of contingent thank-you notes on case managers' visiting residential clients'. *Education and Treatment of Children*, 11(1), 45–51.

Cliteur, P. B. (1999). *De Filosofie van Mensenrechten*.

Cohen, D., et al. (2017). 'Defining social class across time and between groups'. *Personality and Social Psychology Bulletin*, 43(11), 1530–45.

Cohen, G. L., et al. (2007). 'Bridging the partisan divide: self-affirmation reduces ideological closed-mindedness and inflexibility in negotiation'. *Journal of Personality and Social Psychology*, 93(3), 415.

Cohen, G. L., Aronson, J., and Steele, C. M. (2000). 'When beliefs yield to evidence: reducing biased evaluation by affirming the self'. *Personality and Social Psychology Bulletin*, 26(9), 1151–64.

Collins, N. L. (1996). 'Working models of attachment: implications for explanation, emotion, and behavior'. *Journal of Personality and Social Psychology*, 71(4), 810–32. https://doi.org/10.1037/0022-3514.71.4.810

Collins, N. L., et al. (2006). 'Working models of attachment and attribution processes in intimate relationships'. *Personality and Social Psychology Bulletin*, 32, 201–19. doi: 10.1177/0146167205280907.

Collins, N. L., and Read, S. J. (1990). 'Adult attachment, working models, and relationship quality in dating couples'. *Journal of Personality and Social Psychology*, 58(4), 644–63. https://doi.org/10.1037/0022-3514.58.4.644

Csikszentmihalyi, M. (1998). *Finding Flow: The Psychology of Engagement with Everyday Life*. London: Hachette.

Csikszentmihalyi, M., and Seligman, M. E. (2000). 'Positive psychology: an introduction'. *American Psychologist*, 55(1), 5–14.

Darwin, C. (1871). *The Descent of Man, and Selection in Relation to Sex*. London: John Murray.

Davis, M. A. (2009). 'Understanding the relationship between mood and creativity: a meta-analysis'. *Organizational Behaviour and Human Decision Processes*, 108(1), 25–38.

De Tocqueville, A. (1835). *Democracy in America*. Columbia University Press.

De Waal, F. B. (1997). 'The chimpanzee's service economy: food for grooming'. *Evolution and Human Behavior*, 18(6), 375–86.

De Waal, F. B., and Berger, M. L. (2000). 'Payment for labour in monkeys'. *Nature*, 404(6778), 563.

Dickinson, R. L., and Beam, L. (1931). *A Thousand Marriages*. Baltimore: Williams and Wilkins.

Donthula, D., et al. 'Does intolerance of uncertainty affect the magnitude of limitations or pain intensity?', *Clinical Orthopaedics and Related Research*, 478(2), 381.

Drehle, D. (2021). 'What 500,000 Covid-19 deaths means'. Retrieved 14 Mar. 2021 from https://www.washingtonpost.com/opinions/what-500000-covid-19-deaths-means/2021/02/19/8492c9b0-72e1-11eb-b8a9-b946751ofofe_story.html

Dreyer, A. S., and Wells, M. B. (1966). 'Parental values, parental control, and creativity in young children'. *Journal of Marriage and the Family*, 28(1), 83–8.

Duckworth, A. (2016). *Grit: The Power of Passion and Perseverance*. New York: Scribner.

Dweck, C. S. (2006). *Mindset: The New Psychology of Success*. New York: Random House Digital, Inc.

Eigen, M. (2012). *Kabbalah and Psychoanalysis*. New York: Routledge.

Emmons, R. A., and McCullough, M. E. (2003). 'Counting blessings versus burdens: an experimental investigation of gratitude and subjective well-being in daily life'. *Journal of Personality and Social Psychology*, 84(2), 377–89.

Emmons, R. A., and McCullough, M. E. (eds.) (2004). *The Psychology of Gratitude*. New York: Oxford University Press.

Empson, W. (1947). *Seven Types of Ambiguity*, 2nd edn. London: Chatto and Windus.

Erikson, E. H. (1963). *Childhood and Society*. New York: W. W. Norton.

Esposito, P., Collignon, S., and Scicchitano, S. (2020). 'The effect of immigration on unemployment in Europe: does the core-periphery dualism matter?', *Economic Modelling*, 84, 249–58.

Fahmy, D. (2020). 'Americans are far more religious than adults in other wealthy nations'. Retrieved from https://www.pewresearch.org/fact-tank/2018/07/31/americans-are-far-more-religious-than-adults-in-other-wealthy-nations/

Farr, K. (2018). 'Adolescent rampage school shootings: responses to failing masculinity performances by already-troubled boys'. *Gender Issues*, 35(2), 73–97.

Feeney, B. C., and Van Vleet, M. (2010). 'Growing through attachment: the interplay of attachment and exploration in adulthood'. *Journal of Social and Personal Relationships*, 27(2), 226–34. https://doi.org/10.1177/0265407509360903

Fischerauer, S. F., et al. (2018). 'Pain anxiety differentially mediates the association of pain intensity with function depending on level of intolerance of uncertainty'. *Journal of Psychiatric Research*, 97, 30–37.

Foy, D. W., Drescher, K. D., and Watson, P. J. (n.d.). 'Religious and spiritual factors in resilience'. *Resilience and Mental Health*, 90–102. doi: 10.1017/cbo9780511994791.008.

Frankel, E. (2017). *The Wisdom of Not Knowing: Discovering a Life of Wonder by Embracing Uncertainty*. Colorado: Shambhala Publications.

Frankl, V. E. (2006). *Man's Search for Meaning: An Introduction to Logotherapy*. Boston: Beacon Press.

Fredrickson, B. (2009). *Positivity*. New York: Harmony.

Fredrickson, B. L., and Branigan, C. A. (2001). 'Positive emotions', in T. J. Mayne and G. A. Bonanno (eds.), *Emotion: Current Issues and Future Developments*. New York: Guilford Press, pp. 123–51.

Freedom House (2019). 'Democracy in Retreat'. Retrieved from https://freedomhouse.org/report/freedom-world/2019/democracy-retreat

Freud, S. (1950). *Collected Papers*. (5 vols.).

Friedman, T. L. 'It's a flat world, after all'. *The New York Times*, 3 Apr. 2005.

Frum, D. (2003). *The Right Man: The Surprise Presidency of George W. Bush*. New York: Random House.

Gable, S. L. (2000). 'Appetitive and aversive social motivation'. Unpublished doctoral dissertation, University of Rochester, New York.

Gergen, K. J., and Gill, S. R. (2020). *Beyond the Tyranny of Testing: Relational Evaluation in Education*. New York: Oxford University Press.

German Propaganda Archive (1998). *Nazi Propaganda: Caricatures from Der Stürmer. Jewish Virtual Library*. Retrieved from https://

www.jewishvirtuallibrary.org/caricatures-from-der-st-uuml-rmer-jewish-virtual-library.

Gerson, M. (2020). 'We've officially witnessed the total failure of empathy in presidential leadership'. *Washington Post*. Retrieved fromhttps://www.washingtonpost.com/opinions/america-needs-empathetic-leadership-now-more-than-ever/2020/04/02/1f6935f2-750c-11ea-87da-77a8136c1a6d_story.html

Gilbert, D. T. (1991). 'How mental systems believe'. *American Psychologist*, 46(2), 107.

Gilbert, D. T., et al. (1998). 'Immune neglect: a source of durability bias in affective forecasting'. *Journal of Personality and Social Psychology*, 75(3), 617.

Gladwell, M. 'The talent myth'. *The New Yorker*, 22 July 2002, 28–33.

Gledhill, R. ' "Multiculturalism has betrayed the English," Archbishop says'. *The Times*, 2 Nov. 2005.

Goethe, J. W. von (1774/1988). *The Sorrows of Young Werther*, trans. Eric Lane. Sawtry: Dedalus.

Gómez, Á., et al. (2017). 'The devoted actor's will to fight and the spiritual dimension of human conflict'. *Nature Human Behaviour*, 1, 673–9. https://doi.org/10.1038/s41562-017-0193-3

Gralewski, J., and Jankowska, D. M. (2020). 'Do parenting styles matter? Perceived dimensions of parenting styles, creative abilities and creative self-beliefs in adolescents'. *Thinking Skills and Creativity*, 38, article 100709.

Grant, J. W. (1998). *The Church in the Canadian Era*. Vancouver: Regent College Publishing.

Greenaway, K. H., Louis, W. R., and Hornsey, M. J. (2013). 'Loss of control increases belief in precognition and belief in precognition increases control'. *PLOS One*, 8(8), e71327.

Greenberg J., Pyszczynski T., and Solomon S. (1986). 'The causes and consequences of a need for self-esteem: a terror management theory', in R. F. Baumeister (ed.), *Public Self and Private Self*. New York: Springer. https://doi.org/10.1007/978-1-4613-9564-5_10

Groh, D. (1987). 'The temptation of conspiracy theory, or: Why do bad things happen to good people?', in C. F. Graumann and S. Moscovici (eds.), *Changing Conceptions of Conspiracy*. New York: Springer, pp. 1–37.

Grotstein, J. S. (2007). 'On: projective identification'. *International Journal of Psychoanalysis*, 88(5), 1289–90.

Haidt, J. (2012). *The Righteous Mind: Why Good People are Divided by Politics and Religion*. London: Allen Lane.

Harari, Y. N. (2014). *Sapiens: A Brief History of Humankind*. London: Random House.

Harley, D. (2016). 'Student raises funds to prevent suicide'. *The Grizzly*, 40(12), 1–2.

Harlow, H. F. (1958). 'The nature of love'. *American Psychologist*, 13(12), 673.

Hayden, J. (2001). *Covering Clinton*. New York: Praeger.

Higgins, E. T. (1998). 'Promotion and prevention: regulatory focus as a motivational principle', in M. P. Zanna (ed.), *Advances in Experimental Social Psychology*, Vol. 30. Cambridge, MA: Academic Press, pp. 1–46.

Hill, P. C., and Pargament, K. I. (2003). 'Advances in the conceptualization and measurement of religion and spirituality: implications for physical and mental health research'. *American Psychologist*, 58, 64–74. http://dx.doi.org/10.1037/0003-066X.58.1.64

Hittner, E. F., et al. (2020). 'Positive affect is associated with less memory decline: evidence from a 9-year longitudinal study'. *Psychological Science*, 31(11), 1386–95.

Hoffer, E. (1951). *The True Believer*. New York: Perennial.

Hofmann, S. G., et al. (2012). 'The efficacy of cognitive behavioral therapy: a review of meta-analyses'. *Cognitive Therapy and Research*, 36(5), 427–40.

Hofstede, G. (2001). *Culture's Consequences: Comparing Values, Behaviors, Institutions and Organizations across Nations*, 2nd edn. California: Sage Publications.

Hogg, M. A. (2012). 'Self-uncertainty, social identity, and the solace of extremism', in M. A. Hogg and D. L. Blaylock (eds.), *The Claremont Symposium on Applied Social Psychology. Extremism and the Psychology of Uncertainty.* London: Wiley-Blackwell, pp. 19–35.

Hong, Y., and Khei, M. (2014). 'Dynamic multiculturalism: the interplay of socio-cognitive, neural and genetic mechanisms', in V. Benet-Martinez and Y. Hong (eds.), *The Oxford Handbook of Multicultural Identity: Basic and Applied Psychological Perspectives.* New York: Oxford University Press. https://doi.org/10.1037/0022-3514.81.1.97

Huntington, S. P. (1996). *The Clash of Civilizations and the Remaking of World Order.* New York: Simon & Schuster.

Huntington, S. P. (1975). 'The United States', in M. Crozier, S. P. Huntington and J. Watanuki, *The Crisis of Democracy: Report on the Governability of Democracies to the Trilateral Commission.* New York: New York University Press.

Ignatius, D. 'How did Covid-19 begin? Its initial origin story is shaky'. *Washington Post*, 2 Apr. 2020. Retrieved from https://www.washingtonpost.com/opinions/global-opinions/how-did-covid-19-begin-its-initial-origin-story-is-shaky/2020/04/02/1475d488-7521-11ea-87da-77a8136c1a6d_story.html

Inglehart, R. F., and Norris, P. (2016). 'Trump, Brexit, and the rise of populism: economic have-nots and cultural backlash'. HKS Working Paper No. RWP16-026. Accessible at https://papers.ssrn.com/sol3/papers.cfm?abstract_id=2818659

IOM (2017) 'Migration, climate change and the environment: a complex nexus'. Geneva: International Organization for Migration.

Jaensch, E. (1938). *Der Gegentypus.* Leipzig: Ambrosius Barth.

James, W. (1890). *The Consciousness of Self*.

Jankowska, D. M., and Gralewski, J. (2020). 'The familial context of children's creativity: parenting styles and the climate for creativity in parent–child relationships'. *Creativity Studies*, 15(1), 1–24.

Johnston, V. B. (1968). *Legions of Babel: The International Brigades in the Spanish Civil War*. University Park, PA: Pennsylvania State University Press.

Jost, J. T., et al. (2003). 'Political conservatism as motivated social cognition'. *Psychological Bulletin*, 129(3), 339–75.

Jotischky, A. (2004). *Crusading and the Crusader States*. London: Pearson Education.

Kanter, R. M. (1968). 'Commitment and social organization: a study of commitment mechanisms in utopian communities'. *American Sociological Review*, 33(4), 499–517. https://www.jstor.org/stable/2092438

Kerns, R. D., Sellinger, J., and Goodin, B. R. (2011). 'Psychological treatment of chronic pain'. *Annual Review of Clinical Psychology*, 7, 411–34.

Kiss, S. (2012). 'On TV Westerns of the 1950s and '60s'. *New York Public Library*. Retrieved from https://www.nypl.org/blog/2012/12/01/tv-westerns-1950s-and-60s.

Kluger, J. (2014). 'FDR's polio: the steel in his soul'. *TIME*. Retrieved from https://time.com/3340831/polio-fdr-roosevelt-burns/

Kruglanski, A. W. (1990). 'Motivations for judging and knowing: implications for causal attribution', in E. T. Higgins and R. M. Sorrentino (eds.), *Handbook of Motivation and Cognition: Foundations of Social Behavior*, Vol. 2. New York: The Guilford Press, pp. 333–68.

Kruglanski, A. W. et al. (2021). 'On the psychology of extremism: how motivational imbalance breeds intemperance'. *Psychological Review*, 128(2), 264–89. https://doi.org/10.1037/rev0000260

Kruglanski, A. W., et al. (2020). 'Terrorism in time of the pandemic: exploiting mayhem'. *Global Security: Health, Science and Policy*, 5(1), 121–32. https://doi.org/10.1080/23779497.2020.1832903

Kruglanski, A. W., Bélanger, J. J., and Gunaratna, R. (2019). *The Three Pillars of Radicalization: Needs, Narratives, and Networks.* New York: Oxford University Press.

Kruglanski, A. W., Gelfand, M., and Gunaratna, R. (2012). 'Terrorism as means to an end: how political violence bestows significance', in P. R. Shaver and M. Mikulincer (eds.), *Meaning, Mortality, and Choice: The Social Psychology of Existential Concerns.* American Psychological Association, pp. 203–12. https://doi.org/10.1037/13748-011

Kruglanski, A. W., Szumowska, E., and Kopetz, C. (2021). 'The call of the wild: how extremism happens'. *Current Directions in Psychological Science*, 30(2), 181–5.

Kruglanski, A. W., Webber, D., and Koehler, D. (2019). *The Radical's Journey: How German Neo-Nazis Voyaged to the Edge and Back.* New York: Oxford University Press.

Kruglanski, A. W., and Webster, D. M. (1991). 'Group members' reactions to opinion deviates and conformists at varying degrees of proximity to decision deadline and of environmental noise'. *Journal of Personality and Social Psychology*, 61(2), 212–25. https://doi.org/10.1037/0022-3514.61.2.212

Lambert, A. J., et al. (2014). 'Towards a greater understanding of the emotional dynamics of the mortality salience manipulation: revisiting the "affect-free" claim of terror management research'. *Journal of Personality and Social Psychology*, 106(5), 655–78. https://doi.org/10.1037/a0036353

Lenferink, L. I. M., et al. (2017). 'Prolonged grief, depression, and post-traumatic stress in disaster-bereaved individuals: latent class analysis'. *European Journal of Psychotraumatology*, 8(1), 1298311. doi: 10.1080/20008198.2017.1298311

Leonard, N. R., et al. (2015). 'A multi-method exploratory study of stress, coping, and substance use among high school youth in private schools'. *Frontiers in Psychology*, 6, 1028.

Leung, A. K.-Y., and Chiu, C.-Y. (2010). 'Multicultural experience, idea receptiveness, and creativity'. *Journal of Cross-Cultural Psychology*, 41(5–6), 723–41.

Levine, A., and Cureton, J. S. (1998). *When Hope and Fear Collide: A Portrait of Today's College Student*. San Francisco: Jossey-Bass Publishers.

Levine, D. N. (1985). *The Flight from Ambiguity*. Chicago: University of Chicago Press.

Liberman, N., et al. (1999). 'Promotion and prevention choices between stability and change'. *Journal of Personality and Social Psychology*, 77(6), 1135.

List of George Floyd protests in the United States (n.d.). Retrieved from https://en.wikipedia.org/wiki/List_of_George_Floyd_protests_in_the_United_States

Liu, M. (2017). 'War and children'. *American Journal of Psychiatry Residents' Journal*, 12(7), 3–5. doi: 10.1176/appi.ajp-rj.2017.120702.

Lord, C. G., Ross, L., and Lepper, M. R. (1979). 'Biased assimilation and attitude polarization: the effects of prior theories on subsequently considered evidence'. *Journal of Personality and Social Psychology*, 37(11), 2098–2109. https://doi.org/10.1037/0022-3514.37.11.2098

Lustgarten, A. 'The great climate migration has begun'. *The New York Times Magazine*, 23 July 2020. Retrieved from https://www.nytimes.com/interactive/2020/07/23/magazine/climatemigration.html

Macron, E. 'Fight against separatism – the Republic in action'. *France Diplomacy*, 2 Oct. 2020. https://www.diplomatie.gouv.fr/en/coming-to-france/france-facts/secularism-and-religious-freedom-in-france-63815/article/fight-against-separatism-the-republic-in-action-speech-by-emmanuel-macron

Mallett, R. K., Wilson, T. D., and Gilbert, D. T. (2008). 'Expect the unexpected: failure to anticipate similarities leads to an intergroup forecasting error'. *Journal of Personality and Social Psychology*, 94(2), 265–77.

Marchlewska, M., Cichocka, A., and Kossowska, M. (2017). 'Addicted to answers: need for cognitive closure and the endorsement of conspiracy beliefs'. *European Journal of Social Psychology*, 48(2), 109–117. https://doi.org/10.1002/ejsp.2308

McAdams, D. P. (2013). *The Redemptive Self: Stories Americans Live By*, revised and expanded edition. New York: Oxford University Press.

McCraty, R. (2003). 'The energetic heart: bioelectromagnetic interactions within and between people'. *Neuropsychotherapist*, 6(1), 22–43.

McCraty, R., et al. (1995). 'The effects of emotions on short-term power spectrum analysis of heart rate variability'. *American Journal of Cardiology*, 76(14), 1089–93.

McGregor, I., and Marigold, D. C. (2003). 'Defensive zeal and the uncertain self: what makes you so sure?', *Journal of Personality and Social Psychology*, 85(5), 838–52. https://doi.org/10.1037/0022-3514.85.5.838

McKinstry, L. 'How the government has declared war on white English people'. *Express*, 9 Aug. 2007.

Mejia, B. (2020). 'Physicians group releases report on psychological effects of family separation'. Retrieved 14 March 2021 from https://www.latimes.com/california/story/2020-02-25/family-separation-trauma

Mellow, J. R. (1974). *Charmed Circle: Gertrude Stein and Company*. London: Phaidon Press.

Mendelsohn, B. (2011). 'Foreign fighters – recent trends'. *Orbis*, 55(2), 189–202.

Merari, A. (2010). *Driven to Death: Psychological and Social Aspects of Suicide Terrorism*. New York: Oxford University Press.

Michael, E. (2020). 'Alcohol consumption during COVID-19 pandemic: what PCPs need to know'. *Healio News*. Retrieved from https://www.healio.com/news/primary-care/20200416/ alcohol-consumption-during-covid19-pandemic-what-pcps-need-to-know

Mikulincer, M. (1997). 'Adult attachment style and information processing: individual differences in curiosity and cognitive closure'. *Journal of Personality and Social Psychology*, 72(5), 1217.

Mikulincer, M., and Shaver, P. R. (2001). 'Attachment theory and intergroup bias: evidence that priming the secure base schema attenuates negative reactions to out-groups'. *Journal of Personality and Social Psychology*, 81(1), 97–115.

Mikulincer, M., Shaver, P. R., and Rom, E. (2011). 'The effects of implicit and explicit security priming on creative problem solving'. *Cognition and Emotion*, 25(3), 519–31. doi: 10.1080/02699931.2010.540110.

Mill, J. S. (1859). *Essay on Liberty*. London: John W. Parker and Son.

Mill, J. S. (1843). *A System of Logic*. London: John W. Parker and Son.

Miller, B. C., and Gerard, D. (1979). 'Family influences on the development of creativity in children: an integrative review'. *Family Coordinator*, 28(3), 295–312.

Mingyur, Y. (2010). *Joyful Wisdom*. London: Bantam.

Mischel, W., and Shoda. Y. (1995). 'A cognitive-affective system theory of personality: reconceptualizing situations, dispositions, dynamics, and invariance in personality structure'. *Psychological Review*, 102(2), 246–68. https://psycnet.apa.org/buy/1995-25136-001

Moebus, J. (1982). 'Über die Bestimmung des Wilden und die Entwicklung des Verwertungsstandpunktes bei Kolumbus', in K. H. Kohl (ed.), *Mythen der Neuen Welt: zur Entdeckungsgeschichte Lateinamerikas*. (Catalogue to the exhibition.) Berlin: Frölich and Kaufmann.

Morgan, G. S., Wisneski, D. C., and Skitka, L. J. (2011). 'The expulsion from Disneyland: the social psychological impact of 9/11'. *American Psychologist*, 66(6), 447.

Mudde, C. (2004). 'The populist zeitgeist'. *Government and Opposition*, 39(4), 541–63. https://doi.org/10.1111/j.1477-7053.2004.00135.x

Muggeridge, M. (1967). *Muggeridge through the Microphone: BBC Radio and Television*. London: British Broadcasting Corporation.

Myers, D. G. (2000). 'The funds, friends, and faith of happy people'. *American Psychologist*, 55(1), 56.

National Academies of Sciences, Engineering and Medicine (2016). *Attribution of Extreme Weather Events in the Context of Climate Change*. Washington, DC: National Academies Press.

Nietzsche, F. (1996). Human, *All Too Human: A Book for Free Spirits*, trans. R. J. Hollingdale. Cambridge: Cambridge University Press.

Nisbett, R. E., and Wilson, T. D. (1977). 'Telling more than we can know: verbal reports on mental processes'. *Psychological Review*, 84(3), 231–59. https://doi.org/10.1037/0033-295X.84.3.231

Orehek, E., et al. (2010). 'Need for closure and the social response to terrorism'. *Basic and Applied Social Psychology*, 32(4), 279–90.

Orehek, E., and Kruglanski, A. W. (2018). 'Personal failure makes society seem fonder: an inquiry into the roots of social interdependence'. *PLOS One*, 13(8). https://doi.org/10.1371/journal.pone.0201361

Padgett, V. R., and Jorgenson, D. O. (1982). 'Superstition and economic threat: Germany, 1918–1940'. *Personality and Social Psychology Bulletin*, 8(4), 736–41.

Pavlov, I. P. (1927). *Conditioned Reflexes: An Investigation of the Physiological Activity of the Cerebral Cortex*. London: Oxford University Press.

Peale, N. V. (1980). *The Power of Positive Thinking*. New York: Random House.

Pettigrew, T. F., and Tropp, L. R. (2006). 'A meta-analytic test of intergroup contact theory'. *Journal of Personality and Social Psychology*, 90(5), 751.

Piketty, T. (2018). 'Brahmin left vs merchant right: rising inequality and the changing structure of political conflict'. WID. world Working Paper, 2018/7.

Piketty, T. (2014). *Capital in the Twenty-first Century*. Cambridge, MA: Harvard University Press.

Pilgrim, D. (2000). 'The Brute Caricature'. Jim Crow Museum. Retrieved from https://www.ferris.edu/jimcrow/brute/

Popova, M. 'Inclining the mind toward "sudden illumination": French polymath Henri Poincaré on how creativity works', *Marginalian*, 28 June 2018. Retrieved from https://www.brainpickings.org/2013/08/15/henri-poincare-on-how-creativity-works/

Popper, K. R. (1971). 'Conjectural knowledge: my solution of the problem of induction'. *Revue internationale de philosophie*, 167–97.

Popper, K. R. (1959). *The Logic of Scientific Discovery*. New York: Basic Books.

Popper, K. R. (1966). *The Open Society and Its Enemies*, rev. edn. New York: Routledge and Kegan Paul.

Psychology Today. (n.d.) *Confidence*. Retrieved from https://www.psychologytoday.com/us/basics/confidence

Puff, R. 'Quieting the monkey mind with meditation'. *Psychology Today*, 19 Oct. 2011. Retrieved from https://www.psychologytoday.com/us/blog/meditation-modern-life/201110/quieting-the-monkey-mind-meditation.

Putnam, R. D. (2007). 'E pluribus unum: diversity and community in the twenty-first century. The 2006 Johan Skytte Prize Lecture'. *Scandinavian Political Studies*, 30(2), 137–74.

Reykowski, J. (2021). 'Right-wing conservative radicalism as a pursuit of a cultural hegemony'. *Nauka*, 2.

Rhodewalt, F. (1994). 'Conceptions of ability, achievement goals, and individual differences in self-handicapping behavior: on the application of implicit theories'. *Journal of Personality*, 62(1), 67–85.

Richter, L., and Kruglanski, A. W. (1997). 'The accuracy of social perception and cognition: situationally contingent and process-based'. *Swiss Journal of Psychology*, 56, 62–81.

Robinson, L., Leibovitz, P., and Diehl, S. (2015). 'Rihanna in Cuba: the cover story'. *Vanity Fair*. Retrieved 5 March 2021 from https://www.vanityfair.com/hollywood/2015/10/rihanna-cover-cuba-annie-leibovitz

Roets, A., et al. (2015). 'The motivated gatekeeper of our minds: new directions in need for closure theory and research', in J. M. Olson and M. P. Zanna (eds.), *Advances in Experimental Social Psychology*, Vol. 52. Academic Press, pp. 221–83.

Roets, A., and Van Hiel, A. (2007). 'Separating ability from need: Clarifying the dimensional structure of the need for closure scale'. *Personality and Social Psychology Bulletin*, 33(2), 266–280.

Roig-Franzia, M. 'A British actor left Hollywood to fight ISIS. Now he's marooned in Belize. It's quite a story'. *Washington Post*, 15 Oct. 2019. Retrieved from https://www.washingtonpost.com/lifestyle/2019/10/15/british-actor-left-hollywood-fight-isis-now-hes-marooned-belize-its-quite-story/

Roney, C. J., Higgins, E. T., and Shah, J. (1995). 'Goals and framing: how outcome focus influences motivation and emotion'. *Personality and Social Psychology Bulletin*, 21(11), 1151–60.

Rosenblatt, A., et al. (1989). 'Evidence for terror management theory: I. the effects of mortality salience on reactions to those who violate or uphold cultural value'. *Journal of Personality and Social Psychology*, 57(4), 681–90.

Russo-Netzer, P., and Ben-Shahar, T. (2011). '"Learning from success": a close look at a popular positive psychology course'. *Journal of Positive Psychology*, 6(6), 468–76.

Sales, S. M. (1972). 'Economic threat as a determinant of conversion rates in authoritarian and nonauthoritarian churches'. *Journal of Personality and Social Psychology*, 23(3).

Salter, M. D. (1940). 'An evaluation of adjustment based upon the concept of security'. University of Toronto Press. (University of Toronto Studies Child Development Series No. 18).

Saphire-Bernstein, S., et al. (2011). 'Oxytocin receptor gene (OXTR) is related to psychological resources'. *Proceedings of the National Academy of Sciences*, 108(37), 15118–22.

Saroglou, V. (2002). 'Beyond dogmatism: the need for closure as related to religion'. *Mental Health, Religion and Culture*, 5(2), 183–94.

Schuster, M. A., et al. (2001). 'A national survey of stress reactions after the September 11, 2001, terrorist attacks'. *New England Journal of Medicine*, 345(20), 1507–1512.

Schwartz, I. (2020). 'CNN's John King: Trump "shameless" for using coronavirus briefing to talk about war on drugs'. *Real Clear Politics*. Retrieved from https://www.realclearpolitics.com/video/2020/04/01/cnns_john_king_trump_shameless_for_using_coronavirus_briefing_to_talk_about_war_on_drugs.html

Seligman, A. B., Wasserfall, R. R., and Montgomery, D. W. (2015). *Living with Difference: How to Build Community in a Divided World*. Oakland, CA: University of California Press.

Seligman, M. E. (1972). 'Learned helplessness'. *Annual Review of Medicine*, 23(1), 407–12.

Seligman, M. E. (2006). *Learned Optimism: How to Change Your Mind and Your Life*. New York: Vintage Books.

Seligman, M. E., et al. (1990). 'Explanatory style as a mechanism of disappointing athletic performance'. *Psychological Science*, 1(2), 143–6.

Shaver, P. R., and Tancredy, C. M. (2001). 'Emotion, attachment, and bereavement: a conceptual commentary', in M. S. Stroebe et al. (eds.), *Handbook of Bereavement Research: Consequences,*

Coping, and Care. American Psychological Association, pp. 63–88. https://doi.org/10.1037/10436-003

Shenk, J. W. (2005). 'Lincoln's great depression'. *Atlantic Monthly*, 296(3), 52.

Sherif, M., and Sherif, C. W. (1953). *Groups in Harmony and Tension: An Integration of Studies on Intergroup Relations.* New York: Harper.

Sherman, D. A., Nelson, L. D., and Steele, C. M. (2000). 'Do messages about health risks threaten the self? Increasing the acceptance of threatening health messages via self-affirmation'. *Personality and Social Psychology Bulletin*, 26(9), 1046–58.

Shimer, D. 'Yale's most popular class ever: happiness'. *The New York Times*, 26 Jan. 2018. Retrieved from https://www.nytimes.com/2018/01/26/nyregion/at-yale-class-on-happiness-draws-huge-crowd-laurie-santos.html?login=email&auth=login-email

Shuster, S. (n.d.). 'The populists'. *TIME Magazine*. Retrieved from https://time.com/time-person-of-the-year-populism/

Smith, A. (1759). *The Theory of Moral Sentiments.* London: Penguin.

Smith, N. (2017). 'Populist attacks on elites are a dead end'. Bloomberg. Retrieved from https://www.bloomberg.com/opinion/articles/2017-05-03/populist-attacks-on-elites-are-a-dead-end

Sorrentino, R. M., et al. (2012). 'Uncertainty regulation across cultures: an exploration of individual differences in Chinese and Canadian children in the classroom'. *Personality and Individual Differences*, 54(3), 378–82.

Sri Dhammananda, K. (2003). *Everything is Changeable.*

Stachel, J. (2002). *Einstein from 'B' to 'Z'.* Boston: Birkhäuser.

Steele, C. M., and Josephs, R. A. (1990). 'Alcohol myopia: its prized and dangerous effects'. *American Psychologist*, 45(8), 921–33. https://doi.org/10.1037/0003-066X.45.8.921

Stein, G. (n.d.), quotation. *Good Reads.* Retrieved from https://www.goodreads.com/author/quotes/9325.Gertrude_Stein?page=2

Stein, G., and Miller, E. (1926). *Composition as Explanation*. L. & V. Woolf at the Hogarth Press.

Strauss, W., and Howe, N. (1991). *Generations*. New York: William Morrow and Company.

Strauss, W., and Howe, N. (2000). *Millennials Rising*. New York: Vintage Books.

Sumner, W. G. (1906). *Folkways: A Study of the Sociological Importance of Usages, Manners, Customs, Mores, and Morals*. Boston: Gin and Company.

Swann, W. B., Jr, et al. (2010). 'Identity fusion and self-sacrifice: arousal as a catalyst of pro-group fighting, dying, and helping behavior'. *Journal of Personality and Social Psychology*, 99(5), 824–41. https://doi.org/10.1037/a0020014

Szumowska, E., et al. (2020). Unpublished data. Jagiellonian University.

Tadmor, C. T. et al. (2012). 'Multicultural experiences reduce intergroup bias through epistemic unfreezing'. *Journal of Personality and Social Psychology*, 103(5), 750–72. https://doi.org/10.1037/a0029719

Thibaut, J. W., and Kelley, H. H. (1959). *The Social Psychology of Groups*. New York: John Wiley and Sons.

Thomsen, C. W. (1987). '"Man-eating" and the myths of the "New World": anthropological, pictorial and literary variants', in C. F. Graumann and S. Moscovici (eds.), *Changing Conceptions of Conspiracy*. New York: Springer, pp. 40–69.

Tossell, C. C., et al. (2022). 'Spiritual over physical formidability determines willingness to fight and sacrifice through loyalty in cross-cultural populations'. *Proceedings of the National Academy of Sciences*, 119(6), e2113076119.

Trivers, R. L. (1971). 'The evolution of reciprocal altruism'. *Quarterly Review of Biology*, 46(1), 35–57.

Trump administration family separation policy (n.d.), in Wikipedia. Retrieved 14 March 2021 from https://en.wikipedia.org/wiki/Trump_administration_family_separation_policy

Twenge, J. M. (2006). *Generation Me*. New York: Free Press.

Valpy, M. (2007). 'Seismic tremors: religion and the law', in J. G. Stein et al., *Uneasy Partners: Multiculturalism and Rights in Canada*. Ontario: Wilfrid Laurier University Press.

van den Bos, K. (2009). 'Making sense of life: the existential self trying to deal with personal uncertainty'. *Psychological Inquiry*, 20(4), 197–217. https://doi.org/10.1080/10478400903333411

van den Bos, K., et al. (2001). 'Uncertainty management after reorganizations: the ameliorative effect of outcome fairness on job uncertainty'. *Revue Internationale de Psychologie Sociale*, 19(1), 145–56.

van den Bos, K., van Ameijde, J., and van Gorp, H. (2006). 'On the psychology of religion: the role of personal uncertainty in religious worldview defense'. *Basic and Applied Social Psychology*, 28, 333–41.

Viola, V., et al. (2014). 'Routes of motivation: stable psychological dispositions are associated with dynamic changes in cortico-cortical functional connectivity'. *PLOS One*, 9(6), e98010.

Wang, C. S., Whitson, J. A., and Menon, T. (2012). 'Culture, control, and illusory pattern perception'. *Social Psychological and Personality Science*, 3(5), 630–38.

Webber, D., et al. (2018). 'Deradicalizing detained terrorists'. *Political Psychology*, 39(3), 539–56.

Webster, D. M. (1993). 'Motivated augmentation and reduction of the overattribution bias'. *Journal of Personality and Social Psychology*, 65(2), 261–71. https://doi.org/10.1037/0022-3514.65.2.261

Webster, D. M., and Kruglanski, A. W. (1994). 'Individual differences in need for cognitive closure'. *Journal of Personality and Social Psychology*, 67(6), 1049.

Webster-Nelson, D. M., Klein, C. F., and Irvin, J. E. (2003). 'Motivational antecedents of empathy: inhibiting effects of fatigue'. *Basic and Applied Social Psychology*, 25, 37–50.

West, E. (2013). *The Diversity Illusion: What We Got Wrong about Immigration and How to Set it Right*. London: Gibson Square.

Wilson, T. D., et al. (2000). 'Focalism: a source of durability bias in affective forecasting'. *Journal of Personality and Social Psychology*, 78, 821–36.

Wilson, T. D., and Brekke, N. (1994). 'Mental contamination and mental correction: unwanted influences on judgments and evaluations'. *Psychological Bulletin*, 116(1).

Wilson, T. D., Gilbert, D. T., and Wheatley, T. P. (1998). 'Protecting our minds: the role of lay beliefs', in V. Y. Yzerbyt, G. Lories, and B. Dardenne (eds.), *Metacognition: Cognitive and Social Dimensions*. California: Sage Publications, pp. 171–201.

Woodzicka, J. A., and LaFrance, M. (2001). 'Real versus imagined gender harassment'. *Journal of Social Issues*, 57, 15–30.

World Bank Group. 'Groundswell: preparing for internal climate migration policy note #3: internal climate migration in Latin America', 16 Mar. 2018. Retrieved from https://documents1.worldbank.org/curated/en/983921522304806221/pdf/124724-BRI-PUBLIC-NEWSERIES-Groundswell-note-PN3.pdf

York, B. 'Bush loyalty test'. *National Review*, 30 Dec. 2008. Retrieved from https://www.nationalreview.com/2008/12/bush-loyalty-test-byron-york/

Index

5-HTTLPR gene 50
7 July attacks 136
9/11 attacks 69, 72, 134, 136
1960s 97–8

abortion 98, 113, 114
Acceptance and Commitment
    Therapy (ACT) 266–7
accidents 6, 260, 273
Adler, Alfred 166
Adorno, Theodor 96
Aeneid (Virgil) 28–9
Afghanistan 24, 93
afterlife 116
ageing 273–4
ageism 80
Ainsworth, Mary 59–62, 77, 82
air industry 279
Albert, Prince 66
alcohol 3, 39, 40, 149–50, 242
All Shall Be Well; And All Shall Be Well;
    And All Manner of Things Shall be
    Well 250
Allport, Gordon 289
al-Qaeda 185
Alternative for Germany (AfD)
    138, 285
alternative lifestyles 97
ambiguity 17, 93–4
American beliefs and spirit
    68–9, 200
amoyotrophic lateral sclerosis
    (ALS) 216
antisemitism 80, 134, 136, 284, 286
antitype 95–6

anxiety 3–4, 9, 64–5, 116, 220, 272
appreciation 253
Argetsinger, Amy 237
Arieli, Inbal 190–2
aristocracy 238
art
    abstract 155–6
    disagreements over 159
Asch, Solomon 159–60
atheism 55, 127
Atonement, Jewish Day of 26–7
Atran, Scott 177–8
attachment 52
    in adults 75–87
    figures 67
    fixed and fluctuating 83
    secure 60–2, 64, 67–8, 73, 75–7, 83,
        85
    testing 77–8
attribution theory 232
audacity 81
Auschwitz 43–44
austerity 97
Australia 69
The Authoritarian Personality 96
autism 145
autocracy 157
awe 200, 268

Babel, Tower of 276
baby boomers 98
Bangladesh 69
Barkshire, C. T. 203
Batman 131
Beam, Lura 31

The Beatles 219
Beck, Aaron 220
Ben, Shahar, Tal 207
bereavement 66–8, 73–4
Berglas, Steve 242
Berlin, Isaiah 129
Berra, Yogi 5
Berretta, Shirley 192
Berridge, Kent 257
Bevan, Aneurin 129
Bibby, Reginald 281
Biden, Joe 56, 217–18
Bion, Francesca 270
Bion, Wilfred 269–70
Black Death (plague) 136
Black Lives Matter 150, 288
black-and-white thinking 127–40,
    151, 163
Blainey, Geoffrey 281
Blair, Tony 283
Boelen, Paul 67
Bolivia 69
Bolsonaro, Jair 157
bond decisions (US courts) 118
Boorstin, Daniel 237
The Bourgeois Gentleman 10
Bowlby, John 60, 62, 64–5, 77, 82
brain, capacity for development 246
brainwashing 143
breastfeeding 58
Brickman, Philip 260
Buddhism 255–9, 265–7, 275
Buffett, Warren 224
Burns, Ken 216
Bush, George W. 24, 52, 54–6

camaraderie 170–3, 288
Campbell, Donald 42
Canada 68, 281
capital punishment 113
Capitol, storming of 29
Carleton, N. R. 3

Carlson, Richard 297
Carnaby Street 98
Carnegie, Dale 144, 154
Carver, Charles 210
caste systems 238
catastrophizing 211, 213, 221
causation 3–4
CEDAR programme 290–2
celebrity 237
certainty
    desire for 38–40, 140
    in relationships 76
    from religious belief 71
Cervantes, Miguel de 220, 222
challenges, approaches to 206, 234
change, discomfort with 273–4
chaos 17
Cheon, Bobby 50
children 107
    abuse of 65n, 170
    educational performance
        248–50
    effect of freedom and responsibility
        190–4
    labelling 251
    learning optimism 222–3
    mother-child relationships 57–8,
        60–4, 73, 77
    socialization of 42
China 150
    blamed for COVID-19 163
    stereotyping of 134
Chirumbolo, Antonio 271
Chiu, Chi-Yue 101
Christianity 68–70, 133
Churchill, Winston 153, 218, 224, 246,
    256, 266
Chutzpah (book) 190
clairvoyance 72
clarity 93–4
Clark, Hewitt B. 203
class, social 121, 158, 238

climate change 277–8
Clinton, Bill 24, 217
    open-mindedness 52–6
Clinton, Hillary 53, 139
Cliteur, Paul 282
closed-mindedness 10, 17, 28
closure, need for 15, 35–6, 39, 42, 46,
        135–6, 296
    and alcohol intake 149–50
    as hardwired 50
    impact on empathy 145–9
    low need for 15, 148
    premature closure ('freezing') 49,
        78, 109
    questionnaire 18–22
    and religiosity 71–2
    situational affordances 105–6
    and social relationships 142–64
    understanding 22–4
clothing 54–5
cocaine 257
cognitive therapy 220
Cold War 134
Collins, Nancy L. 76
communication 152–4, 156–7
compassion 129, 147–8
competition 108, 207, 243, 252, 278
concentration camps 43–6
conceptions, prior 30, 32
confidence 95, 114, 165
    and knowledge 33
    lack of 166–8
    overconfidence 10
    paradox 32–3
    shaken 119–22
confirmation bias 130
conflict resolution 287
consensus, desire for 161–2
conspiracy theories 134–7, 143,
        172, 205
contact hypothesis 289–93
contentment 202, 258–9, 268

cooking 183–4
Cooley, Charles 86
correlation 3–4
Cotton, Tom 163
counterculture movement 97–8
COVID-19 1, 43, 66, 98, 115, 184,
        288, 294
    and alcohol consumption 149
    anxiety about 3–5, 7–8, 80, 148
    conspiracy theories and
        misinformation about 80,
        134–6, 163
    deliberate spreading of 135
    and domestic violence 148–9
    and economic wellbeing 151–2
    and nationalism 163
    protests during 150–1, 288
    Trump's reaction to 145, 163
creativity 268, 271
Crusades 185
Csikszentmihalyi, Mihalyi 198–9
The Cult of True Womanhood:
        1820–1860 165
cultural differences 52, 88–90, 99–101,
        276, 278–86
    learning to live with 291–2, 298
cultural identity 140
cultural norms 91–3, 278
culture, and group membership
        119–22
culture wars 98
Czech Republic 138

Darwin, Charles 91, 177
Dayan, Moshe 27
death 42, 273
    fear of 116–19, 272
    manipulating mortality salience
        118–19
Death of a Salesman 237
decision making 16–17, 36, 55, 70–1, 95
    cultural differences 90–2

Declaration of Independence 200, 238
defensiveness 26, 113–15
democracy 157, 238
Democracy in America 69
Democritus 157
Demosthenes 167
depression 3, 64, 116, 215, 220
  helplessness theory of 199
  major depressive disorder
    (MDD) 67
depth psychology 269
deradicalization 174–6
Descartes, René 93
desires
  limiting 268
  unsatisfied 257–8
detachment 259
Dhammananda, K. Sri 257
Dialectical Behaviour Therapy
  (DBT) 266
Diallo, Amadou 30
Diamond Princess cruise ship 184
Dickinson, Robert L. 31
digital media 98
disability 216, 260
disaster relief 184
discrimination 276, 289
Disney, Walt 218
distractions, avoiding 51
diversity 276, 279–86, 291–3
  suppressing 293
  tolerance of 80, 112
The Diversity Illusion 282
divorce 273
dogs 198–9
  in Pavlov's experiments 37–8
domestic abuse 39, 148–9
dopamine 257
doubt 113–14, 166
  and extreme beliefs 167–70
Drehle, David von 66
drugs 97, 242, 257

Duckworth, Angela 224–5, 227, 228, 247
Duda, Andrzej 157
Dumbledore, Albus 2
Duterte, Roderigo 138, 157
Dweck, Carol 231–6, 239–40, 245–7,
  253–4

Eastern philosophy 255–9
economy 97, 139
Edison, Thomas 218
education systems 248–53
effort 239–40
Egypt, Yom Kippur War 26–8
Einstein, Albert 76, 219, 271
elections 143, 218
elites 137
Ellenberg, Molly 65
Ellis, Albert 220
Emanuel, Rahm 183
Emmons, Robert 202, 204
emotions 110
  positive and negative 206–7
  predicting 261–3, 265
empathy 24, 54, 75, 143–52, 207
  and closure 145–9
  failures in 145–7
encouragement 227
enemies 288
Enright, Michael 185–6
Enron Corporation 236
environmentalism 151
equality 98, 238
Erdoğan, Recep Tayyip 157
Erickson, Milton 205
Ethiopia 3
eugenics 238
European Union 135
evacuation of children (wartime) 63–5
event-related potentials (ERPs) 51
evolution 37, 142
existential dread 42, 116–19
expectancy 186–9

explanatory styles 212–14, 244–5
extremism 167–71, 185, 288
  deradicalization 174–6
  disillusionment with 172
  and long-term conflicts 178
  push and pull factors 172–4

failure 167, 188–9, 218–19, 229,
    237, 242
  explaining 212–13
  externalizing 244
  fear of 231
  and growth mindset 233–5
fairness 111–12, 130
faith, surpassing understanding 268
fake news 136
fame 237
fashion 88, 99
fatigue 39, 147
Faulkner, William 153
fear 116
  existential 42, 116–19
Federal Protective Service 135
Feeney, Brooke 81
feminism 151
Festinger, Leon 107
fiction 131–2
films 131–3, 140
Fishman, Shira 286
Five Star Movement 139
flexibility 51
focus, ability to 51
food 174, 183–4, 257, 276
formality 54–5
Frankel, Estelle 268–9
Frankl, Viktor 43–6
Franklin, Benjamin 6
Fredrickson, Barbara 203, 206
freedom 129, 130
French Revolution 94, 284
Freud, Anna 64–5
Freud, Sigmund 107, 269

Freund, Tali 1
Friedman, Thomas 99, 279
friendships 75, 80
Frum, David 52, 55

Gable, Shelly 200
Gates, Bill 219
Gelfand, Michele 91
generativity 205
genetics 50–1, 211
genius 239–40, 242
geopolitics 139
Gergen, Kenneth 247–8, 252–4
Germany 92, 134, 138, 174, 285
Gibbon, Edward 71
Gilbert, Daniel 261–5
Gill, Scherto 247–8, 252–4
Gladwell, Malcolm 240
global warming 277–8
globalization 98–9, 279
God 68–70, 268
good life 207
government 52–7
Grand Princess cruise ship 184
Grant, John Webster 72
gratitude 202–5
Great Depression 72
grief 67, 73
grit 223–6, 229–30
groups
  centrism 50
  cohesion in 288
  extremist 168–72, 288
  isolation of 173
  out-groups 50
  and peer pressure 160
  push and pull factors 172–4
  in schools 251
  and self-worth 170–2
  social 119–22
  tribalism 157–63
  youth movements 193

growth mindset 231–42, 244
  developing 246–7
  and relationships 240–2
Gulf War 53

Haidt, Jonathan 129–30
happiness 199–201, 205–7,
    259–60
  predicting 261–3
Harari, Yuval Noah 68
Harlow, Harry 57–9, 67
*Harry Potter and the Philosopher's
    Stone* 219
Hawking, Stephen 216–17, 218
health 43, 205, 217–18, 260, 274
  anxiety about 151–2, 272
  and mental state 219
health care 117
heat, influence of 39
Hegel, Georg Wilhelm
    Friedrich 86
helplessness, learned 198–9
Hemingway, Ernest 153–4
Hentoff, Nat 53
Heraclitus 5, 266
heroes 177–8, 228
  in popular culture 131–2
Higgins, Tory 187, 194–5, 267
Hill, Anita 217
Hinduism 133
Hobbes, Thomas 93
Hoffer, Eric 127
Hofstede, Geert 89
homosexuality 80, 98, 101
Hong Kong 150
honour 167
hope 46, 246
horoscopes 72
Houston, Jean 53
*How to Win Friends and Influence
    People* 155
Hume, David 93

hunger strikes 151
Huntingdon, Samuel 283
hypertension 205

IBM 89
ibuprofen 134
idealism 185
idealization 31–2
identity, and group membership
    119–22
ideologies 68, 95, 170
  commitment to 185
  dichotomous 133
IKEA 49
illness *see* health
imaginative tolerance 129
immigration 63, 112, 138, 277–8
  and cultural cohesion 280–2
  melting-pot perspective 290
  and stereotyping 285–6
  see also multiculturalism
inadequacy, feelings of 166–7
Indonesia 120
induction 5–7
Industrial Revolution 94
inferiority complex 166–7
information processing 109–10, 130
  and alcohol consumption 149–50
  see also closure, premature
insecurity *see* uncertainty
internet 98, 279
Iraq 174, 178
Irvin, J. E. 147
Islam 68, 70–1, 127, 133
  and cultural separatism 285
  negative perceptions of 286
Islamic State (IS) 177–8, 185–6
Islamist extremism 133, 174, 177
Israel 101, 150
  parenting styles 190–4
  Yom Kippur War 26–8
Italy 138

Jaensch, Erich 95
Jagiellonian University 51
James, William 42
Jasko, Katarzyna 151
Jewish ghettos 65
job/work 104–5, 111, 151, 218, 262–5
    choosing 224–7
Jones, Edward 242
Jordan, Michael 228, 239
Judaism 68, 84–5; *see also* antisemitism
justice *see* fairness

Kabbalah 268, 269
Keats, John 266
Kelley, Harold H. 31, 107
Kennedy, John F. 136
King, Martin Luther 112
Kipling, Rudyard 266
Kiss, Stephen 131
Klein, C. F. 147
Klein, Joe 56
Klem, Adena 2
Kossowska, Malgorzata 51, 135
Kubo, Tite 3
Kudilah, Battle of 178
Kuhn, Thomas 34

Lakatos, Imre 34
lateness 48
Le Pen, Marine 138
learned helplessness 198–9
Lenferink, Lonneke 67
Leung, Angela K. Y. 101
Lewin, Kurt 106–9
Lewinsky, Monica 24
liberalism 95
Liberman, Nira 196
Lincoln, Abraham 214–15, 218
listening 153–5
lockdowns 149
Locke, John 93
lottery winners 260

love 69, 85, 240–1
Lovecraft, H. P. 3
loyalty 56, 130
LTTE 169
    deradicalization 175–6

Macron Emmanuel 284
Make America Great Again 121
Marchlewska, Marta 135
Marie-Antoinette, Queen 146
Marigold, Denise 113
martyrdom 167, 177–8
Marwan, Ashraf 27
mathematics 93
McAdams, Dan 205
McCullough, Michael E. 204
McEnroe, John 239, 244
McGregor, Ian 113, 119
McKinstry, Leo 282
Mead, George Herbert 86
meaning 115
mediation 54
meditation 258, 267
Meloni, Georgia 138
memory 269, 273
Mensa 238–9
mental contamination 262
mental strength 165–6
Mikulincer, Mario 77–9, 79–80, 81,
    82–5
Mill, John Stuart 81, 128–30
millennials 98
Miller, Arthur 237
mindfulness 266–7
mindsets 231–54
    changing 234, 246–7
    fixed 232–3, 235–6, 238–9, 242–3
mistakes 26–9, 40
moderation 258
Modi, Narendra 138, 157
Molinario, Erica 139
monarchy 238

money 105, 108, 151, 167
monkeys 57–9, 204
Monroe, Marilyn 219
Montgomery, David 290
Moon landings 136
moral foundations theory 129–30
moral relativism 281
morality, black-and-white 129–31
Morgan, G. Scott 287
Mosaic Madness 281
Mosul 178
mother-child relationships 57–8, 60–4, 73, 77
motivation 154–7, 186
    intrinsic and extrinsic 199–200
motor neurone disease 216
Muggeridge, Malcolm 237
Multicultural Experience Survey (MES) 101
multiculturalism 99–102, 139
    criticism of 281–4, 290
murders 148, 150
music 88, 97–8, 99
mysticism 268–9

Nanygang Technological University 50
Napoleon Bonaparte 165, 167
narcissism 162
nationalism 120, 157, 162–3, 174
natural selection 91
    and values 177
The Nature of Prejudice 289
Nazism 65, 95, 127, 134, 167–74, 285
neo-liberalism 138
Netanyahu, Benjamin 138, 157
Newton, Isaac 93
NFCS scale 18–22
Nietzsche, Friedrich 268
Nobel Peace Prize 184
Northern League (Lega) 139
Northrop, J. T. 203

nuclear weapons 27
nurturing, impact of 57–9

Oath Keepers 98, 288
Obama, Barack 57, 81, 183, 218
obsessive compulsive disorder (OCD) 43
oligarchy 157–8
Open Society and Its Enemies 237–8
open-mindedness 53, 56, 95, 97, 161, 296
    and subliminal priming 83–5
Operation Barbarossa 27
Operation Pied Piper 63
optimism 109, 112, 186–7, 204, 210–12, 218–19
    dimensions of 212–14
    learning 219–23, 229–30
order 16–17
Orehek, Edward 286
Oswald, Lee Harvey 136
otherness 50, 101
    fear of or aversion to 276–7, 284–6, 289
out-groups 50
overconfidence 10

pain, chronic 271–3
Pakistan 120
pandemics 41, 66, 109; *see also* COVID-19
paranoia 108
parents 57–65, 73–4, 146
    and promotion focus 188–94
    teaching optimism 222–3
Paris Peace Accords 92
Parker, Kathleen 3
parties 76, 147
passions, following 224–8
patience 92–3
patriarchy 158
patriotism 162, 287

Pavlov, Ivan, experiments with dogs 37–8
Peale, Norman Vincent 201
Pearl Harbor attack 27
peer pressure 160
permanence 212
perseverance 224–5
personality 108
  and environment 107–9
  strength of 165
  uniqueness of 104–5
personalization 213
pervasiveness 213
Peshmerga 178
pessimism 197, 211–12, 230
  banishing 9–10
  disputation of 220–3
Pettigrew, Thomas 289
Philippines 150
philosophy, Eastern 255–9
The Philosophy of Human Rights 282
phobias 220, 231
Piketty, Thomas 139
plagues 136
plane crashes, MH17 (2014) 67–8
Plato 157–8, 237–8, 240
poetry 94
Poincaré, Henri 270
Poland 135, 150
police violence 30, 150–1
political activism 150–1
politicians, and empathy 144
Popper, Karl 5, 34, 154, 158, 237–8
popular culture 88, 99, 140
populism 137–40, 251
positive psychology 198–209
  courses in 207
positivity 187–97
post traumatic stress disorder (PTSD) 63–4, 67
The Power of Positive Thinking 201
Prabhakaran, Velupillai 175–6

praying 68–9
predictability 16–17
prejudice 79–80, 99–101, 289
Presley, Elvis 219
prevention focus 187–9, 194–7, 208, 267
Pride and Prejudice 78
primates 57–9, 204
priming, subliminal 83–5
principles 53–4
prisons 174–5
private sphere 290–1
Privette, Gayle 192
progressive politics 139
promotion focus 187–97, 208
protests 150–1 288
Proud Boys 98, 288
psychic experiences 53, 72
psychology, as a career 228
Puerta, José Ramón Andrés 183–4
punctuality 54
punishment 118–19, 179
purpose in life 228–9
Putin, Vladimir 138
Putnam, Robert D. 283

Quixote, Don 220, 222

racism 30, 80, 134–5, 238
  and stereotypes 100
radicalization 127, 167, 174–6
Rajapaksa, Gotabaya 175
rationality 33, 40, 154, 220
'Rebecca Myth' 31
redemptive sequences 205
refugees 139, 285
rejection 108, 241, 246
relationships 297
  and gratitude 203–4
  with parents 57–65, 73–4, 77, 146, 170, 188–94

relationships – *cont'd.*
  with partners 75–6, 81–2, 85, 146,
    240–1
  security within 60–8, 75–7
  social/friendships 75, 80
  supportive 81–2
  working 262–5
religion 55, 68–72, 75, 112, 120
  and conflict 133
  conversion 127
  in different countries 68–9
  and fear of death 116
  fervour 185
  and stereotyping 133
  see also extremism
renunciation 173
repression 199
resilience 7
responsibility 70–1
retirement 274
Reza, Yasmina 159
Richter, Linda 155
role-taking 144–5
Roman empire, fall of 71
Romanticism 94, 137
Roney, C. J. 195
Roosevelt, Franklin D. (FDR)
    215–16, 218
routines 1
Rowling, J. K. 219
Roy, Travis 6–7
Russians, stereotypes of 134
Ruth, Babe 240

sacred values 177–8
sacrifice 177
Salter, Mary *see* Ainsworth, Mary
'Samson Option' 27
sanctity 130
Santos, Laurie 207
Saphire-Bernstein, Shimon 211n
Sapiens: A Brief History of Humankind 68

Saroglou, Vassilis 72
Sartre, Jean-Paul 142
satisfaction, search for 257–8
Saudi Arabia 174
Schachter, Stanley 107
Scheier, Michael 210
Schurz, Carl 162
science, philosophy of 34
Second World War 63–5, 95, 134
  impact on uncertainty 96–7
Segerstrom, Suzanne 210
self-assurance, developing 59–60
self-awareness 22–5
self-esteem 113
self-handicapping 242–6
self-harm 250
self-help literature 166
Seligman, Martin 198, 212–14, 221,
    244, 247, 253, 290–1
Sentamu, John 282
separation, of children from mothers
    61–5
serotonin 50n
sex/sexual behaviour 114–15, 257
sexism 80
sexual abuse and harrassment 65n,
    217, 261
Shah, J. 195
Shaver, Philip 82–5
Shenk, Joshua Wolf 215
Sherif, Muzafer and Carolyn 287
shopping 48–9
significance, need for 190, 115,
    119–22, 139–40, 151–2, 183,
    185–6
  in educational achievement 249,
    251, 253
  and extremism/radicalization 121,
    169–72, 175–9
  though pursuing a passion 226–30
Singapore 92, 174
situational affordances 105–6

skills, learning 225, 252
Skitka, Linda J. 287
Smith, Adam 202
smoking 3
social brain 142
social class 121, 158, 238
social cohesion 281–4
social identity 119–22
social media 88, 98
social psychology 107, 232
The Social Psychology of Groups (Thibaut and Kelley) 31
socializing 17, 75–6, 142
Socrates 23
South Africa 69
Soviet Union 97
Spanish Civil War 185
Spider-Man 131
Spinozan belief systems 262
sports 228, 244–5
    and fixed mindsets 239
Sri Lanka 169, 175–6
Stein, Gertrude 121, 160, 268
stereotypes 32, 79–80, 99–101, 114, 141, 285–6, 289
    ethnic and religious 133
stigmatising 167
'Strange Situation' test 61–2
strength 165
stress 250
    reducing 205
students
    assessment 248–53
    depression 250
subliminal priming 83–5
success, explaining 212–13
suicide 45, 215, 237, 250
suicide bombers 167, 173, 178
Sumner, William 288
Sunni militia 178
superheroes 131–2, 141
Szumowska, Ewa 197

Tadmor, Carmit T. 99–101
Taliban 93
Tamil Black Tigers (LTTE) 169
    deradicalization 175–6
technology 277, 278–80
Teresa, Mother 228
terrorism 127, 167
    Islamist 133, 174–5
    and need for closure 136
terror-management theory 117–19
testing (education) 248–52
    alternatives to 252–3
The Theory of Everything 217
Thibaut, John W. 31
thinking
    black-and-white 127–40, 151, 163
    'outside the box' 203
Thomas, Clarence 217
time pressures 146
tiredness 39
Tocqueville, Alexis de 69
tolerance
    imaginative 129
    lack of 149
tolerance of 95
Tossell, Chad C. 165
tourism 279
transitions 273–4
trauma 63–4, 63–5, 269
tribalism 157–63
Trojan Horse 28–9
Tropp, Linda 289
Trump, Donald 29, 56, 63, 121, 137–8, 139, 218
    lack of empathy 145
truth
    and conflict 133
    subjective 128–9, 143
Tsofim (Scouts) 193
Tyson, Mike 239

Uganda 60–1
Ukraine war 294
uncertainty
    accepting/tolerating 49, 143,
        210, 234, 247, 252, 266,
        268–70
    aversive 158
    and black-and-white thinking
        127–40
    creating opportunities 184–6
    cultural attitudes to 88–92, 94,
        99–102
    discomfort with 48–9, 65, 99–102,
        109–10
    impact of historical events 96–7
    measuring your need for 15
    mundane 8–9
    negative consequences of 40
    perceptions of 8–9, 46, 183
    personal 110–13, 119–22, 168–9,
        176–7
    and prejudice 99–101
    situational 122
    and social group membership
        119–22
Uncertainty Avoidance Index (UAI)
    89–90
unemployment 278
uniformity 97
University of Maryland 1

validation 158–9
value (desirability) 186–7
values 88–9, 115, 118, 130, 228–9
    and cultural differences 130, 281–3
    inflexible 129
    sacred 177–8
van den Bos, Kees 110–11, 119
Van Vleet, Meredith 81
Victoria, Queen 66–7
Vietnam War 92, 97
Viola, Martha 51

violence 39–40, 148–50, 167
volunteering 185

war 133, 276
    impact on children 63–5
Wasserfall, Rahel 290
Webster-Nelson, Donna 1, 15–16,
    147, 149, 161
weddings 260
Weiner, Bernard 232
Welter, Barbara 165
West, Ed 282
Westerns (films) 131
White supremacism 133, 135
Wilders, Geert 138
Wilson, Timothy 261–5
Winfrey, Oprah 153, 218
wisdom 257, 259
Wisneski, Daniel 287
Wodicka, Tod 250
women
    abuse of 39, 148–9
    harrassment of 261
    ideals associated with 165
    rights 217
    traditional roles 96–7
Woodstock Festival 97
Woodward, Bob 53
work/career 104–5, 111, 151, 218,
    262–5
    choosing 224–7
World Central Kitchen 184
worldviews 115, 118, 119–20,
    160–2

xenophobia 284

Yom Kippur War 26–8
youth movements 193

Zeman, Miloš 138
Zen Buddhism 259, 268